TATTOO

TATTOO

Marcel Brousseau
Nancy Hajeski,
and Lisa Purcell

with photographs by
Jonathan Conklin

and a Foreword by
Troy Timpel

m ɹ

moseley road

moseley road

© 2009 Moseley Road Inc.

MOSELEY ROAD INC.
Publisher: Sean Moore
International Rights Director: Karen Prince
Art Director: Brian MacMullen
Editorial Director: Lisa Purcell
Senior Editor: Suzanne Lander
Designer: Hwaim Holly Lee
Editorial Assistants: Rachael Lanicci,
Jon Derengowski

Photographer: Jonathan Conklin

Cover subject: Seven / Artist: Mony; Natalie Jean
Title page subject: Diana Lozada
Contents pages subject: Guy Fesko

ISBN: 978-1-4351-1969-7

Library of Congress data is available upon request

Printed and bound in China

10 9 8 7 6 5 4 3 2

CONTENTS

▲ After a bike wreck and three months in a coma, the subject chose a tattoo signifying the brush with death and the fight back to consciousness.
Subject: Morgan Deegan / Artist: Troy Timpe

▲▲ A tattoo rich with meaning. The subject noted that "getting the koi swimming upstream represents a second chance that life has given me."
Subject: Tran / Artist: Troy Timpel

▶ A touching tribute to a lost friend. Tattoo artist Troy Timpel fashioned this intricate pattern for a client who "wanted to mix the paw prints of his recently passed-away boxer dog in this large Japanese floral piece."
Subject: Josh / Artist: Troy Timpel
All photographs this page by Troy Timpel

An intriguing medium with a limitless future, tattooing manages to be an art form as old as time and as modern as today. Tattoos have been found on the oldest preserved human remains, and today they adorn bodies in nearly every culture, all over the world.

From the 1940s through the 1970s, tattooing was largely the territory of military and motorcycle subcultures. The familiar old "sailor" tattoos epitomized military tradition and the stereotyping of our men in service. The 1980s brought a bit more of a progression and broader availability of high-tech tattoo equipment. The 1990s saw the beginning of a tattoo renaissance. The introduction of tattoo magazines, the widening outreach of the Internet, and an increase in the number of tattoo conventions got the public's attention and brought this subculture into an ever-widening arena.

The new players in this tattoo rebirth were mostly art school educated, and they started to push the boundaries. Japanese-style tattooing and various tribal patterns were soon

commonplace motifs within the tattoo scene. The new information age awoke interest in both old and new styles of artwork to accommodate the bursting envelope of how to define body art.

Portrait and photorealistic black and gray started to show some of tattooing's true potential. Large-scale tattooing soon became a common sight on an increasing number of individuals. The end of the 1990s saw no stone left unturned. Full bodysuits, mastery of technique, and a flood of equipment developments made tattooing very popular among a huge cross-section of our population.

I started tattooing in 1991, after attending the Milwaukee Institute of Art and Design. I had the pleasure of spending fifteen years (at the time of this book's publication) of tattooing with Philadelphia Eddie. Eddie was a key figure in the development of the tattoo scene from the 1960s to the present. Working with such a legend in the field gave me a true love and understanding of the tatttoo business.

In 1998 I started a tattoo clothing and promotional company called tattooedkingpin. com. We manufacture clothing, accessories, jewelry, and limited edition books. In 2003 we started running the Philadelphia Tattoo Arts Convention. I have since expanded the tattoo convention circuit to include Baltimore, Milwaukee, and Chicago.

The tattoo scene has exploded around me, and it is great to see the worldwide embrace of what was once a small tight-knit subculture. Television documentaries and "reality" shows have given the public an eyeful, providing educational content about this growing art form. I recently had the pleasure of appearing on the History Channel show *The Works*.

This book showcases striking tattoo photos and actual quotes from a broad spectrum of real subjects. I'm happy to be part of this project— it's given me a meaningful glimpse into people's personal feelings about their tattoos.

Troy Timpel

FOREWORD

◄ An ancient human art, both stigmatized and celebrated throughout history, tattooing is more popular today than at any time in recent memory. This expansive tattoo embodies a new chapter in a long history. Though tribal in nature, like ancient Polynesian tattoos, it was presumably not done for ritual purposes, but instead it satisfies the wearer's vision of himself. It has ancient precedents but a fully modern conception and execution.

Subject: Seven / Artist: Mony

AN ANCIENT ART REBORN

In the autumn of 1691, the mysteriously exotic Prince Giolo of the island of Moangis first displayed his patterned body to the "learned virtuosi" and "persons of high quality" inhabiting smoky, crowded, turn-of-the-century London. A South Sea Islander enslaved in the Philippines and eventually sold to a British merchant sailor, Prince Giolo was trumpeted as the "wonder of the age" for the intricate and colorful tattooing that decorated the entirety of his torso and legs. A promotional broadsheet for the "Painted Prince" speculated upon the "wisdom and ancient learning" embodied by the man's tattoos and claimed that the magical ink rendered his skin impervious to snakebite or poison. Despite his apparent powers, the ornately ornamented prince could not withstand the ravages of smallpox, and he died within months of arriving in London.

Prince Giolo, as depicted in a fanciful 1692 broadsheet. The "Painted Prince" made only a fleeting appearance in London—disease ended his difficult life shortly after he arrived in the pestilent city.
Engraving by John Savage (1692)

Nearly eighty years later, Joseph Banks, Captain James Cook's naturalist, made the first record of Polynesian tattooing practices during the HMS *Endeavor*'s maiden voyage to the South Pacific. To accompany his scientific observations, Banks, along with other members of Cook's crew, submitted his own skin to the Polynesian tattooists' whims and sailed home forever marked. Upon the vessel's return to Great Britain, the tales and drawings of the tattooed inhabitants of the South Seas captivated British society much as the ill-fated Prince Giolo had eighty years earlier, and body art became a small-scale fad among both well-heeled Britons and, of course, sailors.

Early Eurasian Tattoos

What eighteenth-century Britons didn't realize was that tattooing was not a novel practice on the British Isles: a millennium earlier, their Celtic and, later, their Anglo-Saxon ancestors had customarily decorated their bodies with ceremonial and familial tattoos. Tattooing had once been common across Europe and Asia among the diverse tribal cultures that populated the vast landmass. The 1991 discovery of Ötzi the Iceman in an Alpine glacier on the Austrian-Italian border gave clear evidence that Neolithic Eurasians had marked their bodies—Ötzi's yellowed skin, preserved in ice for more than five

thousand years, bore multiple small tattoos. Numerous lines were hatched on his lower back. On the inside of his left knee, he wore a small tattooed cross; his ankles were also decorated with clusters of parallel lines. In total, the Iceman wore some fifty-seven tattoos. Their purpose remains conjecture—although some anthropologists link them to social ritual, others believe that some sort of ancient acupuncture, intended to relieve Ötzi's aching joints, left the marks. Whatever the purpose of his tattoos, Ötzi is not alone among the ancients—both his ancestors and his descendents practiced tattooing. Archaeologists have excavated archaic bone needles and clay ink reservoirs at Paleolithic dig sites in Europe.

Eurasian tattooing became far more sophisticated during the millennia after Ötzi perished in the Alps. Tombs discovered in the steppes of southwestern Siberia in the mid- and late-twentieth century revealed remains of the Pazyryk people, who, besides excelling as skilled horsemen and fierce warriors, practiced

intricate, figurative tattooing. One mummy, a sturdy male believed to be a chief, wore a menagerie of animals on his body, all distinctively rendered. His right arm hosted two mighty deer, a donkey, a ram, and a fictitious carnivorous monster. On his chest, two griffins stood in winged splendor, while on his right shin, a fish

"Not one great country can be named, from the polar regions in the north to New Zealand in the south, in which the aborigines do not tattoo themselves."

—Charles Darwin, *The Descent of Man*, 1871

spanned from his ankle to his knee. Despite these and other elaborate designs, the Pazyryk chief also bore a row of circles along his spine, which, not unlike Ötzi's tattoos, were probably intended as a form of physical therapy.

Universal Ink

History reveals tattooing to be a universal human practice. Not only did the Polynesians and ancient Eurasian tribes decorate themselves with abstract designs and elaborate totems, but also the ancient Egyptians, the Inca, numerous American Indian tribes, and ancient Chinese all practiced tattooing. The famous intricacy and lushness of contemporary Japanese tattooing is a result of the culture's long heritage of body art. When European empires began colonizing the South Seas and the New World during the Age of Exploration (from the early fifteenth century to the early seventeenth century), the inked bodies of Polynesians and American Indians should not have seemed as exotic as they did to the colonizers—Europeans might have looked that way too, had they not, centuries earlier, chosen to abandon tattooing as a social norm. What Europeans saw—proudly tattooed bodies—was a mirror of their own distant heritage before it was swayed, like everything else, by the mores of Greek, Roman, Jewish, and Christian culture.

▲ Full-body tattoos on men are a long-standing tradition in Japan. The tattooist commonly uses the entire back as a canvas for intricate, lush depictions of the natural world.
Photograph by Felice Beato, c. 1870

◄ Tattooing in the South Pacific consisted of an array of patterning suited to both the contours of the body and, most surprisingly to European colonizers, the face. Drawings of tattooed islanders amazed European audiences.
Engraving © Jupiter Images

The Battle of Hastings in 1066 saw the Normans conquer the tribal Anglo-Saxons. The Normans brought their Latinate culture north to the British Isles, changing the language and mores of the region. Among the cultural shifts was a cessation in tattooing, which the Normans associated with undesirables.

Fragment of Bayeux Tapestry / Wikimedia

The Greeks were familiar with tattooing, having learned the technique from the Persians, but they were neither enthusiastic nor artistic practitioners. For the cosmopolitan Greeks, a tattooed body was the look of the barbarian tribes that massed across northern Europe. The Greeks thus used tattoos to indicate "barbarians" in their own culture: both slaves and criminals were forcibly tattooed.

The Romans subsequently adopted the Greek stance on tattoos—they tattooed slaves, criminals, and mercenary soldiers. Tattooing was considered anathema in Rome, so much so that its Latin word—*stigma*—is permanently infected with a sense of shame. It is said that the malicious Emperor Caligula would arbitrarily demand that members of his court be tattooed, thus scarring them for life in Roman society.

As Christianity permeated the Roman Empire, tattooing became even more forbidden. Christian culture had adopted the Jewish rule on tattooing as outlined in the Book of Leviticus: "You shall not make any cuttings in your flesh on account of the dead or tattoo any marks upon you." Tattooing, associated as it was with totems and pagan polytheism, had no place in Jewish religion. Likewise, in Christian Europe, tattooing came to be seen as ungodly. Emperor Constantine, who converted the Roman Empire to Christianity in the year 325, even restricted the tattooing of undesirables: slaves and criminals could still be tattooed on the body, but never again could their faces be stigmatized, since they had been "formed in the image of the divine beauty."

Taboo Tattoos

As Christianity swept through Europe, clearing away tribal spirituality, tattooing disappeared. In 787 Pope Hadrian I officially outlawed tattooing, setting a precedent that would last for centuries. In the British Isles tattooing finally seemed to have gasped its last when the Anglo-Saxon King Harold died on the field at Hastings in 1066, his lifeless, tattooed body representing the expiration of an entire culture. Yet tattooing did survive the Middle Ages and the restrictions of Catholicism; indeed, in the service of God, a small tattoo was permissible, such as the tiny crosses that Crusaders inked on their arms before going into battle.

It wasn't the Age of Exploration's rediscovery of tribal tattooing that

> ## "[It was] a narrative of his master's harshness."
>
> **—Greek philosopher Bion of Borysthenes** (circa 300 B.C.), describing the brutally tattooed face of his father, a former slave

> **"My body is a journal in a way. It's like what sailors used to do, where every tattoo meant something, a specific time in your life when you make a mark on yourself, whether you do it yourself with a knife or with a professional tattoo artist."**
>
> —Johnny Depp

pushed body art back toward the mainstream in Western culture after centuries as a stigma. It was scientific innovation—in particular, the electric tattoo needle. As mentioned earlier, after tattooing had reentered the Western consciousness, it became popular among both the aristocracy—who would have their bodies discreetly tattooed in the name of exotica—and seafarers, who would commemorate their voyages. But tattooing by hand, as it had been done for all of human history, was a slow, painful process, and strange as it may seem, a luxury in a modernizing society, due to the time, care, and money

involved. In 1891, Samuel O'Reilly, a British immigrant living in New York, patented a tattoo machine based on an electric pen that had been devised fifteen years earlier by none other than Thomas Edison. O'Reilly's machine revolutionized tattooing—now fast and affordable, tattooing attracted curious individuals from the lower classes, which alienated the rich, who began to shun body art.

During the first half of the twentieth century, the purpose of tattooing shifted. Sailors and soldiers were still regular patrons, requesting insignias indicating their patriotism, inky reminders of loved ones, or scantily clad beauties to gaze upon during lonely nights far away. More markedly, though, modern, electric tattooing developed its own subculture of well-decorated artists and patrons, men—and women—who saw unadorned bodies as blank canvases

The electric tattoo needle transformed body art in the West from a wealthy lark to an everyman art. Today tattoo technology is both enabling and benefiting from the popularity of body art. More tattoos mean more money for innovation. Despite all the gadgets, some adhere to an older way, particularly in Japan, where traditional tattooists decorate great swaths of skin with just needles, inks, and no electricity.

Photograph by David Brimm / Shutterstock

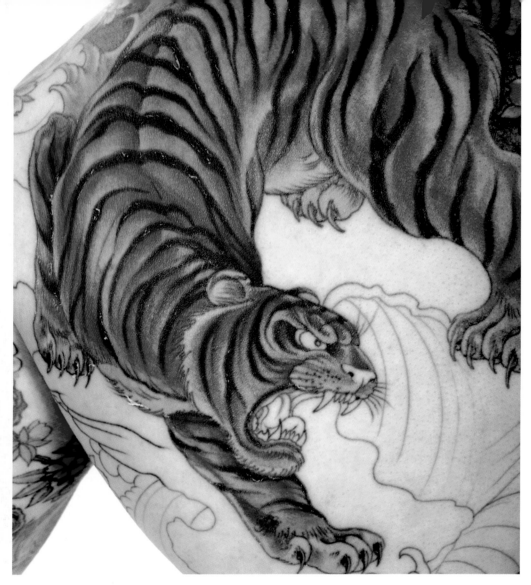

> "The human body is always treated as an image of society."
>
> —Anthropologist Mary Douglas

▲ Modern tattooing shows a synthesis of disparate cultural styles. Here a tiger is inked in the sinuous Japanese manner.

Subject: Tommy Shaun / Artist: Greg James, Sunset Strip Tattoo

▶ This person opted for a medieval-style crest, reminiscent of old European shields.

Subject: Johnny Directions

▶▶ This tattooist has created a unique image with a sensibility all its own.

Subject: Josh / Artist: Chop Chop Shop Tattoos

waiting to be colored with the tattooist's whims. The electric needle also led to the reemergence of tattooing as an art form, particularly in the United States, where in keeping with the nation's heterogeneous character, multiple tattoo cultures began to hybridize into wide-ranging styles. Crests and crosses of European heritage merged with tribal abstractions, Polynesian patterns, and the undulating animal forms of China and Japan. Fused by the fine-art ambitions of a handful of prominent twentieth-century tattooists, these disparate strands emerge today on people's bodies as elaborate, tattooed manifestos, ornate indications of heritage, or simply flashes of beauty and whimsy enlivening the skin.

Outcast or Mainstream?

Today tattooing is more popular in Western culture than it has been for perhaps a millennium. Participation and acceptance of tattooing has spread across class and gender boundaries. Once considered the domain of certain subcultures—sailors and soldiers with anchors and "Mother" scrawled across their arms, criminals etched with crude jailhouse tattoos, or carnival "freaks" decorated head to toe with impenetrable designs—tattoos decorate a substantial portion of society today. Some call it a resurgence of tribal culture; others call

it a fad. Some see the popularization of tattooing as a cooption of working-class habits by the middle class; others see it as a surging new arena for fine art. Some see it as indicative of the undimmed human desire for exotica amid a bleak existence; others see it as a gesture of commitment and self-expression. Of course, some still feel it is purely the domain of misfits. Yet, regardless of theories, the reasons and inspirations for tattoos are deeply personal: everyone has a unique reason for tattooing his or her body. No longer the requirement of a ritual culture or the stigma of a parochial society, tattooing is more than ever before a choice, though not one to be taken lightly. When the needle pierces the skin, the whims of an artist and his or her subject become permanently embedded in the body. This book explores the nature of that experience through the photographs and recollections of myriad decorated individuals who continue to propagate one of the oldest and most controversial modes of human artistic expression.

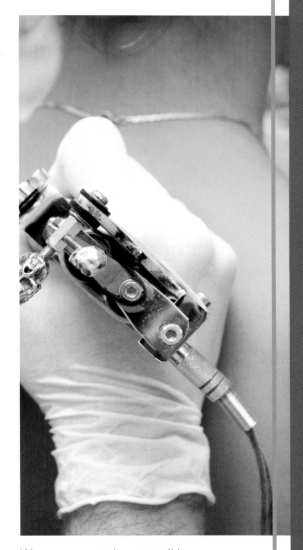

"For someone who likes tattoos, the most precious thing is bare skin."

—Cher

Women are greatly responsible for the current resurgence of tattooing. They are decorating their bodies more today than at any time in recent history. The rise of tattooed women has coincided with a rise in female tattoo artists.

Photograph by Dima Kalinin / Shutterstock

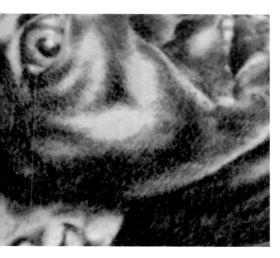

◀ The bearer of this sinister tableau gave his tattooist free rein to create a horrifying image.
Subject: Steve Bregenzer / Artist: Brian Donovan, Mercury Tattoo

▽ There's a method to this madness—this full-back tattoo recounts its wearer's life story.
Subject: Jason Bergmann / Artist: Jonathan Linton

Tattoos have always been emblems of fantasy. Centuries ago the tattooist and the tattooed were fantastic individuals dwelling in an exotic world at the far edge of the oceans. Today the tattooist is an entrepreneur and an artist who works with his or her clients to conceive bizarre worlds and give them life under shallow skin. Some people request malevolent totems to convey their comfort with the underside of life—skulls, ghouls, dragons, avenging angels. Others submit their skin to the sinister imagination of the tattooist; on the planes of their body entire worlds of macabre frenzy emerge, as grim and intricate as Bosch or Brueghel landscapes. Tattooing is a painful process; these tattoos give form to that pain. The bodies here are canvases haunted with shadows and monsters. Born from the brains of the artist and the client, dark fantasies come alive on the skin.

DARK FANTASIES

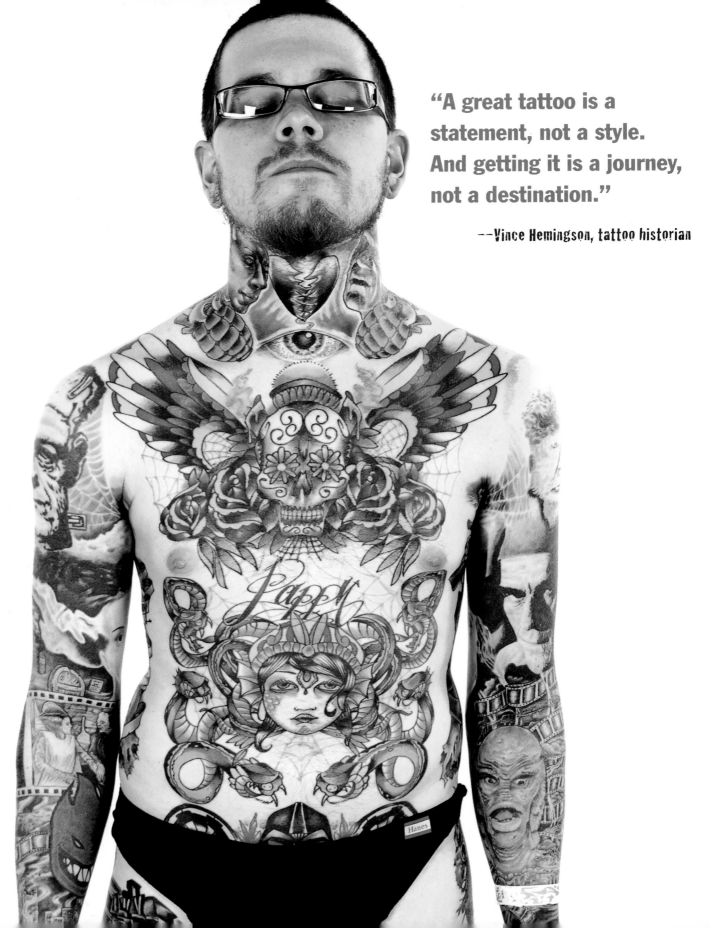

"A great tattoo is a statement, not a style. And getting it is a journey, not a destination."

--Vince Hemingson, tattoo historian

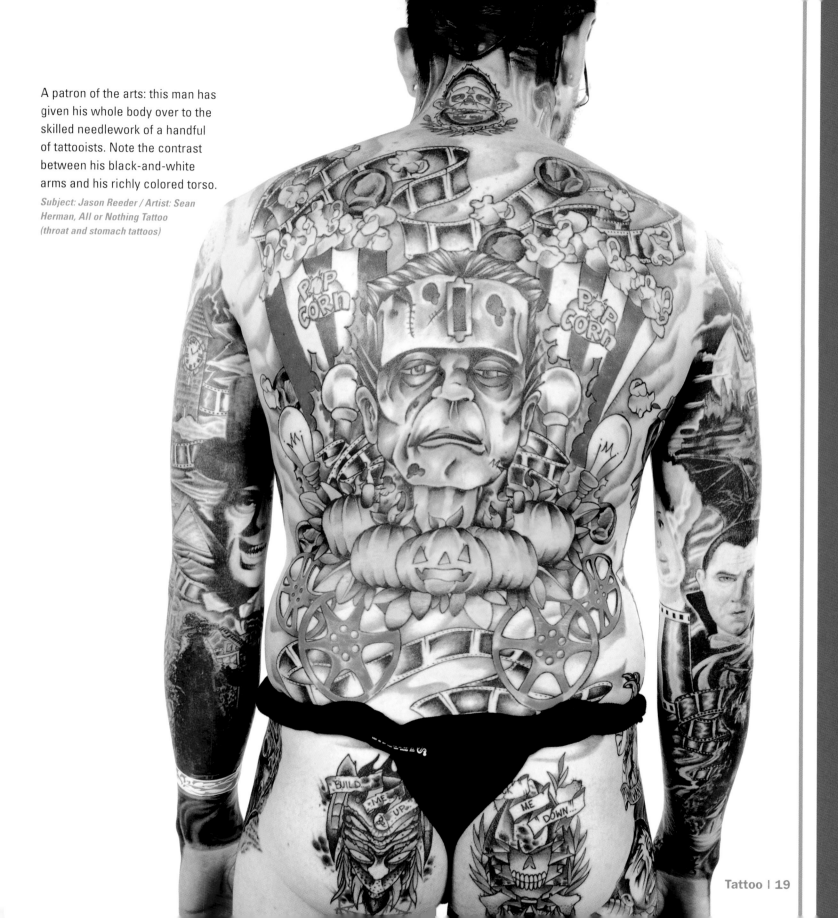

A patron of the arts: this man has given his whole body over to the skilled needlework of a handful of tattooists. Note the contrast between his black-and-white arms and his richly colored torso.

Subject: Jason Reeder / Artist: Sean Herman, All or Nothing Tattoo (throat and stomach tattoos)

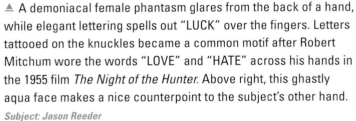

▲ A demoniacal female phantasm glares from the back of a hand, while elegant lettering spells out "LUCK" over the fingers. Letters tattooed on the knuckles became a common motif after Robert Mitchum wore the words "LOVE" and "HATE" across his hands in the 1955 film *The Night of the Hunter.* Above right, this ghastly aqua face makes a nice counterpoint to the subject's other hand.

Subject: Jason Reeder

▷ Among this man's myriad tattoos, some may be inspired by the artists' whims, while others may carry a personal meaning. Each image harmonizes with not only the curves of this man's body but also with the borders of each adjacent image.

Subject: Jason Reeder

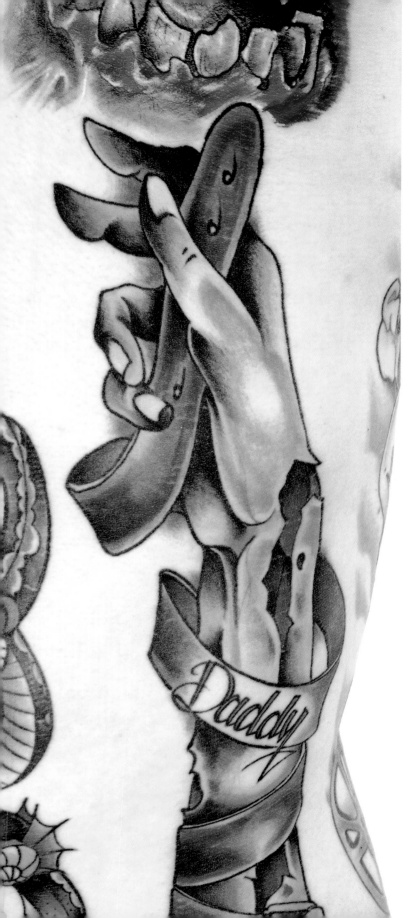

◄ A ghastly green severed arm wrapped in a belt slides upward on the rib cage, dangerously close to a tooth-filled maw.
Subject: Jason Reeder / Artist: Thomas Kenney, Classic Electric Tattoo

▽ A red-eyed demon stares out from underneath the subject's arm.
Subject: Jason Reeder / Artist: Thomas Kenney, Classic Electric Tattoo

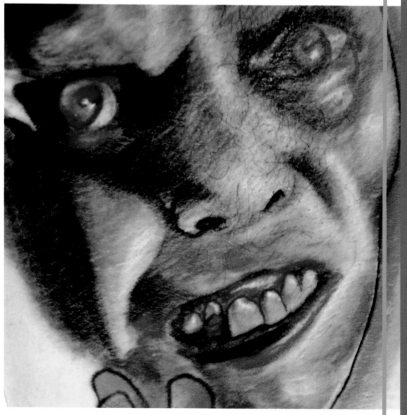

◀ This woman color-coordinated her ensemble to match the brilliant hues of her tattoos.
Subject: Tania

▼ Symbols of life, roses, mingle with imagery of death, a skull, in this boldly drawn tattoo.
Subject: Tania

▶ Not your ordinary Kabuki face—this one, dripping with blood, has met a gory fate.
Subject: Tania

▼ Beauty and the beast combined in one grim visage. It is a ghoulish turn on Picasso's trick of combining a profile and a whole face.
Subject: Tania

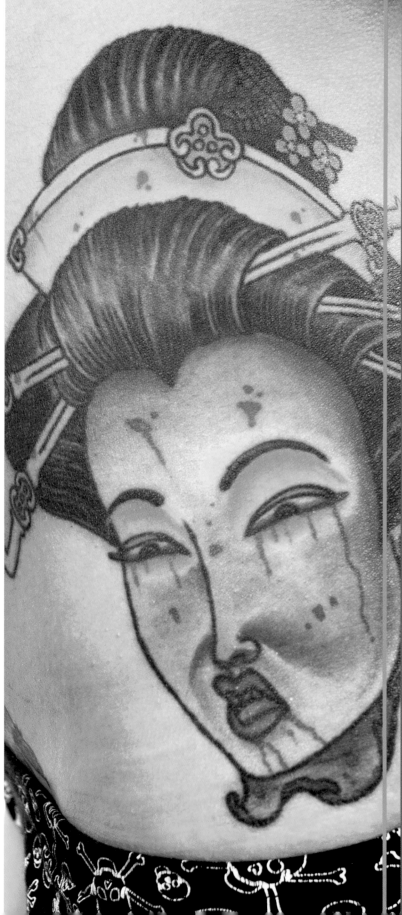

Whether leering, snarling, or pointing tongues, demon faces are meant to elicit fear, but they also give tattoo artists opportunities to create images of ominous beauty. Demons have been a popular subject of artists for centuries. In the Middle Ages they were used in the allegorical paintings of Hieronymus Bosch and Pieter Brueghel the Younger and even adorned churches in the form of hideous gargoyles. In modern times demons populate horror films and dark-themed comic books. Demon faces will likely remain a staple of tattoo culture, a blend of grinning evil and amazing ink.

▶ The skin of this sinister face has been flayed down to the muscle—note the intricately drawn sinews.

Subject: Tommy Visconto / Brian Donovan, Mercury Tattoo

▶▶ A ghoulishly green demon skull. The skull is a universal symbol for death.

Subject: Casper / Artist: Adam Bruce

▶▶▶ Opposite page left, a red face, flaming hair, piercing stare, little beard—Satan, in the flesh! Center, in myth, long noses and pointed chins often carry sinister connotations—as does, of course, a mouthful of sharp teeth.

Subject: Stephen Lyte

▶▶▶▶ A bestial, feral, yet almost human creature illustrates the subject's sense of "the evil inside of me."

Subject: Alid Marquez / Artist: Alex Alien, Aztec Roots Tattoo

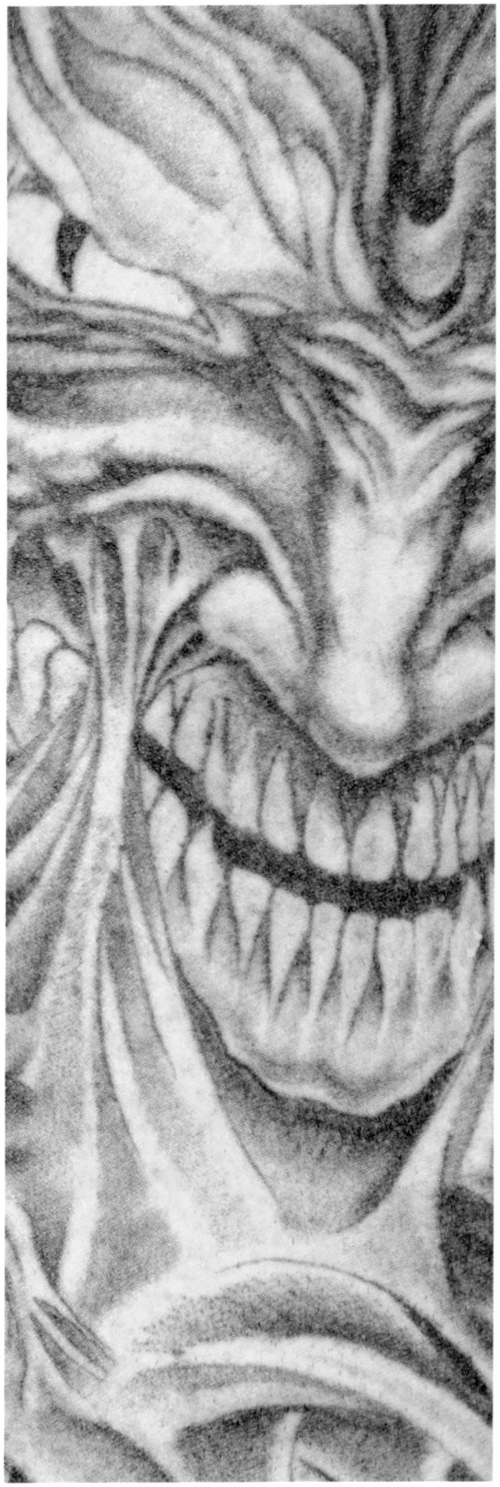

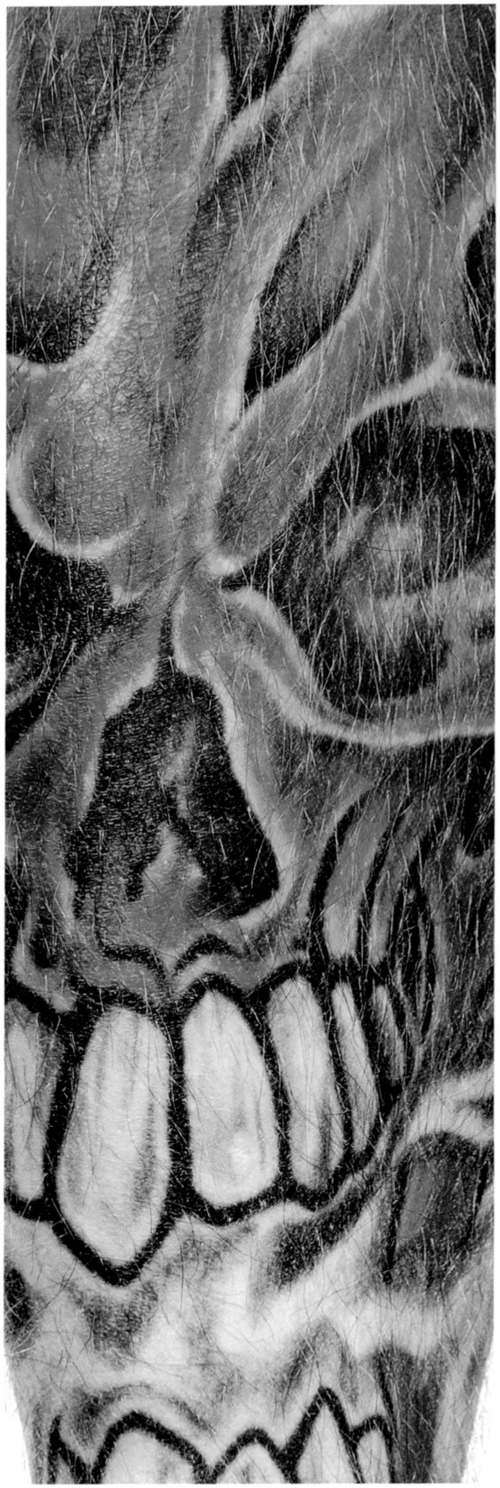

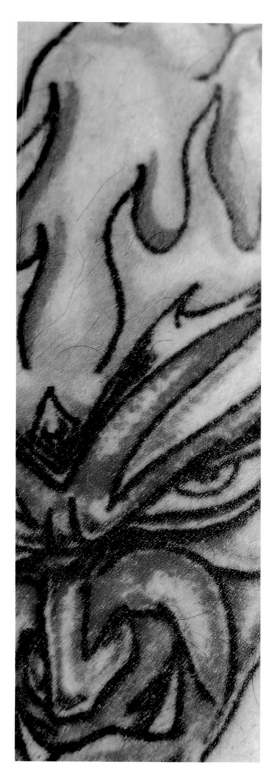

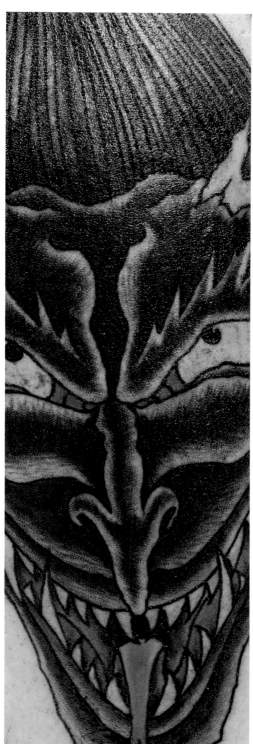

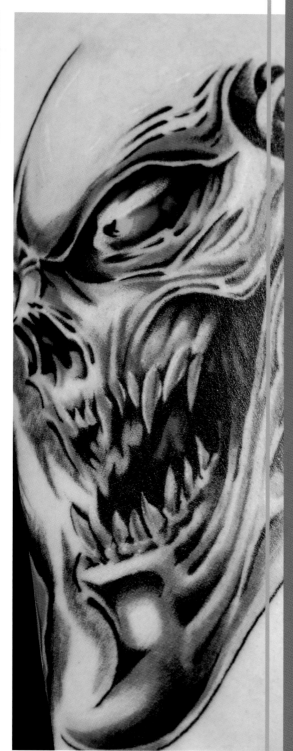

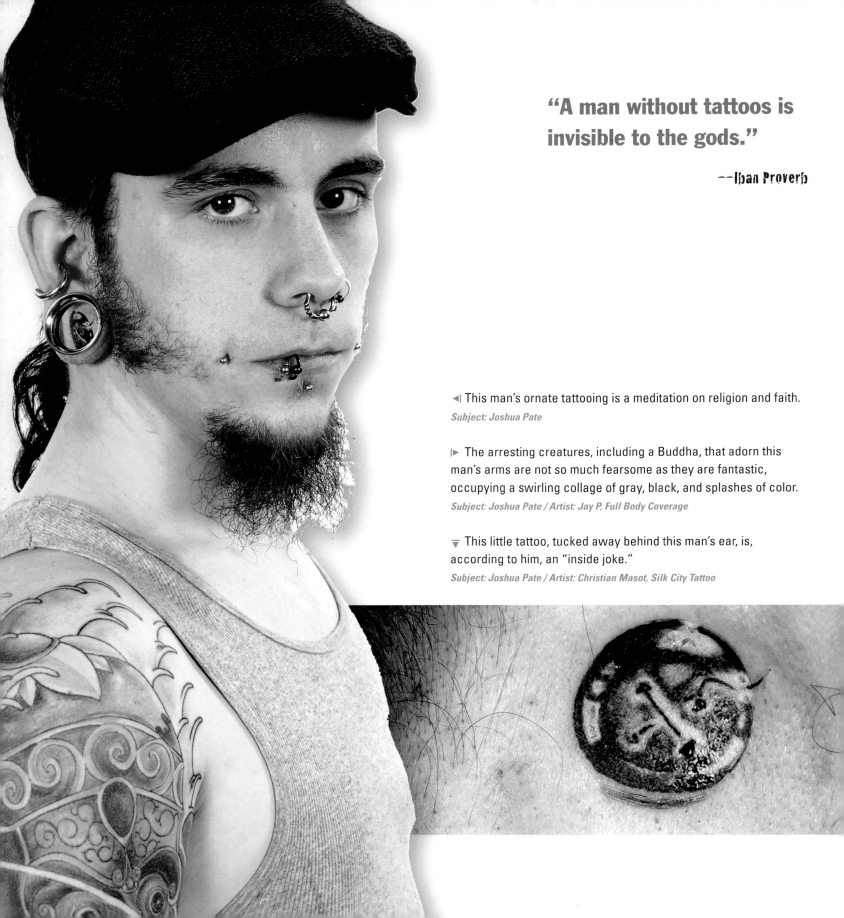

"A man without tattoos is invisible to the gods."

—Iban Proverb

◄ This man's ornate tattooing is a meditation on religion and faith.
Subject: Joshua Pate

▶ The arresting creatures, including a Buddha, that adorn this man's arms are not so much fearsome as they are fantastic, occupying a swirling collage of gray, black, and splashes of color.
Subject: Joshua Pate / Artist: Jay P, Full Body Coverage

▼ This little tattoo, tucked away behind this man's ear, is, according to him, an "inside joke."
Subject: Joshua Pate / Artist: Christian Masot, Silk City Tattoo

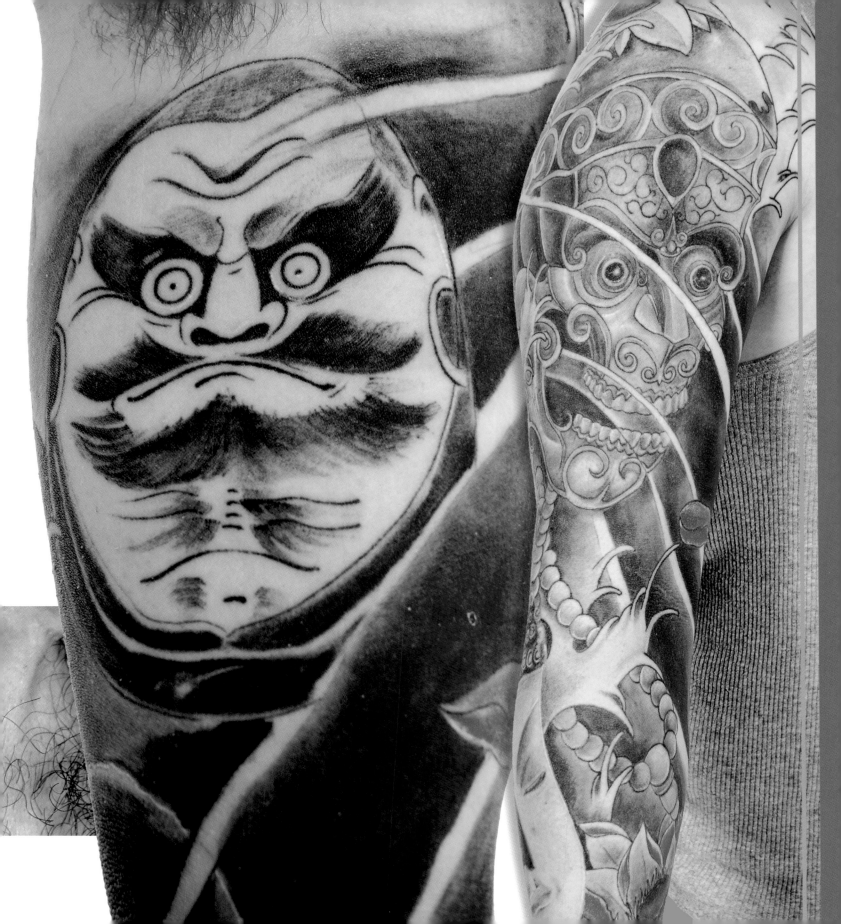

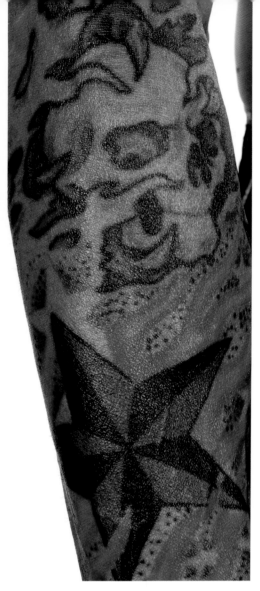

▲ A tortured Jesus is captured in all of his agony on this man's upper chest.

Subject: Noel Roman Velez

▲ Rosary beads amid tendrils of flame pattern this man's chest.

Subject: Noel Roman Velez

▲ Abstract shapes contrast colorfully with a sharply rendered five-pointed star.

Subject: Noel Roman Velez

▶ An array of styles—cartoonish, surreal, realistic, abstract—decorate this man's skin, but the overall mood is macabre.

Subject: Noel Roman Velez

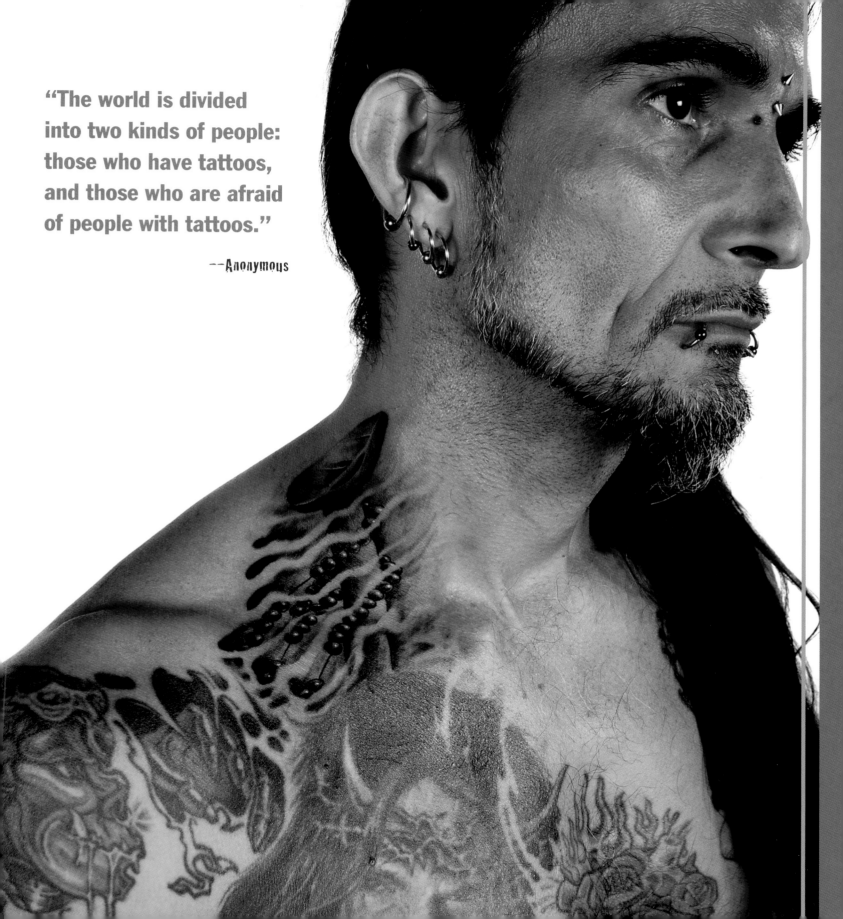

"The world is divided into two kinds of people: those who have tattoos, and those who are afraid of people with tattoos."

—Anonymous

▲ Lost among the gallery of ghouls? Former Unites States president George W. Bush is flanked by question marks.
Subject: SHORT / Artist: Bob Tyrrell

▶ A tearfully tragic beauty hovers, bleeding, above a bandaged skull.
Subject: SHORT / Artist: J. Ranno

◀◀ This man opted for simplicity in the creation of some of his tattoos.
Subject: SHORT

◀ This rendering of the infamous vampire Nosferatu, is figuratively precise. Nosferatu hides beneath a colorful and chaotic right arm.
Subject: SHORT / Artist: Dave Tedder

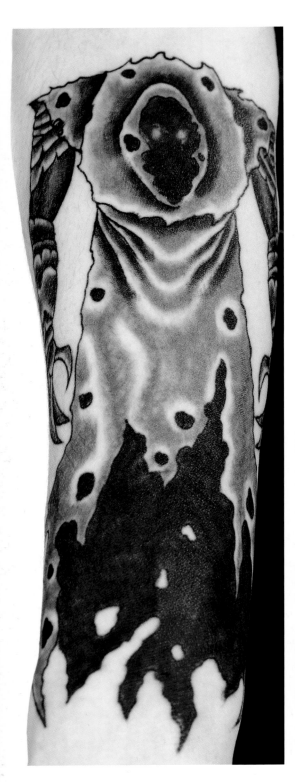

◀ Purple, black, and a little bit of green were all the colors needed to make this ghoulish specter, which hovers, tattered, over the subject's forearm. This hulking, faceless apparition appears riddled with bullet holes. Those undead guys just refuse to die!

Subject: Derek Vile / Artist: Ozzie Perez

▶ The Rocket from the Crypt . . . fresh from underground, this combo Bride of Frankenstein / sexy mummy glows with electric energy and seems ready to leap from her skull-adorned coffin.

Subject: Tim Fisher / Artist: Smitty

▼ A richly colored and rendered golden tiger pays homage to Japanese tattooing. It rises menacingly from searing waves of crimson and violet.

Subject: Cal / Artist: Brian Donovan, Mercury Tattoo

◄ The fearsome "Lord of the Dead" finds himself inked on the subject's right foot.
Subject: Jim / Artist: Paul Acker

▷ "The horror! The horror!" This man's body is a gallery of gore, some of it inspired by the movies, some of it totally original.
Subject: Jim

▽ Mixed messages: evil Darth Vader from *Star Wars* looks over at a banner-entwined heart that reads "Hopeless Romantic."
Subject: Jim / Artist: Paul Acker

◀ Much of the subject's back is devoted to Leatherface, the chainsaw-wielding maniac of *The Texas Chainsaw Massacre*. Note the chainsaw-chain border.

Subject: Jim / Artist: Paul Acker

▶ Nightmares and dreamscapes. From a diabolical clown face to a demon baby, the detail of this man's tattoos is extraordinary.

Subject: Jim

"You may lose your most valuable property through misfortune in various ways. You may lose your house, your wife and other treasures. But of your *moko*, you cannot be deprived except by death. It will be your ornament and companion until your last day."

-- Netana Whakaari of Waimana tattoo

This man sports a veritable shirt of tattoos, each one blending into the text to form an intricate, colorful mosaic of fantastically sinister body art. At left, a golden, grinning skull occupies the center of the man's well-decorated torso.

Subject: Vincent Gallo / Artist: Mike LeBoffe, Baker Street Tattoo

Scenes of mayhem and mortality swirl across this man's skin. Both his left and right arms bear colorful designs of chaotic skulls, while at the far right, his entire back tells an exotic story of destruction in rich black and white. Perhaps, in time, it too will be colored in.

Subject: Vincent Gallo / Artist: Mike LeBoffe, Baker Street Tattoo

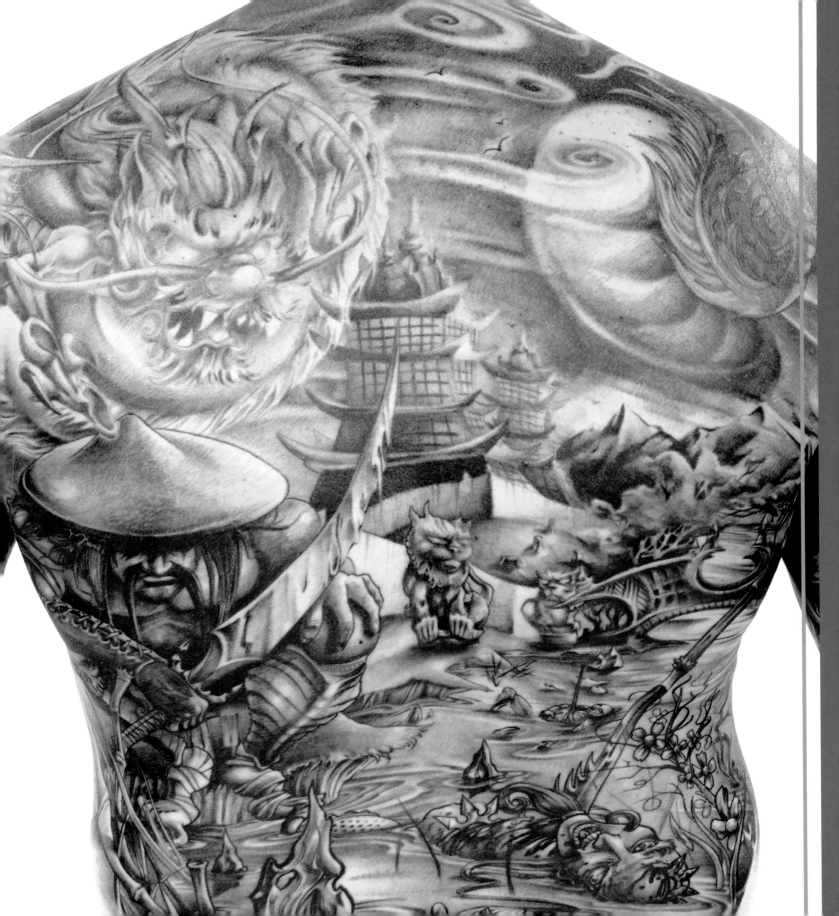

◄ A classic skull image with a yellow-eyed rat atop was lifted from the subject's own drawings.
Subject: Josh N. Brader / Artist: Juan (Spare)

▶ Another vintage tattoo motif—skulls and roses— takes on a new dimension. Is that the skull's eyes or something a bit more amorous?
Subject: Angela Bibey / Artist: Ink Bitch

▶▶ A checkerboard sleeve ends in a grim skull visage.
Subject: Chuck

▼ Fierce in its framing, this militant skull glares out menacingly from a shield-like background.
Subject: Stephen Lyte

"I'm a tattoo artist myself, and these tattoos on my body were my personal drawings. My art inspires me, and now it's on my body forever."

—Josh N. Brader

"There's more to the skull
than meets the eye."

—Angela Bibey

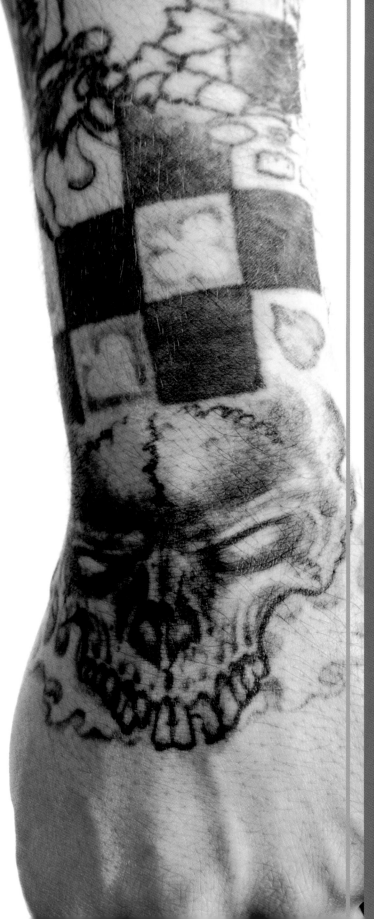

Here is a great body of work, all of it done by one artist. A fantastical array of creatures, from tigers and leopards to serpents and spiders weave from head to toe. A samurai vanquishing a tiger forms the centerpiece of this man's full-body coverage. Often, tattooists form long-standing relationships with their customers, adding a new piece to the living canvas year after year.

Subject: Catman / Artist: James Vond, Straight A Tattoo

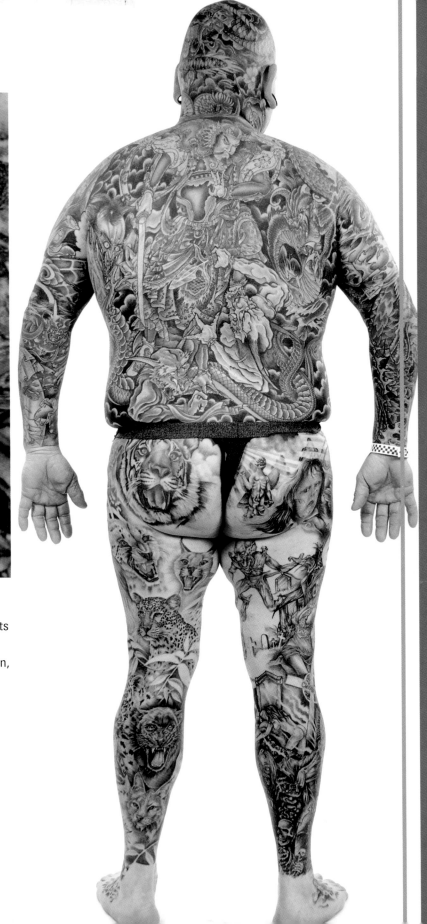

"Tattoos aren't meant for every-body and they're too goddamn good for some people."

--Lyle Tuttle, tattoo artist, author, and lecturer

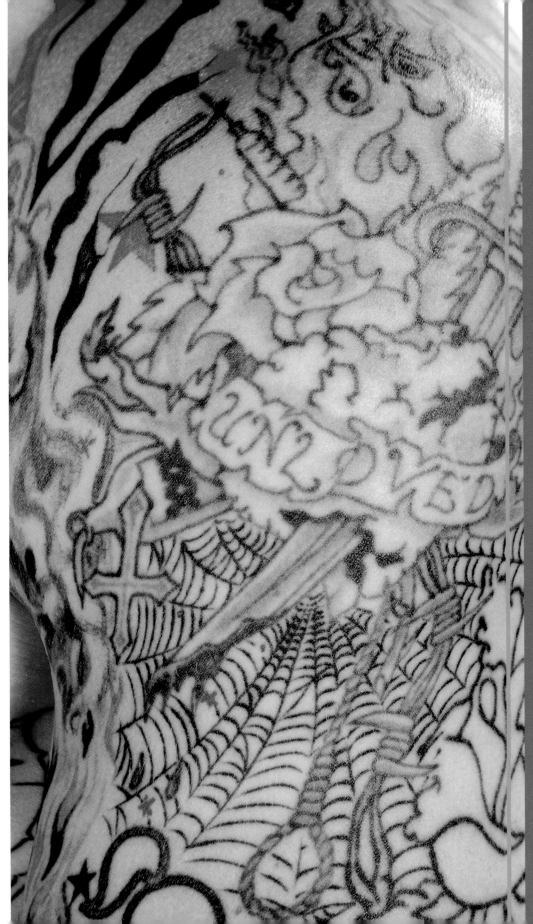

A stark palette of red and black explodes into intricate scenery on this man's arms and torso. Woven into the dense pattern are radiating cobwebs, a swirling dragon, and cascading stars.

Subject: Chuck / Artist: Whatever Tattoo

◄ The back makes a large, flat, unbroken canvas, well suited to ambitious tattoos.
Subject: Jen

▷ "Life's struggle and the appearance of evil" inspired this hanya mask tattoo. Kabuki theater uses hanya masks to represent a woman so consumed with jealousy that she transforms into a hideous demon.
Subject: Chris / Artist: Troy Timpel, Philadelphia Eddie's

◄ Colors give a tattoo depth and set its mood. At left, reds and yellows alternate with gray and a sudden splash of cornflower blue.

Subject: Lenny Breaks / Artist: Kevin LeBlanc, White Lotus Tattoo

▷ At right, the ghoul's sienna eyes illuminate this stormy pattern of murky grays and black.

Subject: Lisa Zelenak / Artist: Khaoz

▷▷ At far right, this dragon is highlighted by well-handled washes of fluorescence.

Subject: Anthony Colonnello

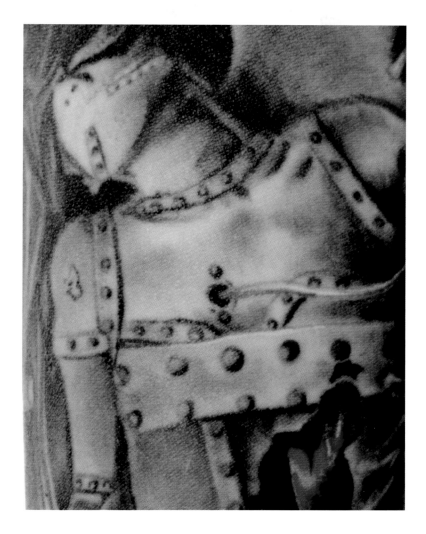

▲ Visions of the scary and the surreal: the steel encased, riveted torso in this dramatic tattoo is cut away to reveal an organic heart.

Subject: Stephanie Campbell / Artist: Joe John's

◂ On this subject's left arm, an android's pretty face is cut open; lifelike skin no longer covers the internal matrix of guts and gears.

Subject: Robbo / Artist: Steve Monie, Pinz & Needlez

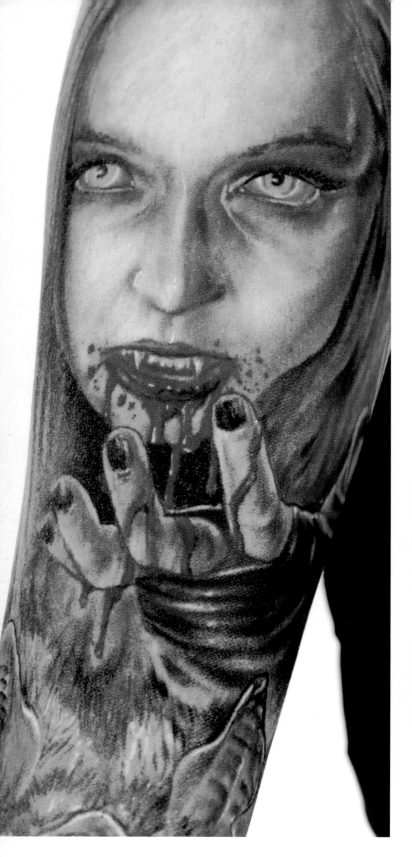

"I love horror. I love my dog."

--Kristin Maszkiewicz

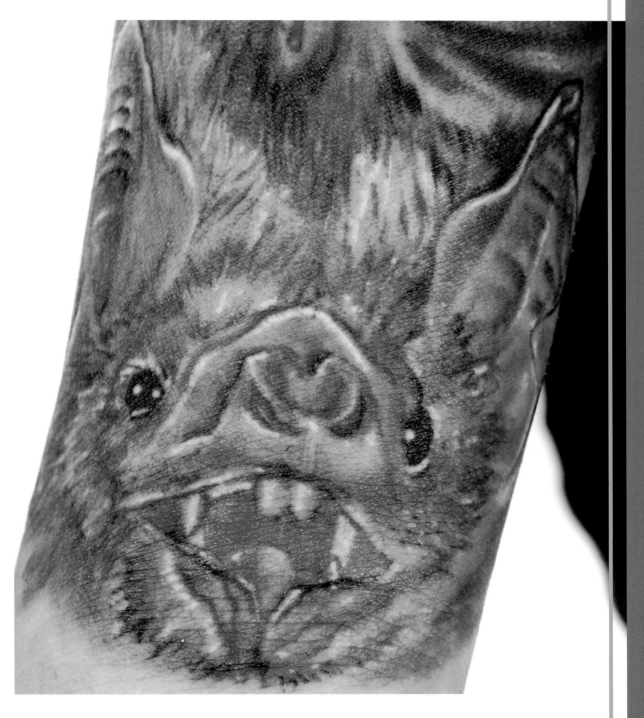

◀◀ A blue-eyed, bloodthirsty female vampire looms above a tattoo of a source of the legend, the vampire bat.
Subject: Kristin Maszkiewicz / Artist: Paul Acker

◀ A skillful rendering of the subject's dog, Pee Wee Martini, a Chinese crested, shows the lolling tongue typical of the breed. Chinese cresteds often win "ugliest dog" contests, but their owners find them charming.
Subject: Kristin Maszkiewicz / Artist: Shane O'Neill

▶ A close-up of a vampire bat, showing the razor-sharp teeth. Although fierce looking, these flying mammals feed mainly on dozing cattle, not human prey.
Subject: Kristin Maszkiewicz / Artist: Paul Acker

◄ This man's love for the movie *The Nightmare Before Christmas* compelled him to permanently decorate his skin with the film's distinctive characters.
Subject: Matt Mauro / Cort Bengtson, Corts Royal Ink

▽ This woman inked a gentle, light-hearted reminder to herself and others to try to relax a little amid the "hardships of life."
Subject: Big Johnson / Artist: Meghan Patrick

Today a tattoo is no longer a ritual mark. It is a form of self-expression, and when it comes to expressing themselves, some people just want to have fun. For a nominal fee you can walk into the tattoo parlor, endure an hour or so of creative needlework, and emerge wearing the characters from your favorite movie, rock gods or real gods, pithy quotes or words of wisdom. These bodies are collages of diverse enthusiasms; these tattoos map people's passions in washes of color and delicate hatching and affix their mottoes permanently, never to be forgotten. Tattoos are commitments—these tattoos show people's faith in their inspirations and reveal them as conduits of creativity—the art that moved them is reproduced on their skin so that it may move others to think, or even to laugh.

LIGHTER LOOKS

◀ Flash from the past. Tattoo trendsetter Sailor Jerry never imagined this forearm would be the site of one of his nubile nymphs, but this is classic Jerry—from the knowing look in the lively eyes to the signature all-caps warning below.

Subject: Christina Ginger

▲ Another vintage look, this time with a macabre twist. A delicate fan forms the backdrop for a floral frame of violets and a rose that surround a pair of skulls. The skulls' gazes draw the eye to the tarantula in the center.

Subject: Christina Ginger / Artist: Sara Purr

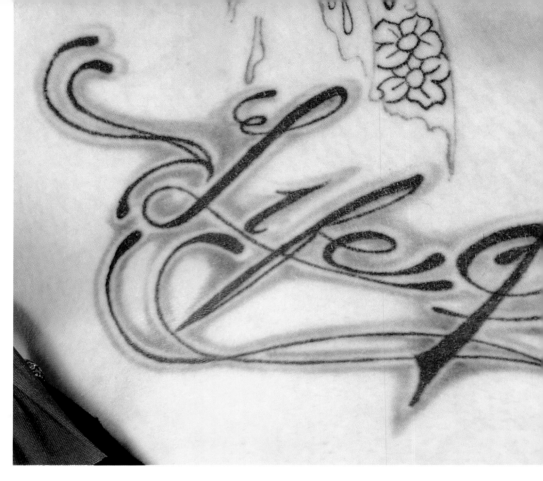

"I got 'Life Is Beautiful' written across my chest as my first tattoo when I was eighteen—it was kind of like motivation for me after I got out of the hospital. I deal with depression and drug issues in my life, and it just helps to remind me that there is beauty in this world worth living to see."

--Shannaan

▲ This life-affirming message has motivated its wearer to deal with the difficulties of her life, and to see past them to the underlying beauty in this world.

Subject: Shannaan / Ian Greenings, Artistic Integrity

▶ A glorious mess. This woman wears the cluttered paraphernalia of modern life.

Subject: Jessica Dibala / Adam Pietras

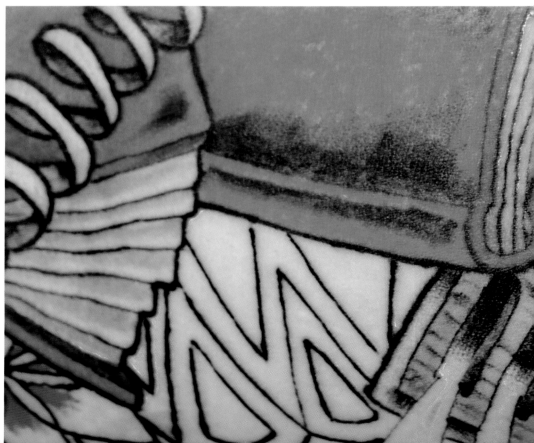

◀ A jolt of lightning and the turn of a skull-inscribed skeleton key, and this monster of a heart comes to life in full color.
Subject: Antietam

▼ Another, more sober, more figurative take on the trials of the heart. Each tattoo reveals the perspective of its wearer.
Subject: Bunny

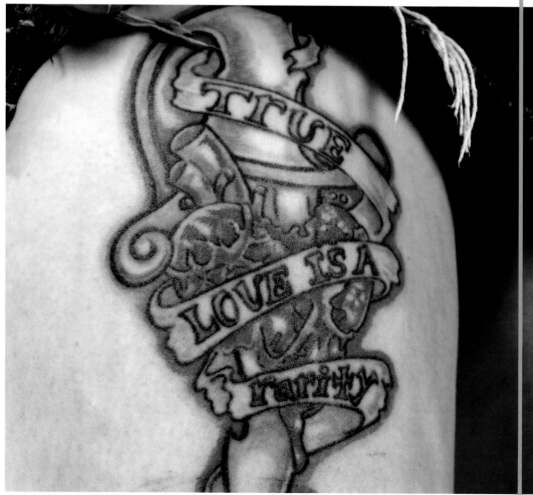

"A tattoo is a true poetic creation, and is always more than meets the eye. As a tattoo is grounded on living skin, so its essence emotes a poignancy unique to the mortal human condition."

--V. Vale and Andrea Juno, *Modern Primitives*

This man's chest is alive with classic tattoo symbolism. Scythes frame a skull clock that sits amid cobweb-backed wings and roses.

Subject: Raymond Baranowski

Although the art of tattoo is most often associated, and rightly so, with intricate and beautifully rendered images, words are increasingly moving to center stage—or center skin. It's certainly not new to include words and lettering in tattoo designs; for example, subjects have long chosen to pay homage to mothers, lovers, military units, and hometowns by naming them by name. These days, though, the words themselves are often the entire tattoo, written clearly for all the world to see. Simple affirmations such as "Just Go For It" or "Life Is Beautiful" and proud proclamations such as "Drug-free" draped across chests or snaking around waists and legs, show that ink truly forms the message.

This woman doesn't limit her manifesto—a belief that love is worth the work—to one part of her body. The words "If love is a labor, I'll slave till the end" circle her hips like a belt.

Subject: Lacey Villareal / Artist: Chris Lowe, Naked Art Tattoos

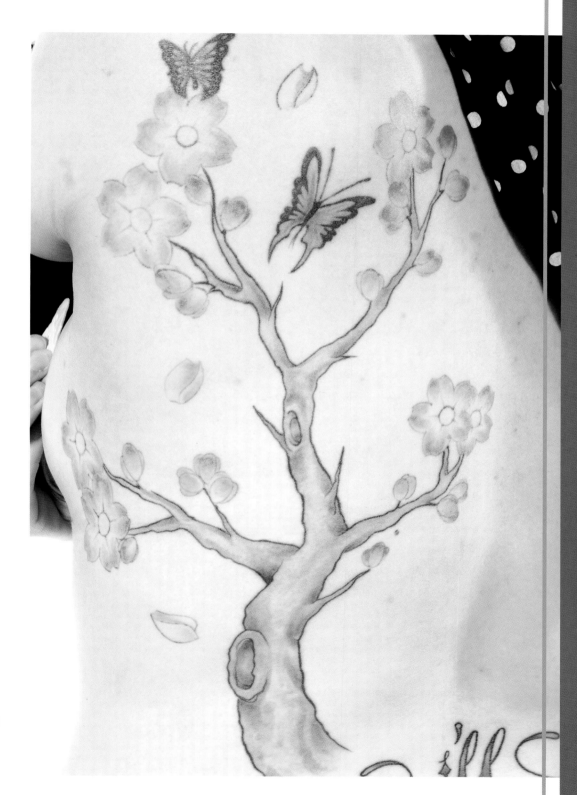

◄ Colorful, cartoonish, and well-rendered imagery decorates much of this woman's body. A self-affirming ode to the band Hole decorate one leg, far left. And echoing the rich palette of the opposite leg, a beatific Buddha smiles serenely while clasping Roman Catholic rosary beads.

Subject: Lacey Villareal / Artist: Chris Lowe, Naked Art Tattoos

▷ An homage to spring: graceful butterflies and delicate cherry blossoms.

Subject: Lacey Villareal / Artist: Orlando, Creative Visions

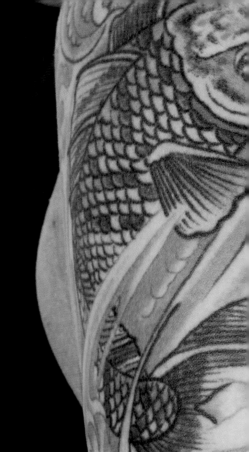
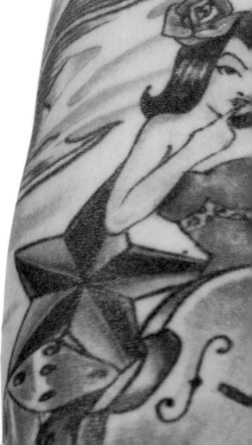

Though modern tattoos run the gamut from fun to funky to downright fierce, for centuries these old standbys topped the charts—hearts, often featuring the name of a loved one; nautical tattoos, including anchors, mermaids, and sailing ships; and flowers, especially red roses, which symbolize true love. More recently there were the ever-popular "souvenir" tattoos—hula dancers from Hawaii, tumbling dice from Vegas, and palm trees and exotic birds from the tropics. Cheesecake tattoos, such as pin-up girls and saucy nudes, were also a key part of the ink tradition. Not surprisingly, many of these vintage tattoos have been making a comeback. Sometimes you just can't beat a classic.

This woman and her tattooist have collaborated a number of times to create a pastiche of colorful scenery, ranging from a new take on the trusty old anchor motif to wildlife imagery to a pretty jazz musician amid skulls and stars.

Subject: Linh Le

▲ This couple shows two different approaches to tattooing—he decorates himself with sprawling dense-coverage scenes, while she favors isolated images, such as a finely drafted chrysanthemum.

Subjects: Rebecca Kolodziejczak and Nick Less

◀ This man wears dragons on both his chest and his back, but the styles diverge—one is in lush color and the other in stark black.

Subject: Nick Less / Artist: Troy Timpel

"Everybody gets the tattoo they deserve."

--David Duchovny, actor

"Who doesn't love
chicks that scrap?"

--Short

▲ Pure cheesecake flash with a 1940s feel features a card-dealing cutie baring her best from a lucky horseshoe.

Subject: Amanda Doran / Artist: Jim Weiss, Slinging' Ink

◄ Miss "Tuff Love" looks like she's ready to take on all the bad boys—and keep smilin' while she kicks some butt.

Nicholas S. Grandinetti "Short" / Artist: Christian Masot, Silk City Tattoos

◄◄ This sexy portrait tattoo of a pouty brunette beauty makes full use of the subject's hand and wrist.

Subject: Aaron Michalovski / Artist: Mike Comp

▶ In typical pin-up girl fashion, this curvy graduate flashes her ample assets and stoops to conquer.

Subject: Pearl Donovan / Artist: Capt. Gordon Staub

This woman commemorates her favorite pop culture figures, including cartoon stars Ren and Stimpy, at top left; fashion doll Barbie, top right; and the characters from the film *Beetlejuice*, at bottom.

Subject: Debbie Monie / Artist: Steve Monie

Note the rich coloring—several hues, ranging from ink black to cotton candy pink, combine to form an arresting portrait of Jerry Springer.

Subject: Debbie Monie / Artist: Aaron

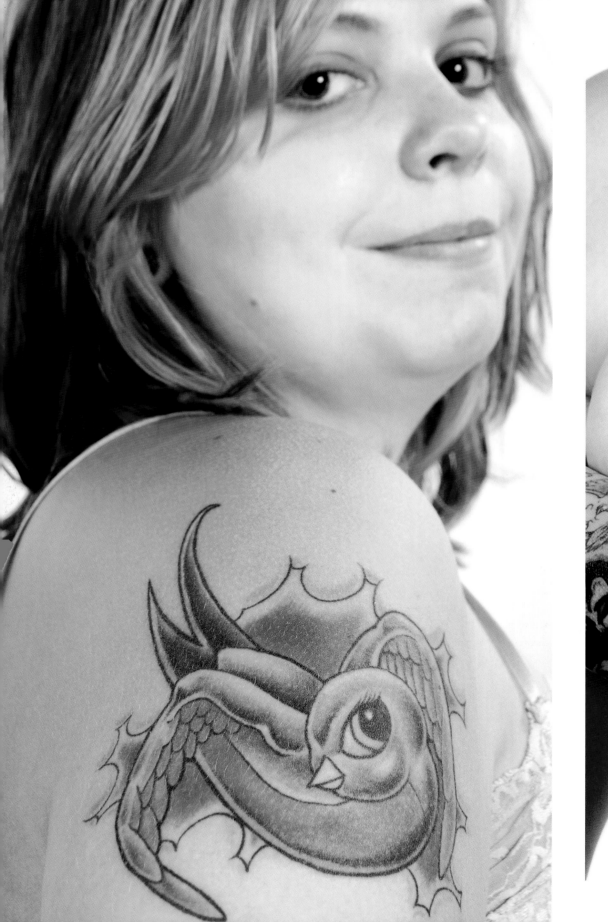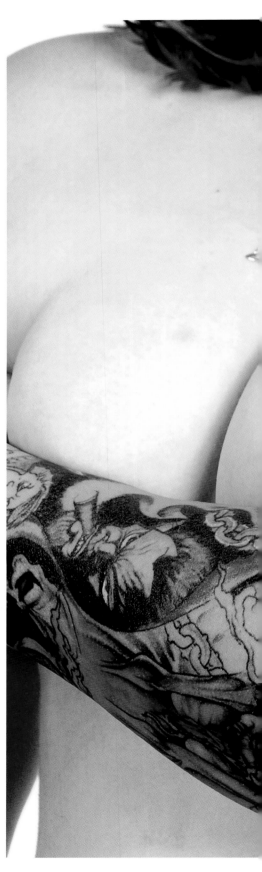

▲ The pretty but surreal occupies one side of this woman's body, while the savage and surreal consumes her other half. Her left arm abruptly changes from a soft blue butterfly to a scene of monstrous terror in black and white with highlights of red and yellow.

Subject: Risa / Artist: Trey, Baltimore St. Tattoos

◄│◄│ The serene multi-hued bird on her right arm seems to merely smirk in response to the chaos wreaking havoc on the other side.

Subject: Risa / Artist: Mr. Jason, Baltimore St. Tattoos

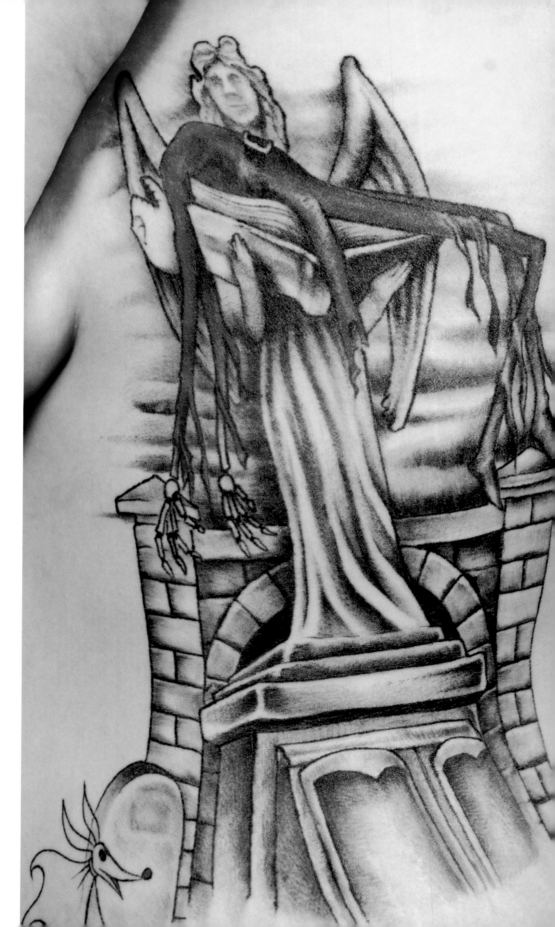

▐► Miniatures of the macabre and the mischievous adorn this woman's body, including a vignette from the film *The Nightmare Before Christmas.*

Subject: Risa / Artist: Mr. Jason, Baltimore St. Tattoos

▐►▐► Opposite, a couple of unique penguins take up residence on her limbs. A fierce crested rockhopper penguin stands framed by a knife and fork, above; while below a seemingly angelic emperor penguin seems to have hit the bottle a bit too hard.

Subject: Risa / Artist: Missi Blue, Baltimore St. Tattoos

▐►▐►▐► Minimalist effects: a simple woebegone stick figure and an elegant monogram trail down her back, while a grinning jack o' lantern hides behind her ear.

Subject: Risa / Artist: Matted Ink

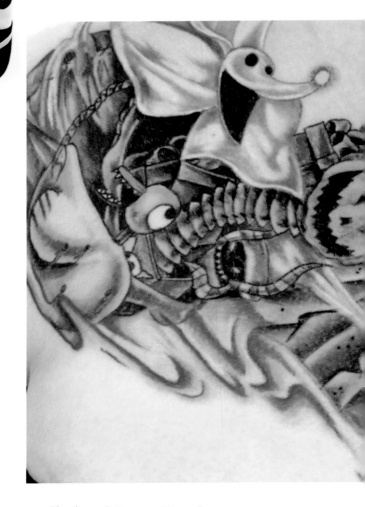

Whether it's Disney, Pixar, Looney Tunes, Hanna-Barbara, or Tim Burton's animation, fanciful cartoon characters have always been popular as tattoos, especially with women and with men who aren't looking for that Goth/biker gang effect. Cartoons allow ink artists to use the brightest of colors and "inject" humor into their tattoos, while allowing the bearer to make a statement that is playful rather than predatory.

◄ Alice, the Mad Hatter, and the Cheshire Cat tumble down the subject's leg in this paean to the Lewis Carroll classics *Alice in Wonderland* and *Through the Looking Glass* as adapted by the Walt Disney animation studio.

Subject: Candice Martell / Artist: Meghan Patrick

▲ The weirdly wonderful characters of Tim Burton's *The Nightmare Before Christmas* flow across this woman's skin, each rendered with fine detail and rich color. Thankfully, copyright protection hasn't stymied body art.

Subject: Candice Martell / Artist: Meghan Patrick

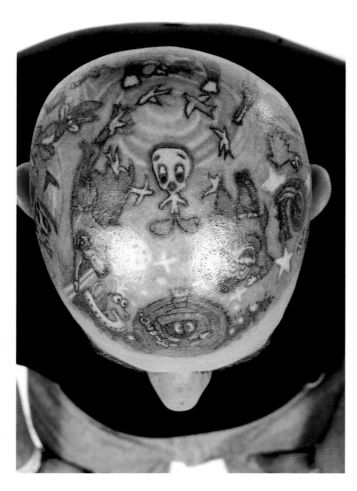

▲ Surrounded by Bugs Bunny, Yosemite Sam, Sylvester, and other cartoon favorites, Tweety Bird takes center stage in one man's full-head homage to Looney Tunes and Merrie Melodies.

Subject: The Boo

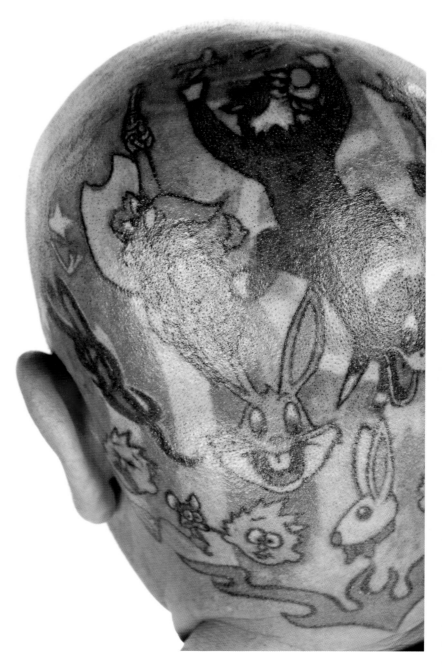

▶ For the truly dedicated, no spot of skin should go undecorated, including the top of the head. This model's dragon tattoo is lush and detailed.

Subject: Catman / Artist: James Vond, Straight A Tattoo

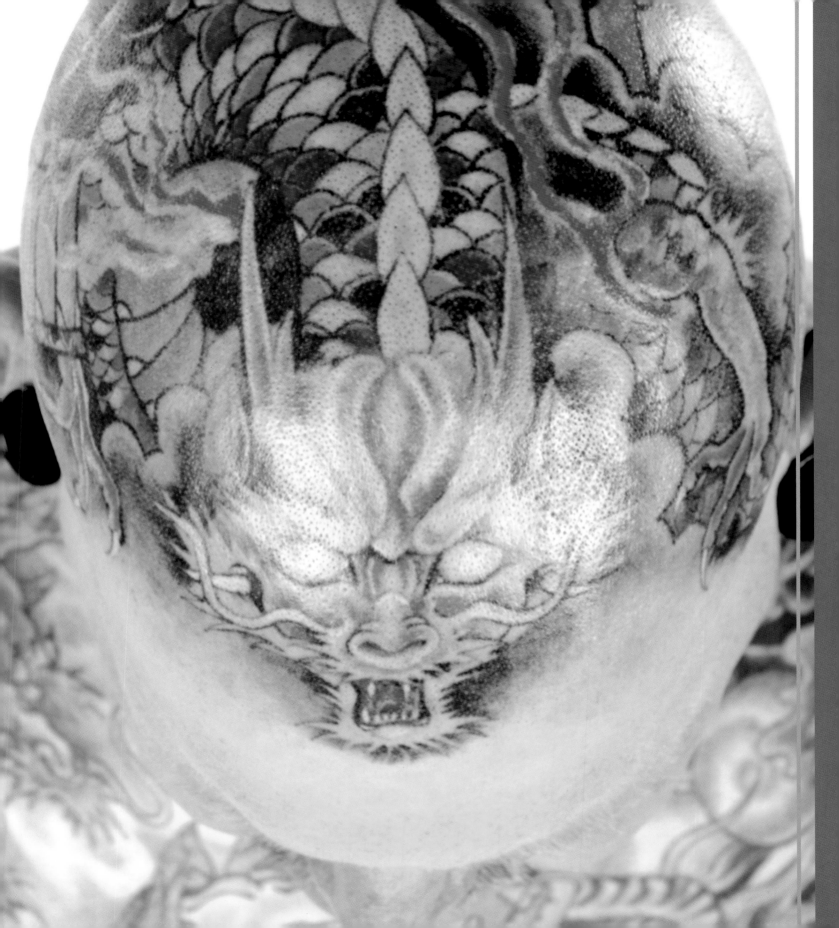

"Be who you are and say what you feel because those who mind don't matter and those who matter don't mind."

--Dr. Seuss

Three of Dr. Suess's most beloved creations parade along the subject's arm: the cherry-red Fox in Socks, a happy Who, and, of course, the Grinch—whose heart was three times too small until he discovered the true meaning of Christmas.

Subject: Brian Doebler / St. Marq, New Breed Tattoo

> "I am not strange, I am just not normal."
>
> --Salvador Dali

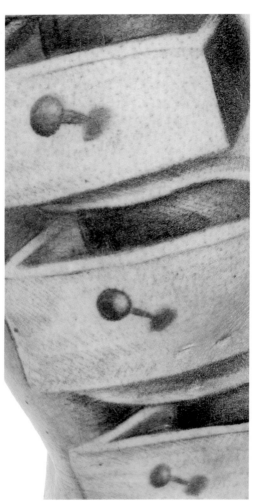

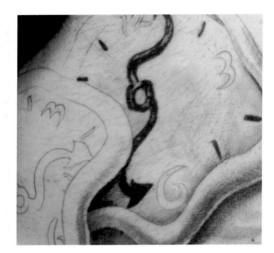

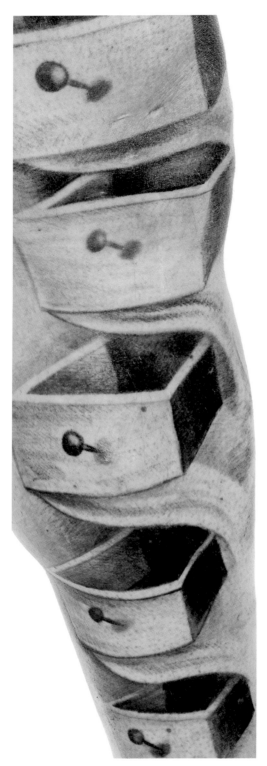

This man pays enthusiastic homage to the master of Surrealism, Salvador Dali, picturing both the artist, opposite page, and his creations, such as a take on the "melting clocks" from his famous 1931 painting *The Persistence of Memory*, above left. Above and right is an ink interpretation of Dali's enigmatic lithograph *Drawers of Memory*.

Subject: Brian Doebler / St. Marq, New Breed Tattoo

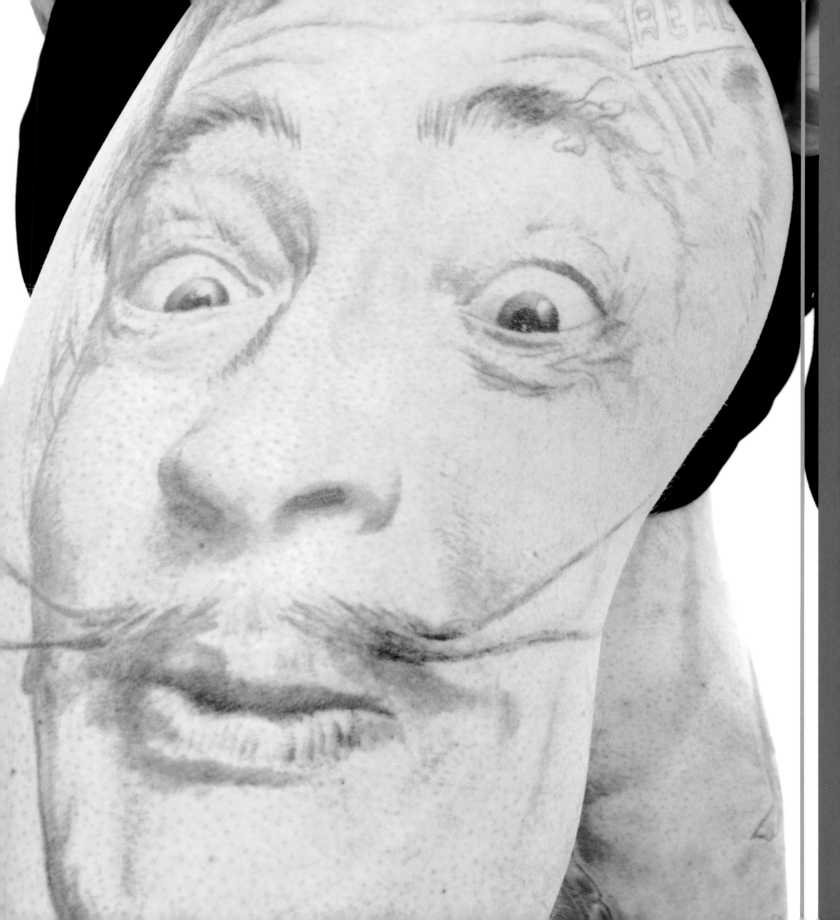

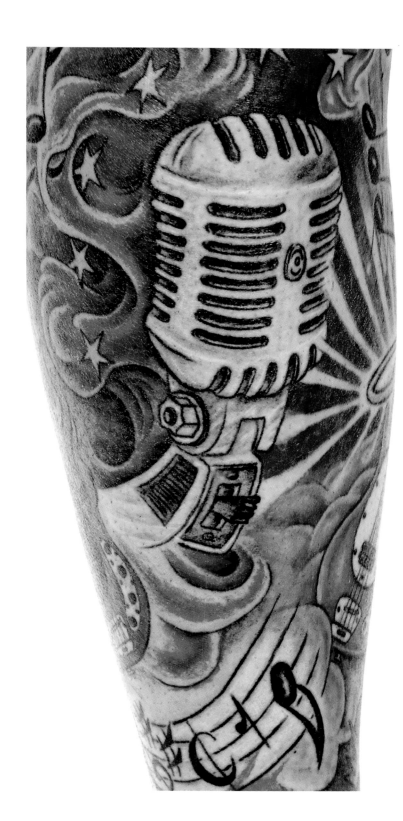

◁ Like an inky explosion of vibrant color, this tattoo homage to pop music—with its oversize microphone, electric guitars, and sheet music—is awash with dazzling, saturated hues.
Subject: Johnny Directions

◁◁ This unique image of an oversized and big-eyed carp taking a ride on an overburdened ox is taken from the tattoo artist's sketchbook. It shows both rich color choices and masterful shading.
Subject: Matthew DesOrmeaux / Artist Jeff Paetzold

◁◁◁ Color . . . astonishing, vivid color . . . is key in all of these lively tattoos. Deep emerald green sails make this square-rigged ship seem to surge upward from the subject's skin.
Subject: Matt Bernard / Artist: Miami, Miami's Tattoos

Aliens are among us! And they're right there on our arms, legs, and torsos. Space creatures became popular tattoo subjects during the 1950s, when science fiction movies were the rage, and have never lost their appeal. Whether it's the gut-busting creature from *Alien*, sweet, googleeyed ET, or Marvin the Martian, these space invaders have won us over. Surrender Earthlings!

▼ ALF, the famous alien life form from TV makes an amusing tattoo. His hairy coat is rendered with a soft pastel effect.

Subject: Alicia "Koala Kid" Collins / Artist: O, Oxygen Tattoos

▼ Another tribute to childhood idols: Transformer autobot Bumblebee stalks this subject's skin in a colorful blaze of shaded yellows and black.

Subject: Johnny Directions

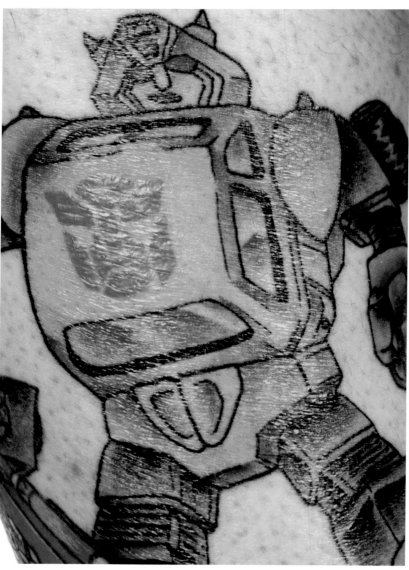

▽ This childlike alien scene features a flying saucer, a panicked human, and several super heroes zooming around in the sky.

Subject: Starr DesOrmeaux

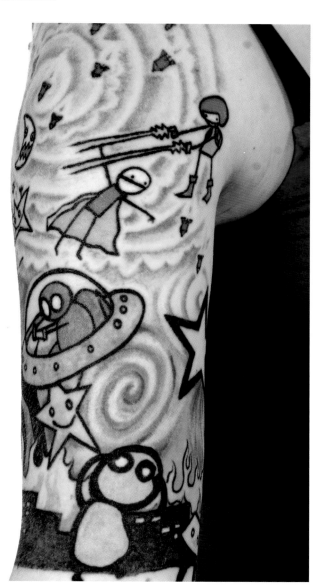

▽ Comical one-eyed spacemen fend off a huge, spewing caterpillar, proving that even aliens need a reliable exterminator.

Subject: Christopher Merker / Artist: Amber, Blue Velvet

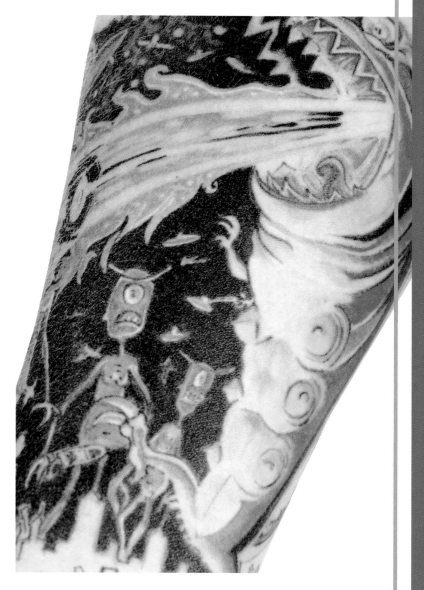

▲ An uncomplicated, but vivid, burst offers simple, but effective advice.

Subject: Rebecca Kolodziejczak

Words and pictures: this woman affirms her identity
and attitude with a series of colorful tattoos.

Subject: Cherry Von Jersey

"I wanted my arms to be so saccharine sweet, you puke when you look at them."

—Antietam

▲ Simple lines form a heart-wearing teddy bear.
Subject: Antietam

◀ A polka-dotted fawn epitomizes "sweet."
Subject: Antietam

⬥ Using color brilliantly, this tattoo remains adorable and perky—even if it does point out that love is like getting a pencil in the eye.

Subject: Jamie Margera / Artist: Bill Bill, Imperial Design Tattoo

⬥ Possibly a tribute to the subject, this winsome rabbit is well served by its bold use of scarlet and baby blue.

Subject: Bunny / Artist: Jime Litwalk

"The love between the mermaid and the merman reminds me of the love and desire my parents always had. It just reminds me that real love exists and does stand the test of time."

--Shannaan

Mermaid tattoos have always been popular motifs with sailors, representing both longing for love after lonely months at sea and the threat of being lured to a watery grave. This tattoo of a mer-couple is an example of a soft-focus treatment that also creates a wonderful spatial quality.

Subject: Shannaan / Artist: Rachel Telles, Side Show Tattoos & Piercings

◀ A great horned owl in full stretch decorates the entirety of this man's upper back. The bird's plumage is well depicted in only shades of black and brown.
Subject: Michael Leaver / Artist: Jackie Jennings, Ink Bitch

▼ A fluorescent garden decorates a chest, with numerous flowers realistically rendered.
Subject: Lauren Sears / Artist: Jon Jon, Cutting Edge Arts

The patterns of nature have seemingly always poured forth from the tattooist's needle. More than a millennium ago the Pazyryk people in what is now Russia regularly decorated themselves with ink animalia, both real and imagined. Today it is not uncommon to see bodies that are galleries of beasts—carnivores and herbivores, fish and fowl. Tigers bare their fangs and stare menacingly through yellow eyes from forearms and thighs; eagles and owls stretch their wings across shoulder blades and scapulae; water flows down the skin in inky rivulets, sheltering frogs in lilied pools. These bodies are worlds unto themselves—sinuous trees hold clouded skies aloft, flowers spread, dragons emerge from the vaunted deep. To be somehow more than human is a dream of some—to wear the patterns and camouflage and color of wild fauna and flora. Here the mysterious designs of nature are harnessed by the tattooist and recreated in ink upon bare skin.

THE WILDLIFE

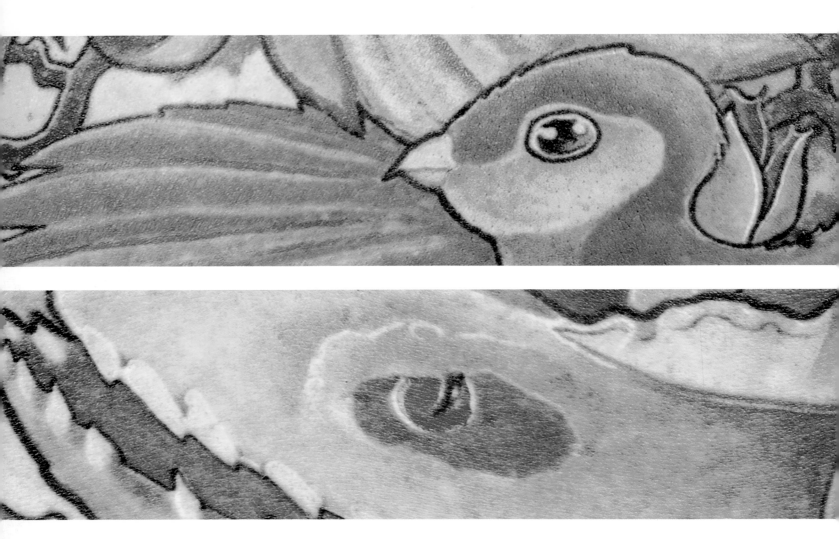

"I like the way getting a tattoo feels.
If I'm depressed, it's nice to get one
and deal with the pain. "

--Megan Fox, actor

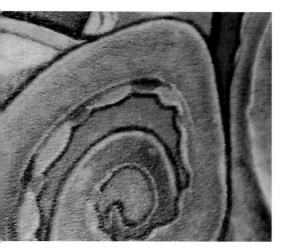

For millennia, humans have used tattooing to invoke the qualities of wild animals. Personal struggle inspired this couple to get their tattoos, and they chose animal images that evoke beauty, grace, and strength.

Subjects: Kim Edwards and Todd Glover

Intense ink coverage is the theme at left , as flying stars and shooting flames appear to have erupted around the older, more humble, heart tattoo commemorating the subject's parents. Below left: The carefully delineated lines of this koi are filled in with burnished golden hues interspersed with jet black and shimmery silver markings, which pop against the cerulean and aqua hues of the water.

Subject: Todd Glover / Artist: Tara Goshow, Phenom-A-Bomb Tattoo

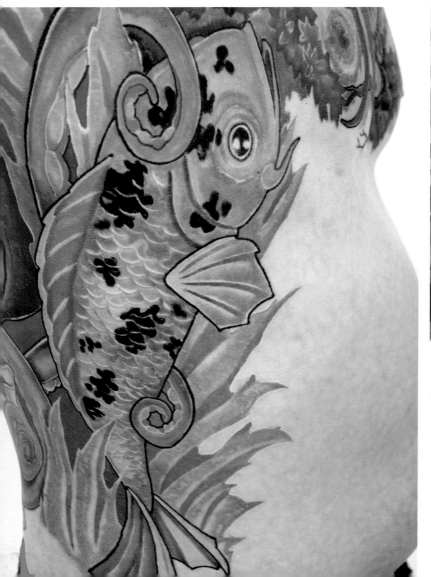

This striking chest panorama, below, features an adult eagle about to feed its young with a writhing snake. The color choices, graphic symmetry, and naturalistic treatment of the animals are all outstanding. At right, nautical motifs appear in adjoining chest and arm tattoos—and include a galleon, the U.S. Navy anchor and line, and a mermaid surrounded by curious sea creatures.

Subject: Todd Glover / Artist: Tara Goshow, Phenom-A-Bomb Tattoo

Leviathans abound on this man's back, amid a diverse underwater environment. To wear an animal on your body is to identify with its attributes.

Subject: Todd Glover / Artist: Tara Goshow, Phenom-A-Bomb Tattoo

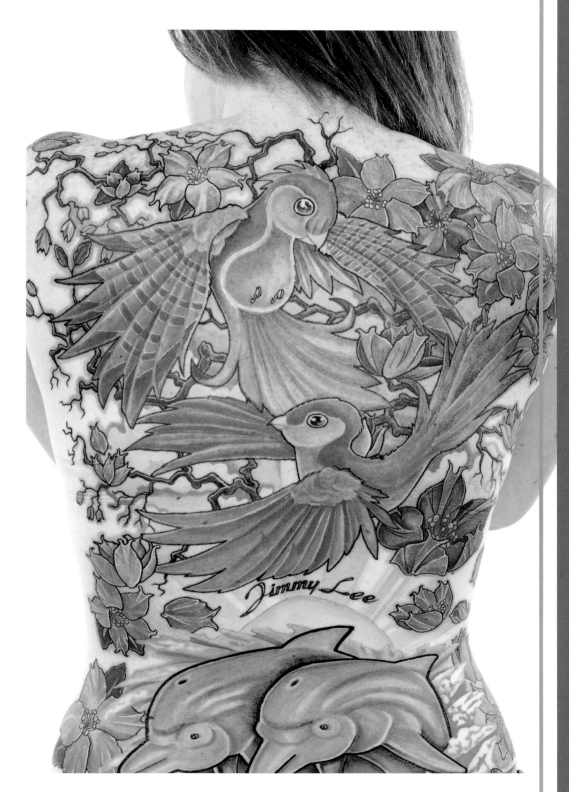

The same artist has richly decorated this woman's back, though she has crafted a more placid scene of brilliant cerulean bluebirds and cavorting dolphins

Subject: Kim Edwards / Artist: Tara Goshow, Phenom-A-Bomb Tattoo

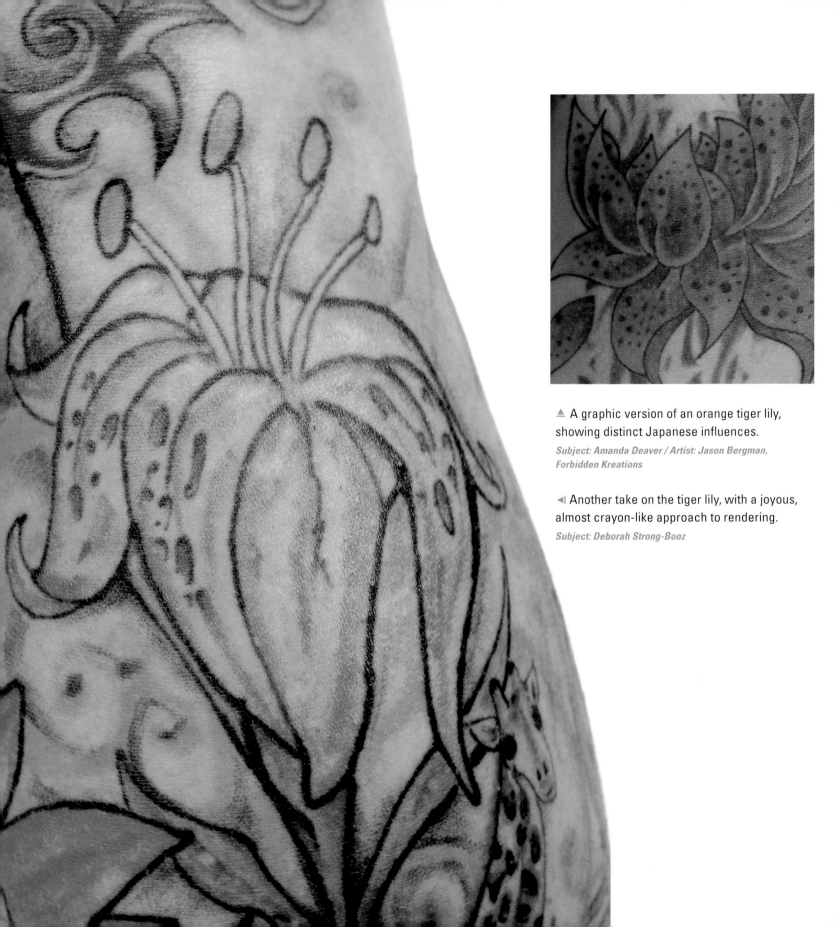

▲ A graphic version of an orange tiger lily, showing distinct Japanese influences.

Subject: Amanda Deaver / Artist: Jason Bergman, Forbidden Kreations

◁ Another take on the tiger lily, with a joyous, almost crayon-like approach to rendering.

Subject: Deborah Strong-Booz

▲ A glowing fire flower in Day-Glo bright colors evokes flames and peacock plumage.

Subject: Rio Rivera / Artist: Jon Jon, Cutting Edge Body Art

▲ Serene Chinese lilies take on a watercolor serenity in verdant greens and blushing pinks.

Subject: Karen Herb / Artist: Christopher Depinto, Shotsie's Tattoo

▮▶ Masterful control of cool color and subtle shading gives these moody cobalt and azure blue roses an airbrushed lightness.

Subject: Mark Peck / Artist: Eric Willis

"Show me a man with a tattoo, and I'll show you a man with an interesting past."

--Jack London, writer

This man goes by the moniker "Jungle Jim," and it's easy to see why. The sheer density of the imagery is astonishing. It will probably only get denser—he appears to be running out of room.

Subject: Jungle Jim / Artist: Matthew Amey, Independent Tattoo

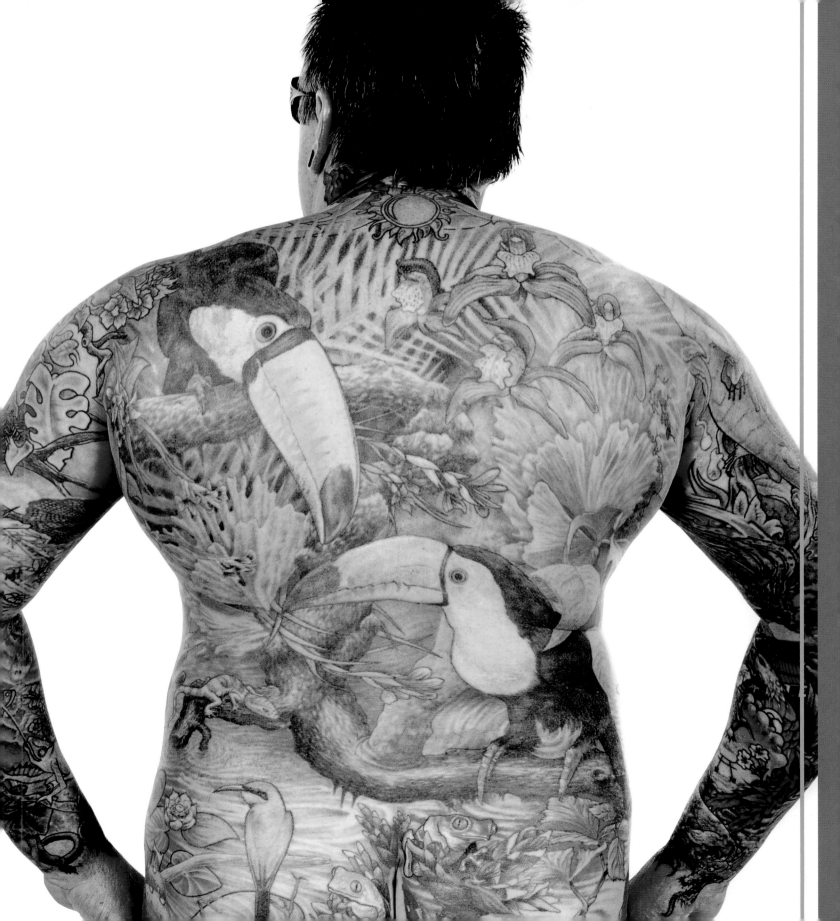

Some more of Jungle Jim's lush tattooing. The expansive world on his skin even includes a well-populated ocean, below, frogs leaping lily pads, right, and a dazzling variety of flora interwoven everywhere.

Subject: Jungle Jim / Artist: Matthew Amey, Independent Tattoo

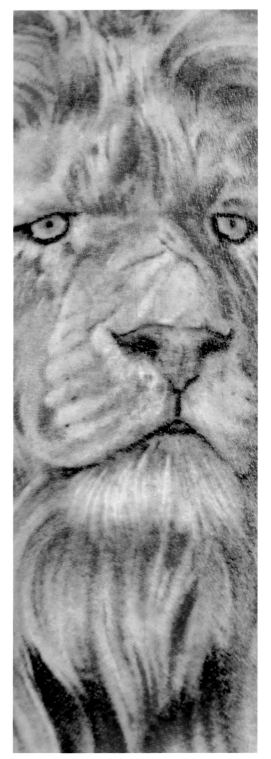

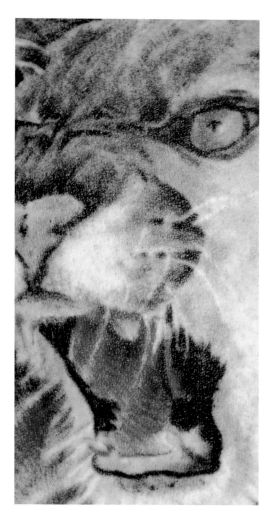

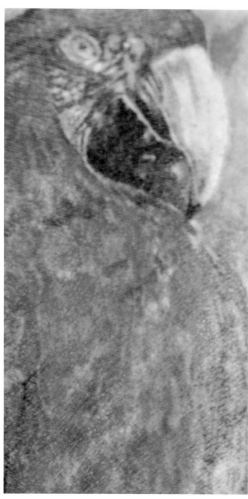

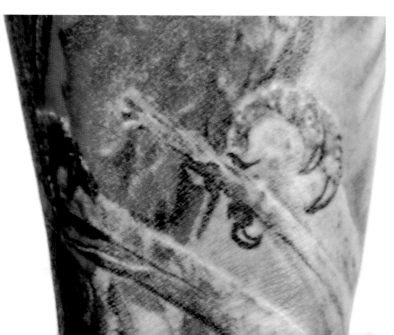

Lions and tigers and parrots, oh my! The handsome, stately, and savage features of a big cat always make for a striking tattoo, whether it's a tiger pictured in repose or a leopard in full snarl. The rich plumage of a parrot also lends itself nicely to body art.

Subject: Curly / Artists: Paul Acker and Mike Hull, Deep Six Laboratory Tattoo Shop

▶ Old-school flash suits this owlish intellectual.
Subject: Hannah G. Lilly / Artist: Rodrigo Melo

▼ Unexpected flashes of heliotrope pink and lazuline blue makes this a bird of distinction.
Subject: Curly / Artists: Paul Acker and Mike Hull,
Deep Six Laboratory Tattoo Shop

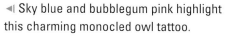 Sky blue and bubblegum pink highlight this charming monocled owl tattoo.
Subject: Jody Warner / Artist: Matt Zimmerman

 An Asian-influenced owl in fierce tones of chrome yellow and cherry red on black.
Subject: Joseph Sanbrotti / Artist: Casey

"I love how smart owls are. Rainy days in tattoo shops = owl tattoos."

—Jody Warner

Beautiful wings and feathers grace this woman's body, which is dominated by an ambitious Art Deco back piece. It is still a work in progress—her lower back remains an uncolored outline.

Subject: Mum / Artists: Dan Gilsdorf, Spike, Gary Cosmonaut, and Atom Grey (arms); VyVyn Lozanga (stomach); back fill-in by Bugs

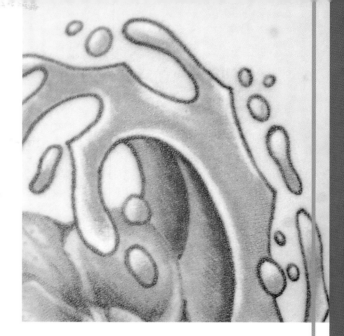

Water, water, everywhere. Just as the ocean can be both calm and turbulent, so can the tattoos that depict it. This subject chose swirling designs of wave-swept orchids and lilies for her body, while sinuous palms frame a purple sunrise over a serene sea.

Subject: Sue Gertner / Artist: Guy Aitchison (arm); Dustin McAndrew, The Ultimate (ribs)

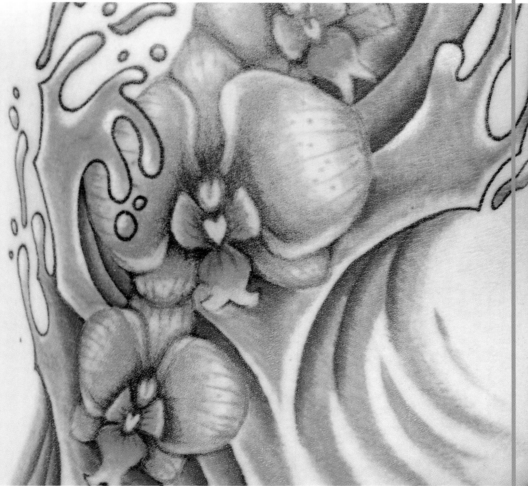

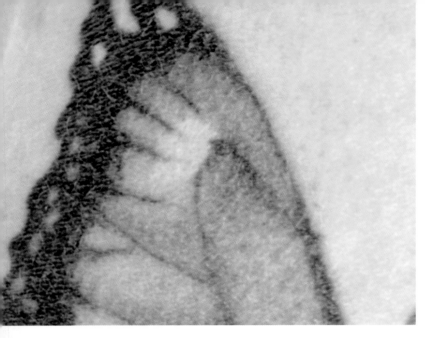

Colorful, boldly rendered scatterings of butterflies, from blue morphos to monarchs decorate this subject's body.

Subject: Angela Bibey / Artist: Ink Bitch

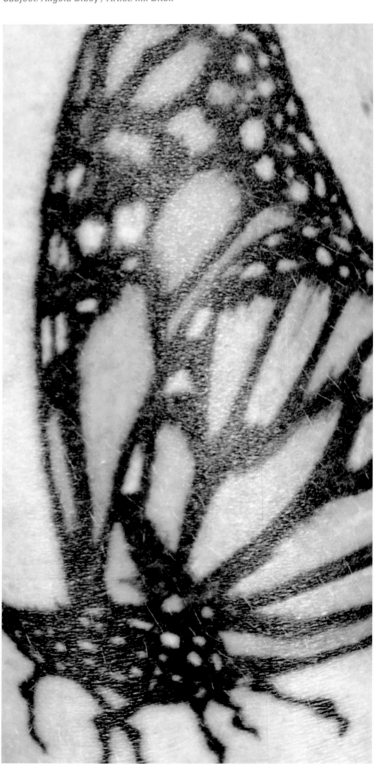

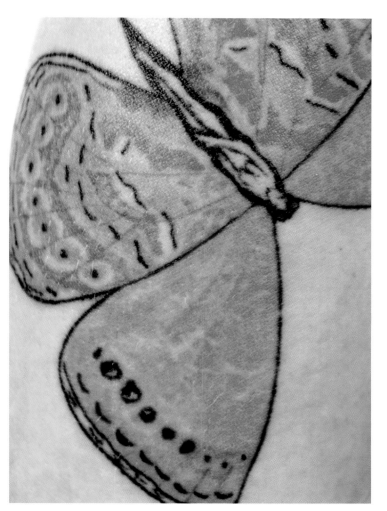

◁ Winsome woman or beautiful butterfly? It takes a careful look to reveal the female form between these orange and turquoise wings.
Subject: Angela Bibey / Artist: Ink Bitch

▽ Butterflies convey beauty and grace amid a rough, ugly world. This is especially exemplified by the elaborate back piece below, in which a butterfly flits freely among a tangled, thorny garden.
Subject: Angela Bibey / Artist: Gil

◀ Nature imagery abounds on this woman's body, including fanciful fire engine red fish swimming through inky blossoms.
Subject: Rachel Riley

▼ Scarlet skulls center the blue-tinged orchids that guard the exposed heart across her chest.
Subject: Rachel Riley

▼ The barest hint of pale aqua and breathy tints of smoky amethyst color graphic feathery wings on her shoulder.

Subject: Rachel Riley

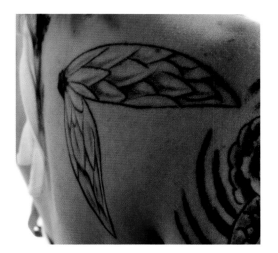

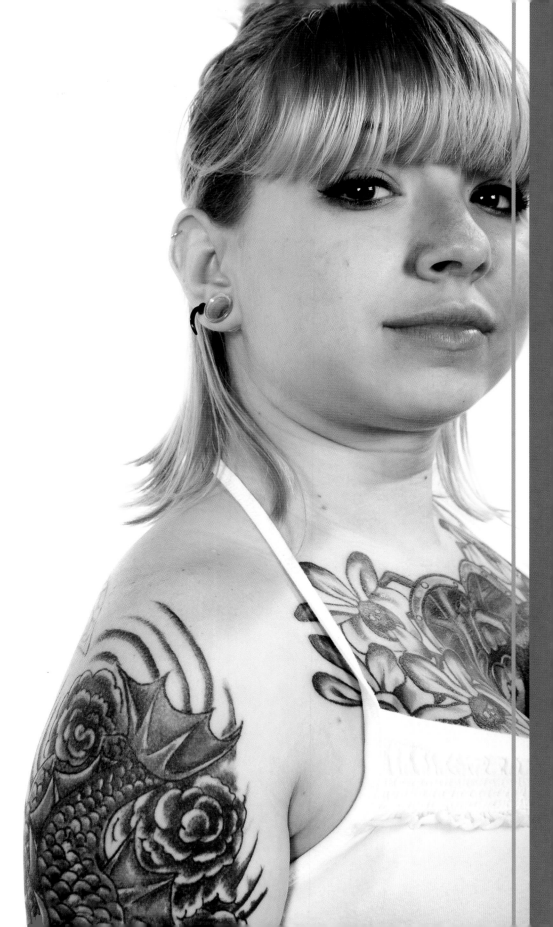

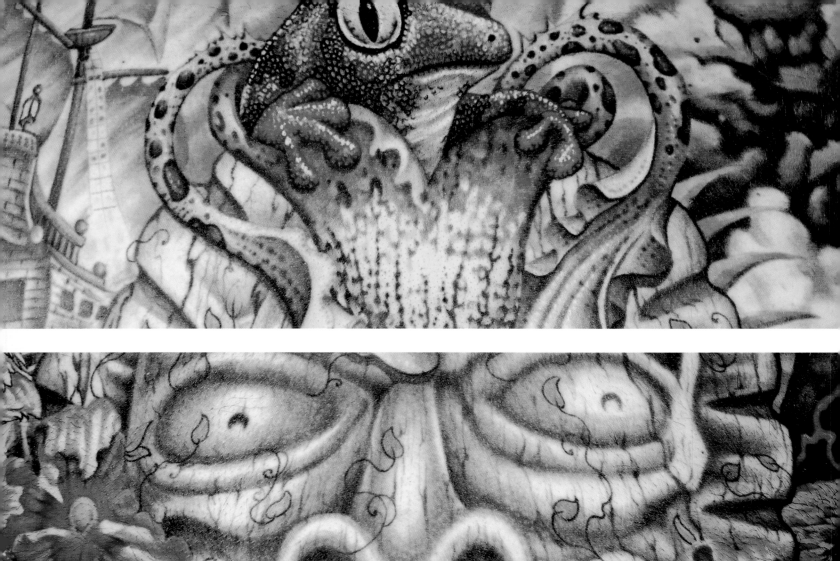

This man states that the "rain forest makes him think of vacation." Examining the imagery on his back is certainly an escape from the mundane.

Subject: Matt Mauro / Artist: Cort Bengtson, Corts Royal Ink

"I saw the duckling at the curiosities exhibit and fell in love."

—Beth Neronski

▽ A quirky but lovable two-headed duckling, finely rendered and shaded in elegant earth tones, is offset with luminous lavenders.

Subject: Beth Neronski / Artist: Kevin Berube, Art for Life

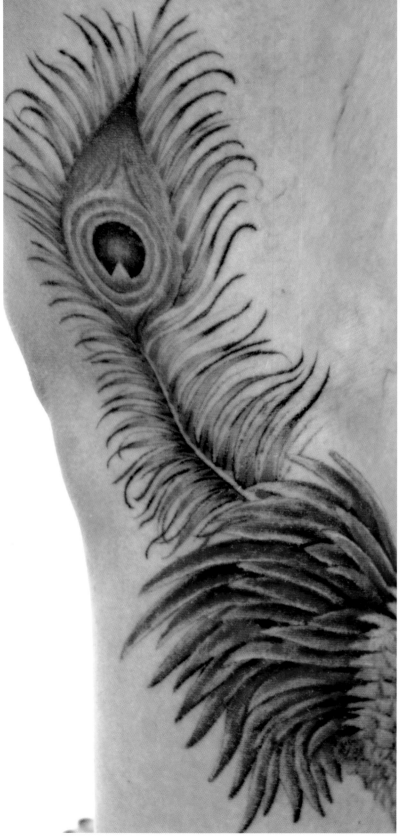

▶ This mauve-headed bird seems to glow from within, with fine feather gradations of deep carmine red to bright cadmium yellow.
Subject: Vinnie Greer / Artist: Meghan Patrick

▼ Colorful and slightly surreal—a proud rooster, below and left, waves a delicately rendered peacock feather within its already splendid plumage. His comb is edged in nearly neon yellow.
Subject: Rebecca Kolodziejczak

▲ Intricate details flourish amid the swirling nature-inspired collages on this model's legs. The black-and-white areas may eventually be colored in, but as they are, they do offer a nice contrast to the vivid flowers and leaves.

Subject: Cyndi Pape

▼ The closer one gets to a piece, the more impressive the draftsmanship appears. On full-body designs, tattooist artists must become masters of collage, blending and harmonizing images with uncommon skill.

Subject: Cyndi Pape

▲ A school of fish conveys the mysteries of underwater life on this woman's body.

Subject: Siobhán A. Counihan

▶ Was the subject feeling "koi" when it came to choosing to this exotic fish tattoo with its vivid colors and Asian influence?

Subject: Rich / Carol Oddy, Medusa Tattoo

"This is an homage to Long Beach Island, New Jersey. I spent every summer of my life there, my grandparents live there; it's the only real home I've ever known."

--Siobhán A. Counihan

◀ This tattooist has deftly colored this koi fish, highlighting the variegated scales to convey the reflection of light. The natural color of a model's skin is among the hues a tattoo artist can work with.
Subject: Sara Purr

▼ Scales and petals alike receive the same meticulous attention to detail, with well-chosen variations of the same hues to form flowers, fish, and trees in this dense tattoo.
Subject: Cal / Artist: Brian Donovan

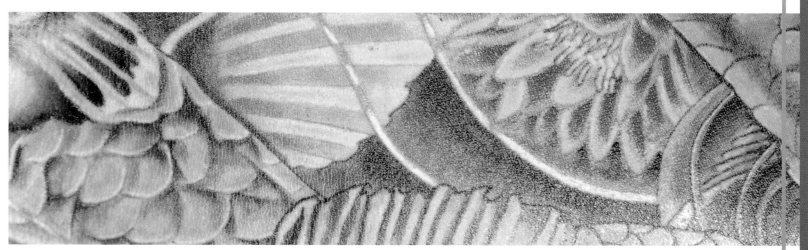

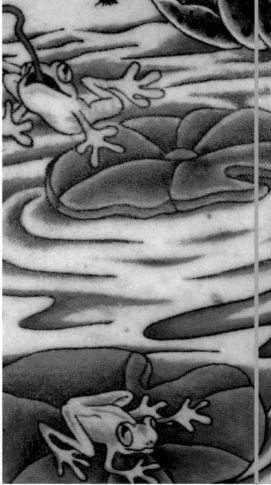

"Up high, the flies are playing, and frolicking, and swaying. The frog thinks: Dance! I know You'll end up here below."

— Wilhelm Busch, painter and poet

A vision of both peace and whimsy: the placid nature of this woman's lower back is belied by the frog leaping and snaring a fly on her upper back.

Subject: Cherry / Artist: Brandon Hamilton, Skin Images

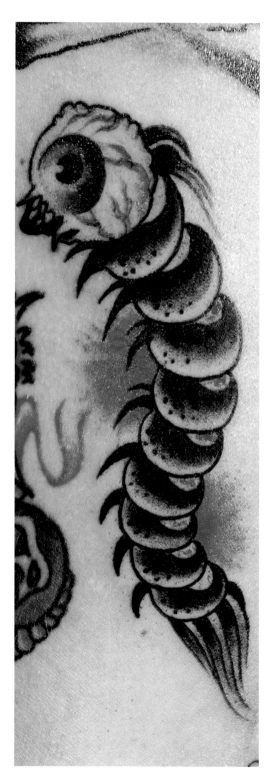

▲ A menagerie of fantastic animals decorates this man's body. A sinuous dragon occupies beastly waters on his right arm.

Subject: Raymond Baranowski

◄ A slinky centipede fronted by a bloodshot eyeball creeps across his skin, far left; while at near left, a ghoulish octopus swims across the underside of his left arm.

Subject: Raymond Baranowski

◄◄ Opposite page, a Canada goose toting a sickle and sporting wings inhabited by skulls takes flight across his upper back.

Subject: Raymond Baranowski

▲ This dragon, balled up amid fire and smoke, shows a nice combination of precision and abstraction.

Subject: Toonbrian

▲▲ A green and gold dragon bares its teeth as it snakes up the subject's upper arm to swoop downward across his chest.

Subject: John Baird / Artist: Joe Lasheski, Squid Ink

▲ With long, intricate, serpentine bodies and bestial but personified faces, dragons make eye-catching tattoos.

Subject: John LaForgia / Artist: Steve Bolt

▷ Some variant of the dragon inhabits the legends of most every culture around the world. Dragons with long, ribbonlike bodies are descended from Chinese lore.

Subject: Laura / Artist: Deirdre Aikin

Dragons appear in many tattoos, and why not? These fabulous creatures of legend are visually stunning, whether they are patterned after the benevolent water-dispensing creature of Eastern tradition or the malevolent fire-breather of Western myth. With scaly, serpentine bodies, leonine claws, and gigantic wings, dragons lend themselves to multitudinous interpretations and treatments, in pallets as vivid or as muted as the wearer chooses.

"I love vampires, kitty, and ivy."

—Kelley Treat

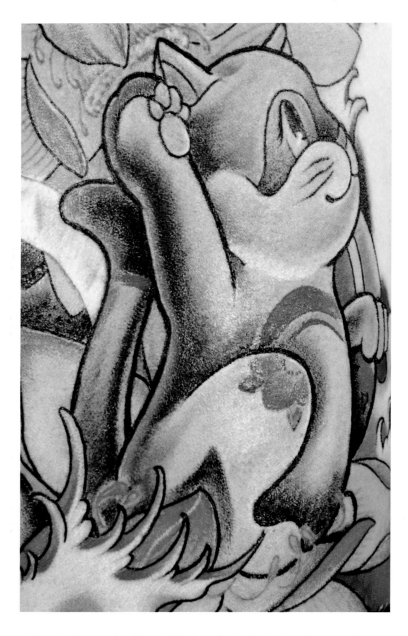

▲ A variation on the *Maneki Neko*—the lucky beckoning cat—is done in lollipop pastels to create a cute but not cloying tattoo.

Subject: Kelley Treat / Artist: "Kitty Love" by Mike Connors

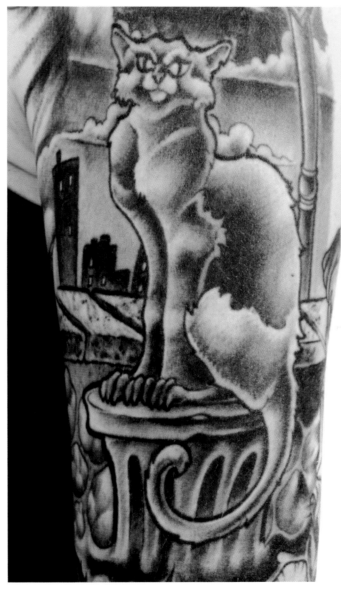

▲ Lean and hungry but still sitting proud and tall—the hard-luck life of the city stray is done in film-noir black and white.

Subject: Cat Golden / Artist: David Blake

◄ "Such is life." A technicolor take on the same theme. Stray cats, a midnight black and an orange ginger, stake out fence-side seating to their favorite garbage can.

Subject: Rebecca Kolodziejczak

"New life with the lotus . . . the doves are my parents watching over me."

--Willis

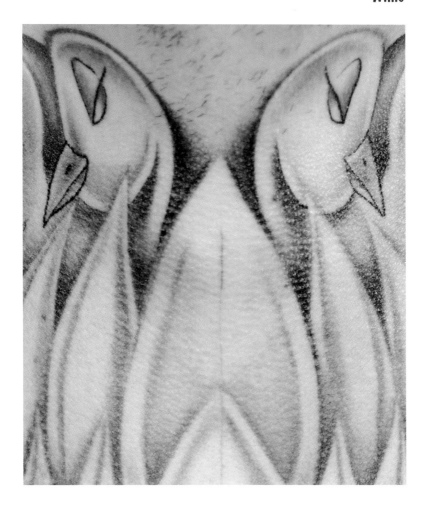

▲ Graceful lines form these doves nestled in lotus petals.

Subject: Willis / Artist: Tony, Lady Luck Tattoo Gallery

◀ Commanding in its elegant simplicity, this monochrome rhinoceros, with its impressive tusk, takes up the entirety of this subject's torso.

Subject: Brian Doebler / Artist: St. Marq, New Breed Tattoo

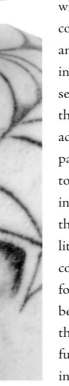

◀ Self-expression is an important facet of tattoo culture and can be conveyed with phrases as well as graphics. "Drug Free" likely indicates a personal epiphany.
Subject: Miss Mac the Knife / Artist: Jon Morse

▽ "American Classic" could either refer to nostalgia for the past or to a strong identification with the U.S.A.
Subject: Spider

It goes beyond to be or not to be. To be, you must answer the question, who am I, really? And here, the answers come in manifestos of embedded ink. In ancient Polynesian cultures the tattooist introduced his tattooees to their true selves—with needles and dye, he found the people they were meant to be and adjusted their bodies accordingly. The patterns that defined them were not theirs to choose. Today in the West, we believe in choosing our own identities—here then, are bodies wearing their identities literally on their sleeves. These tattoos are commitments to personal principles—forms of fidelity to certain experiences or beliefs. They are inked as words or scenes; they are both symbols of the past and the future. They answer questions of self in indelible ink that will last a lifetime.

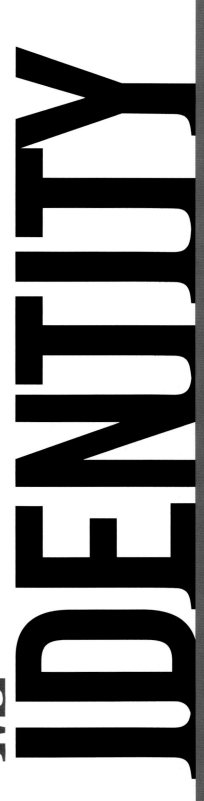

MY IDENTITY

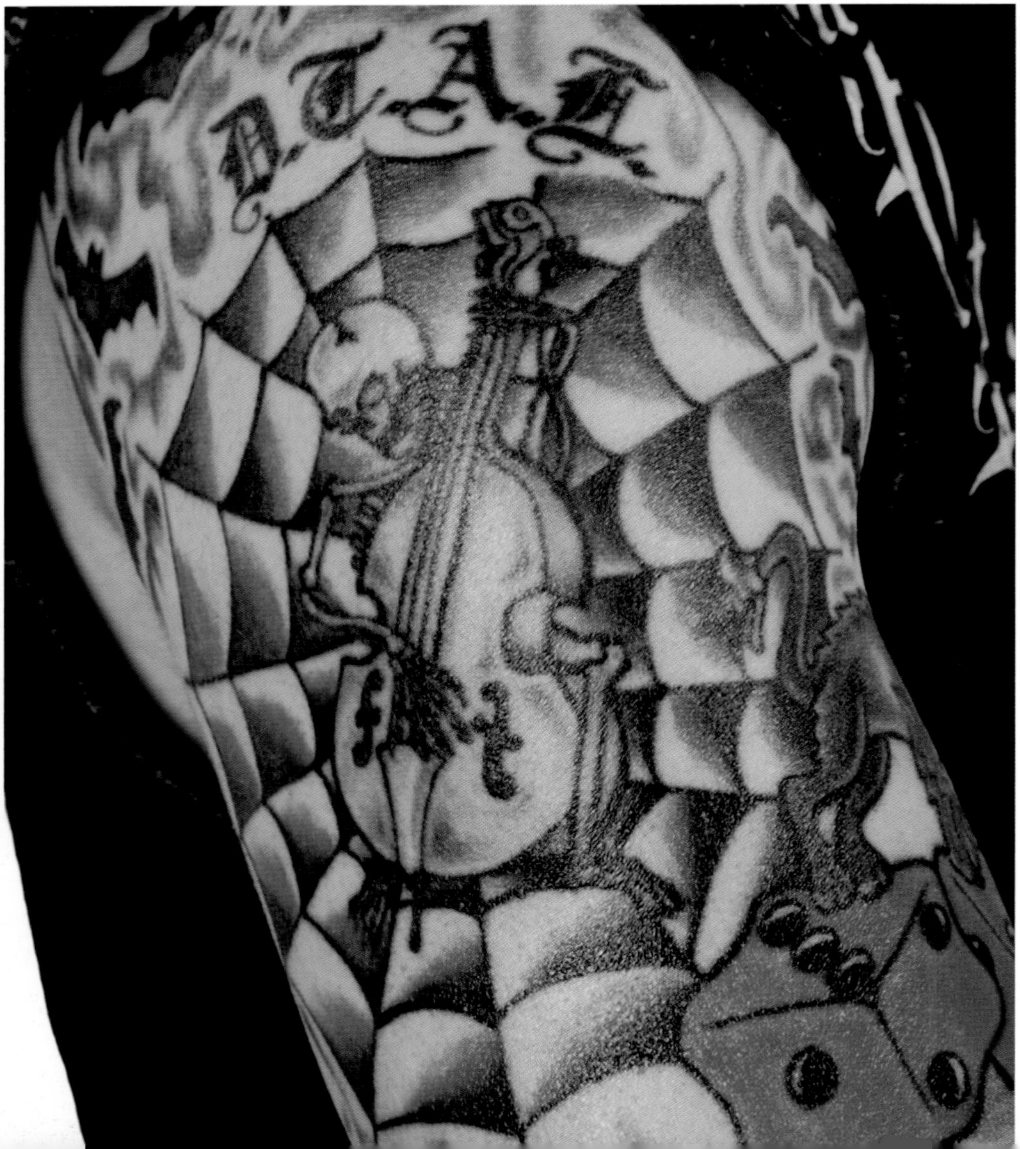

▲ Dark sentiments expressed with words and images have always attracted rebels and renegades. "Living in Darkness," spelled out in gothic letters across this man's shoulders, offers a very specific worldview.
Subject: Vic Victor

◄ A skeleton playing an upright bass on the subject's arm is both macabre and whimsical, while a black cat straddling red dice could symbolize bad luck at the gambling table.
Subject: Vic Victor

► This striking chest tattoo features a bat-winged skull wearing a crown. The Latin phrase below it, *mors ex supera*, appropriately means "death from above."
Subject: Vic Victor

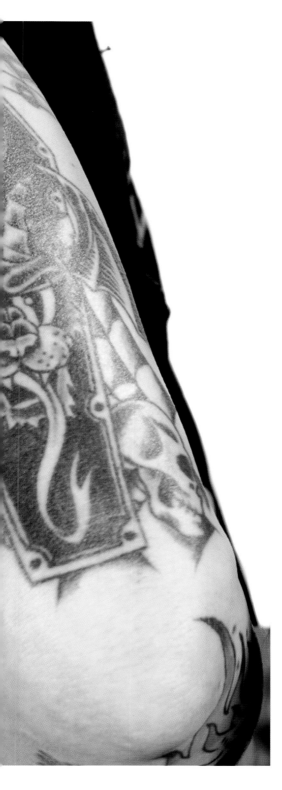

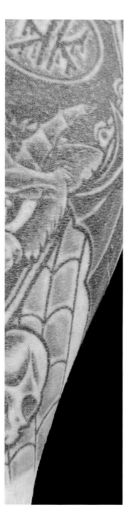

Two variations on a theme: these men show off the same Koffin Kats logo tattoo, a horned beast inside a coffin, but demonstrate how color choice can affect the outcome. The all-black version is punk-Goth intense, while the brightly colored and beautifully inked version replaces some of its wicked punch with a jolt of psychobilly humor.

Subjects: Vic Victor and Tommy Koffin / Artist: Sam Wolf

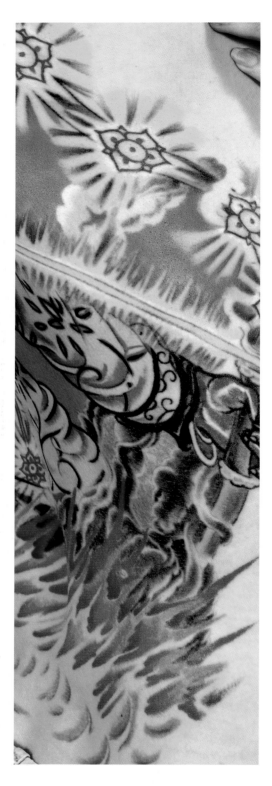

The semi-fierce goddess Vajra-yogini—or female Buddha—shown in these tattoos represents the feminine manifestation of Divine Wisdom. Hindus in Nepal also revere her under the name Chinnamasta. There are many other powerful female images women choose as tattoos: the Egyptian goddess Isis or Queen Cleopatra; the Greek love goddess, Aphrodite, or their goddess of wisdom, Athena. From Hindu mythology comes the ferocious goddess Kali and the mother goddess Shakti. There are lethal lady pirates and female figures from the Tarot: the High Priestess, the Empress, or Justice holding the scales. Even Lady Liberty appears. From dark fantasy comics there is Vampirella, Red Sonja, and Lady Death. These images all represent female empowerment and the strength of the feminine in male-dominated cultures.

The female Buddha Vajra-yogini appears here in all her glory. This subject chose to decorate herself with Vajra-yogini because of the goddess's "strong female energy—plus it's badass."
Subject: Lela Simon / Artist: JJ Simon

▲ Even traditional images of Hindu deities depicts them as fantastical creatures of brilliant color. Here Shiva, the destroyer or transformer, appears in his blue-skinned incarnation.
Subject: Mayimbe181

◄ Saraswati, the Hindu goddess of knowledge, music, and the arts is rendered here in a sultry comic-book style.
Subject: Hannah G. Lilly / Artist: C-Jay, Rising Dragon Tattoos

"She is the goddess of arts and intellect, and I'm an artistic smartass."

--Hannah G. Lilly

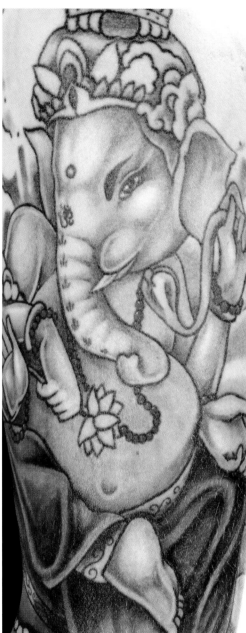

⬥ One of the easiest to recognize of the Hindu gods—the elephant-headed Ganesha, who is often called the "lord of beginnings" or a remover of obstacles. This version uses a basic gray-black palette subtly enhanced with touches of magenta and yellow.

Subject: Melissa / Artist: Ruler, Silk City Tattoo

▷ "Overcoming incredible odds" inspired this subject's vibrantly colored take on Ganesha. With skin a sea-tinted blue and a bejeweled headdress of gold, the god sits on splendid royal plum–colored drapery.

Subject: Miss Amanda / Artist: Colby Long

⬥ A very flash interpretation of the hindu goddess Kali shows this consort of Lord Shiva in her blue-hued, many-armed form. Her azure skin is offset with gold adornments and purple and red finery. Despite her associations with death and destruction, recent movements have reimagined Kali as a benevolent goddess of change.

Subject: S.C. Gypsy Queen Aurora / Artist: Margo

▲ Color-saturation tattoos are not for the faint of heart. This charming Hello Kitty Geisha in pink is a virtual arm painting, complete with fully inked-in background.
Subject: Krista Ruttman / Artist: Frankie G.

◄ Another example of intense inking, this tropical floral tattoo showcases a rich, color-splashed airbrushed effect.
Subject: Krista Ruttman / Artist: Frankie G.

▮► With billowing sails, a square-rigged ship skims a frothy sea along the subject's arm, above. Below, Day of the Dead–style male and female skulls adorn the subject's feet.
Subject: Krista Ruttman / Artist: Frankie G.

▲ Like nonstop eye candy, this collection of small tattoos covers the inner arm.

Subject: Krista Ruttman / Artist: Frankie G.

▲ Knuckles are popular for in-your-face message tattoos: why wear a medic alert bracelet when you can wear a warning on your skin?
Subject: Frankie G. / Artist: Marcus Koch

▶ Two very traditional tattoos are shown here—the ubiquitous "Mom," with hearts and flowers, and a "Dad" banner with an anchor.
Subject: Frankie G.

▶ Mexico's Day of the Dead is commemorated in bright colors with this iconic tattoo of the Virgin Mary with a skull head.
Subject: Frankie G. / Artist: Mark Cornwall

▶ Both halves of this couple are fans of heavy-coverage inking. Her lady pirate stands before a red Jolly Roger and straddles a treasure chest. His neck tattoo confesses that he's a "Hopeless Romantic."
Subjects: Krista Ruttman and Frankie G. / Artist: Frankie G. (her); Civ (him)

"Love lasts forever, but a tattoo lasts six months longer."

--Anonymous

▲ Her divorce inspired this woman's rainbow-hued "Forgive and Forget" heart-within-a-heart chest tattoo.

Subject: Megan Velazquez / Artist: Pork Chop, Chop Shop Tattoos

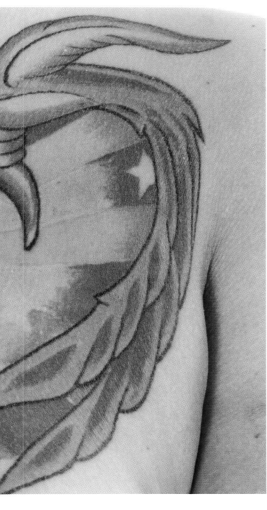

▶ Like a tattoo riff on *Dr. Strangelove*, a sexy female soldier rides a bomb while the Stars and Stripes billow in the background.

Subject: Megan Velazquez / Artist: Pork Chop, Chop Shop Tattoos

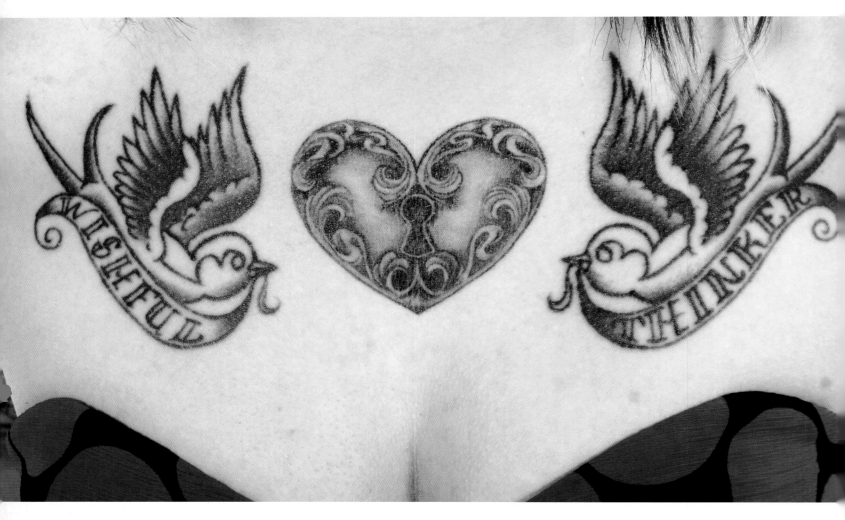

"Jem is my favorite cartoon and my role model. When I was little, I wanted to be her when I grew up."

--Mikey A

▲ All-black tattoos can be surprisingly feminine—if they are approached delicately. This "Wishful Thinker" chest tattoo of birds surrounding a heart-shaped lock has a definite Victorian feel.

Subject: Mikey A / Artist: Meghan Patrick

▮▶ Above right, another graceful monochrom tattoo, skeleton keys strung on a winding ribbon. The subject explains its meaning: "The keys to my heart can be unlocked. The keys on my hips read: 'Friends, family, music.'" Many tattoos contain ironic symbolism, such as this hand grenade show below right, which comes wrapped in a pink bow and with a heart-shaped pull ring.

Subject: Mikey A / Artist: Meghan Patrick

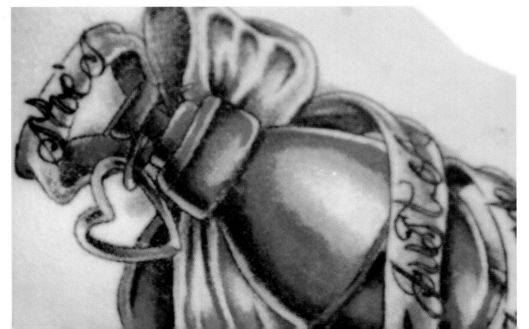

▲ This attention-grabbing comic book–style scene features animated pop stars Jem and the Holograms and other symbols of stardom.

Subject: Mikey A / Artist: Alex Feliciano

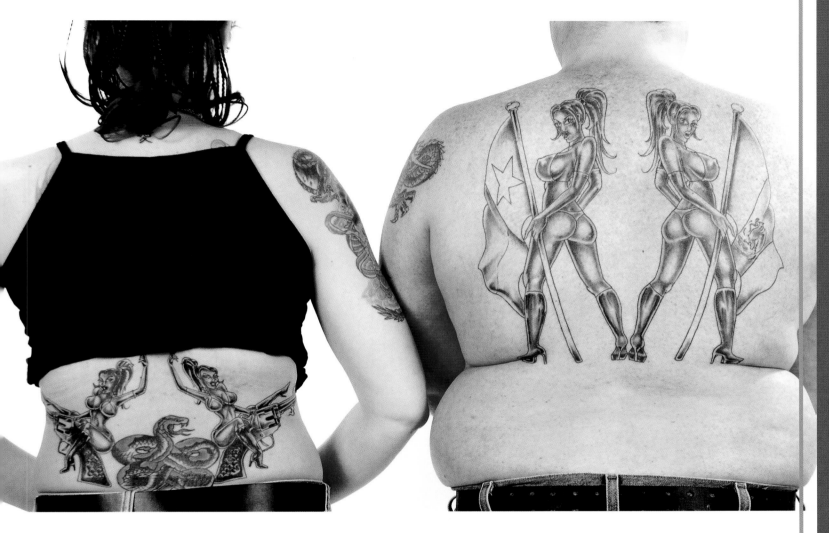

▲ Identity tattoos don't need to be somber or scary—many are playful even as they relate to the serious sides of life. Here, a husband and wife show off matching bikini babes—a redhead and a brunette—across their backs. Her pistol ridin' mamas bookend a coiled snake, while his two ladies wave the flags of Texas and Mexico, representing his son's heritage.

Subjects: Pearl and Shane Donovan / Artist: Jason "Bug Juice" Nightingale, Tiki Tattoo

◄ This couple sport Chinese-style dragons on their upper arms. Her dragon, in shades of teal, gold, and red, wraps around a knife-wielding female pearl diver—a symbol of her successful struggle against depression. His pair of scarlet serpents twining around each other are again for his son, who was born in the year of the dragon.

Subjects: Pearl and Shane Donovan/ Artist: Annette LaRue (her); Cameron Sweet (him)

> ## "The pearl diver symbolized the struggle with depression and overcoming it."
>
> —Pearl Donovan

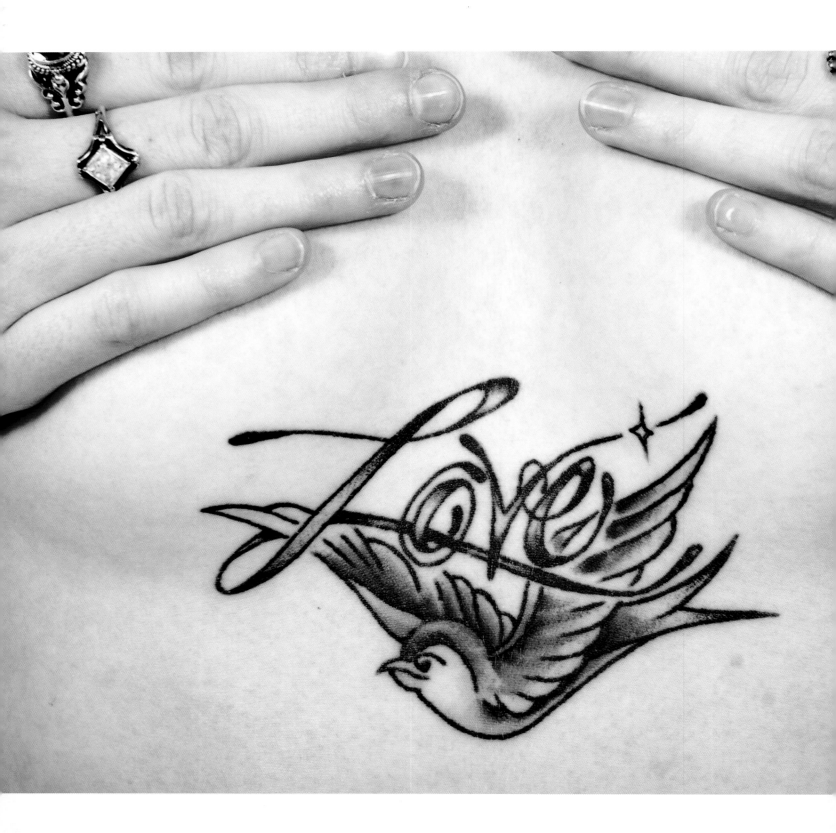

"The tattoo is a strong reminder to live fully in the moment and never have regrets"

--Angelina Jolie, actor

◄ At left, a lovely bluebird takes flight, carrying its simple but heartfelt message.
Subject: Whitney Valentine / Artist: Ed Glassner

▼ A snarling tiger lurks amid hot pink tropical flowers, hoping for a meal.
Subject: Whitney Valentine / Artist: Justin Valentine

▲ This naughty girl is putting her best feet forward and tellin' it like it is.

Subject: Whitney Valentine / Artist: Justin Valentine

◀ Her thigh-high message, embellished with a cerulean snub-nosed pistol, leaves little to the imagination.

Subject: Whitney Valentine / Artist: Ed Glassner

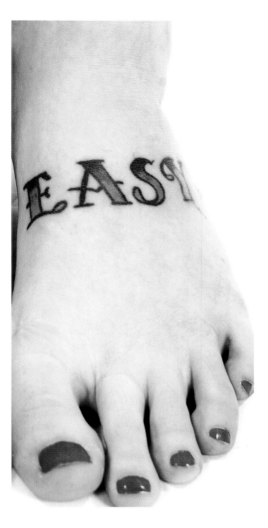

▶ A female silhouette from a popular trucker's mud flap is paired with a "tongue in cheek" affirmation.

Subject: Whitney Valentine / Artist: Jimmy Aguliar

Across the shoulders and even down to the hand and fingers, classic tribal designs, stark in coal black, are joined on the torso by a sinuous Asian dragon with highlights of blood-red ink.

Subject: Seven / Artist: Mony (tribal); Natalie Jean (dragon)

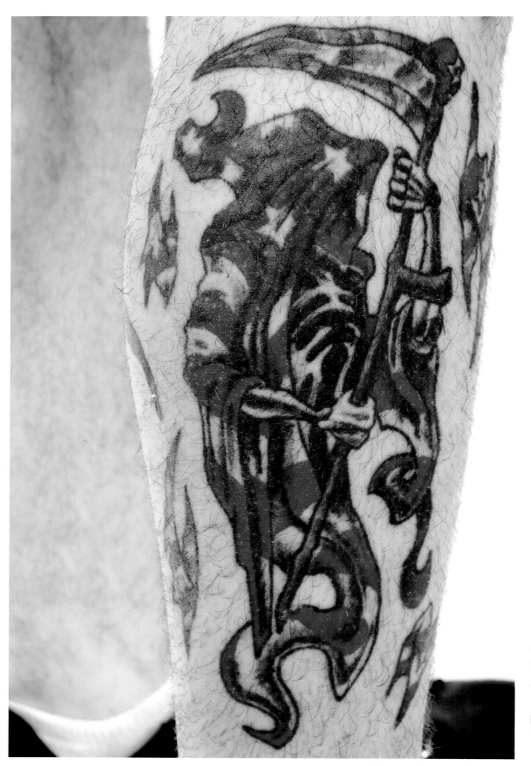

◀ Is the grim reaper wrapped in Old Glory sending a mixed message? At least that's not the case with the phrase on his other leg.
Subject: Bill Taylor

▶ So, tell us, was Daddy's blue-eyed (and blue-haired) son really "Made in the USA"?
Subject: Little Billy and Father

◀ Some people so identify with their hometowns that they want them inked permanently onto their bodies. This subject's pride in Philadelphia takes the form of a well-crafted collage of the city of brotherly love's distinctive skyline.

Subject: Anthony Lipczynski / Artist: Brian Donovan

▶ Other people may identify far more easily with a place "somewhere over the rainbow," as in this subject's finely detailed and sensitively shaded rendition of another famous skyline—the city of Oz.

Subject: Azad "Az" Shirozoau / Artist: Joe Lasheski, Squid Ink Tattoo

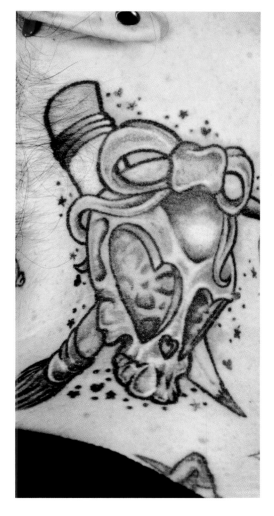

▲ Ink images wrap around the subject's neck from ear to ear. Starting under her right ear, an artist's insignia features a crossed pencil and paintbrush behind a beribboned blue skull. Sassy hot pink brass knuckles adorn her throat. Shown far right is like something from a cryptic dream: a skull and crossbones with a pink bow floats above a flaming lock.

Subject: Kristel Oreto

◀ Idle hands look like they are certainly the devil's playground when they're adorned with a pair of spooky girl and boy waifs.

Subject: Kristel Oreto / Artist: Gunnar (hands); Jason Leigh (knuckles)

"The brass knuckles are a reminder as a woman tattoo artist to be strong every day when I look in the mirror in this man-based industry."

--Kristel Oreto

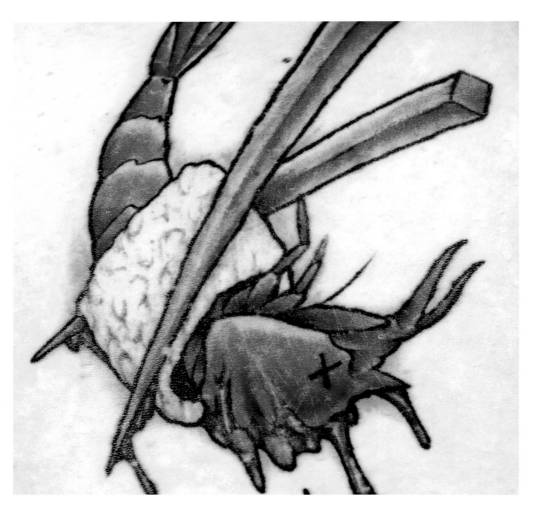

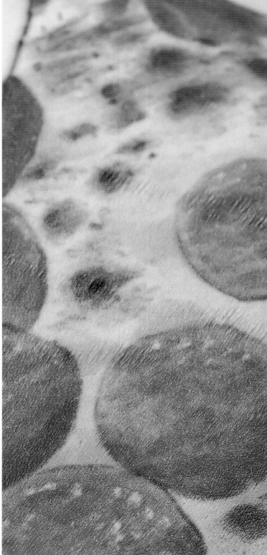

▲ Sushi, anyone? This tattoo features strong graphic lines and neon-bright color ink.
Subject: Kristel Oreto / Artist: Matt

▶ When a tattoo hits your eye like a big pizza pie, that's amore!
Subject: Kristel Oreto / Artist: Chris Bliston

▶▶ This squash may have a runny center, but the complementary color combination works great. Fitting for a woman who is writing a cookbook, these vibrant food tattoos circle the subject's waist.
Subject: Kristel Oreto / Artist: Chris Slota

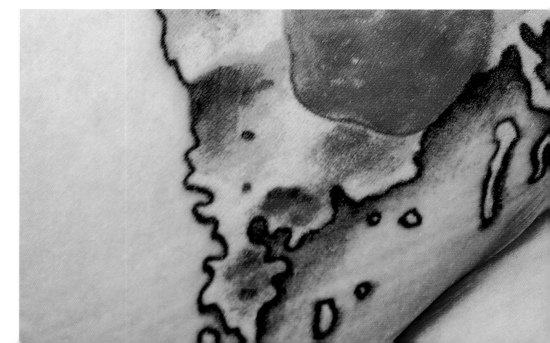

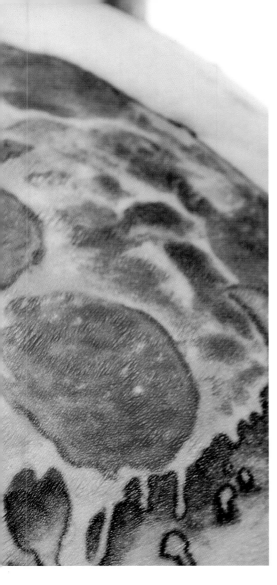

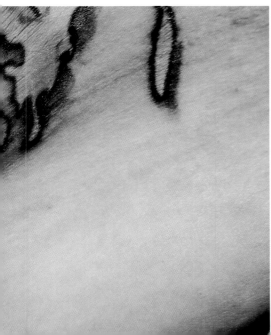

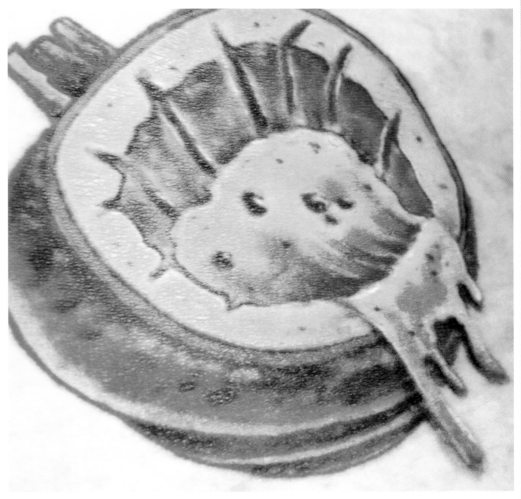

"Having my kid's art on my body forever is awesome."

--Kristel Oreto

These seemingly random tattoos, a mix of writing and colorful imagery, create the dreamy effect of children's drawings, which is exactly what they are based on.

Subject: Kristel Oreto / Artist: Angel and Lucca

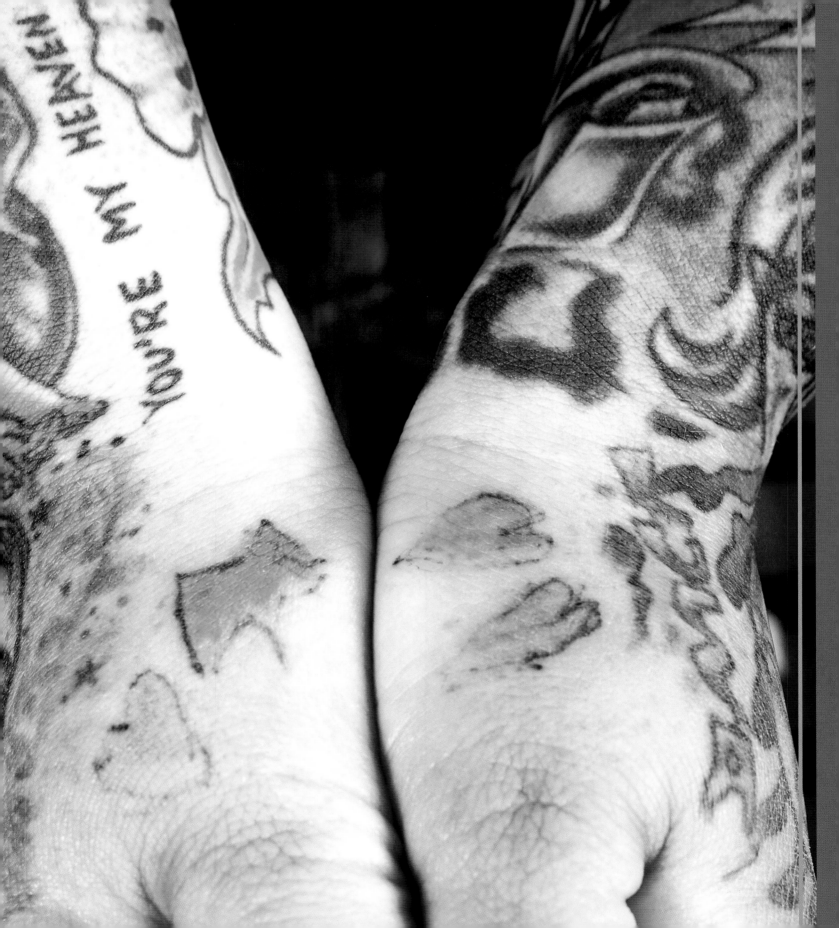

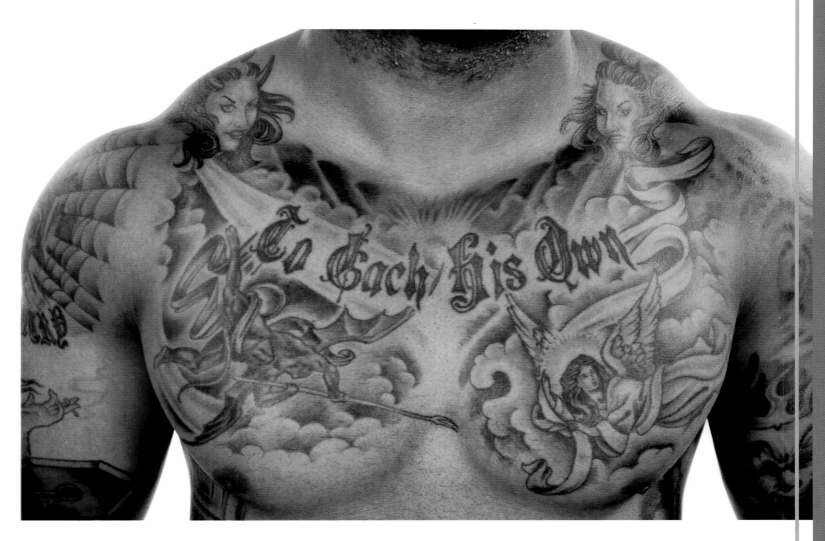

▲ A celestial battle between good and evil takes place on the subject's chest. The full scope of the battle scene—and the graphic intensity of the remarkable tattoos—can be appreciated in this upper-body view.

Subject: Carl Smith / Artist: Jason, Tattoo World

◀ In close-up, a devil in a jester's cap grins wickedly at the violence ensuing below him, all taking place under the banner, "To Each His Own."

Subject: Carl Smith / Artist: Jason, Tattoo World

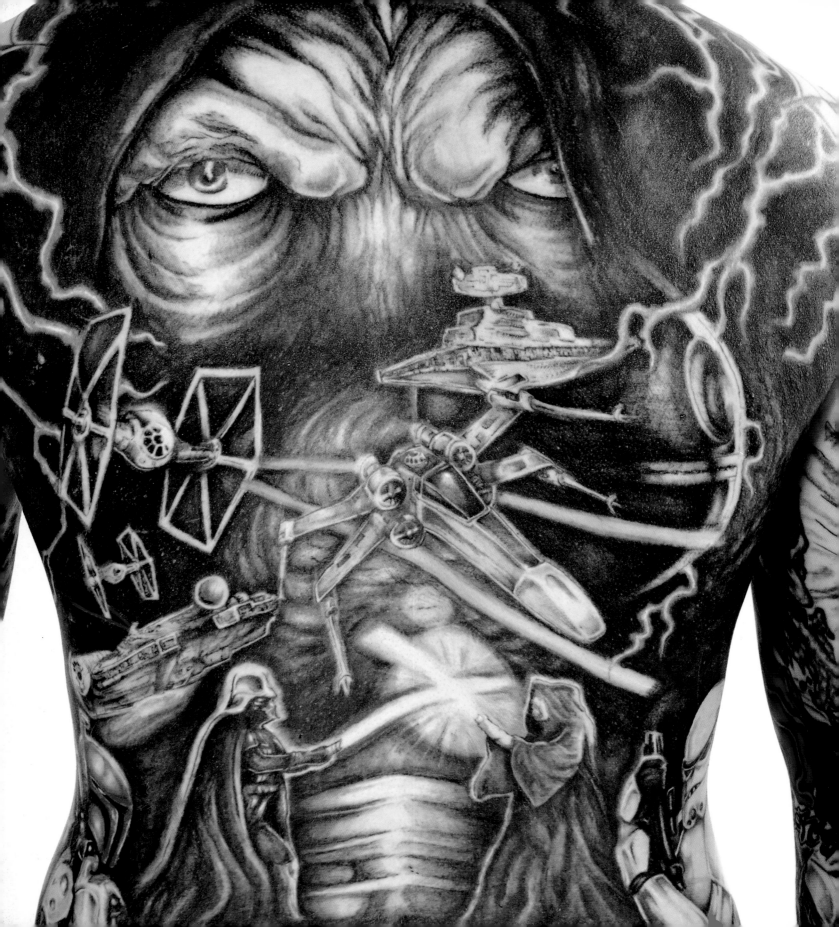

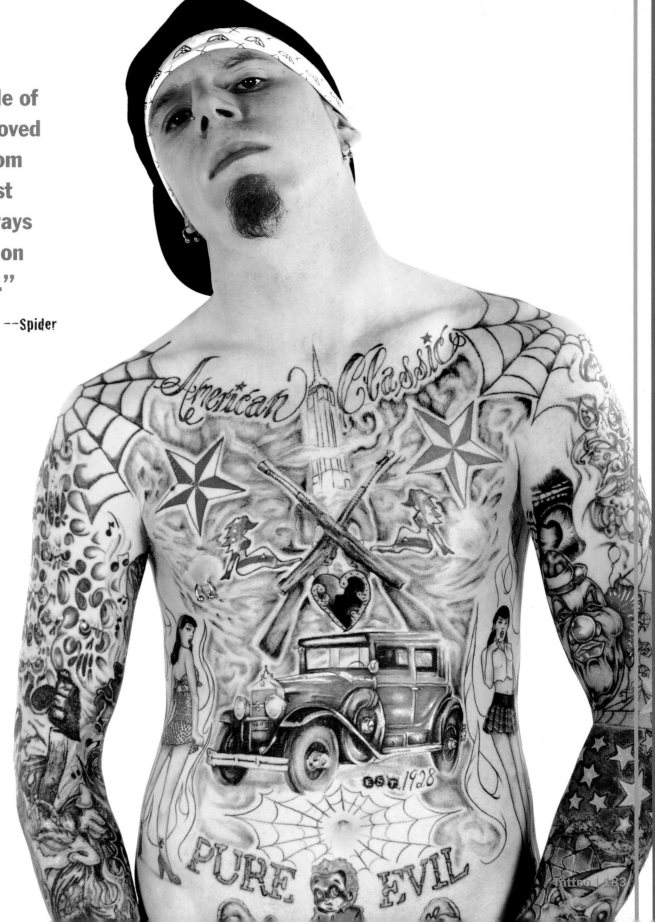

"The dark side of *Star Wars*. I loved that movie from childhood, just because I always wanted to be on the dark side."

--Spider

◄ This detailed *Star Wars* homage includes a looming Emperor Palatine and Darth Vader locked in a light saber duel with Obi Wan Kenobi.

Subject: Spider / Artist: Tommy Skoon, Ink Asylum

▶ This full-chest tattoo creates a vivid panorama of "American Classics," including the Empire State Building and a 1928 Model-T Ford.

Subject: Spider

A sad child-woman with her wounded teddy bears. Sometimes tattoos can tell a very personal story or mark a victory.

Subject: Nikki Sparks / Artist: Jose Garcia

"I was anorexic for seven years, and this tattoo is an ode to beating it."

—Nikki Sparks

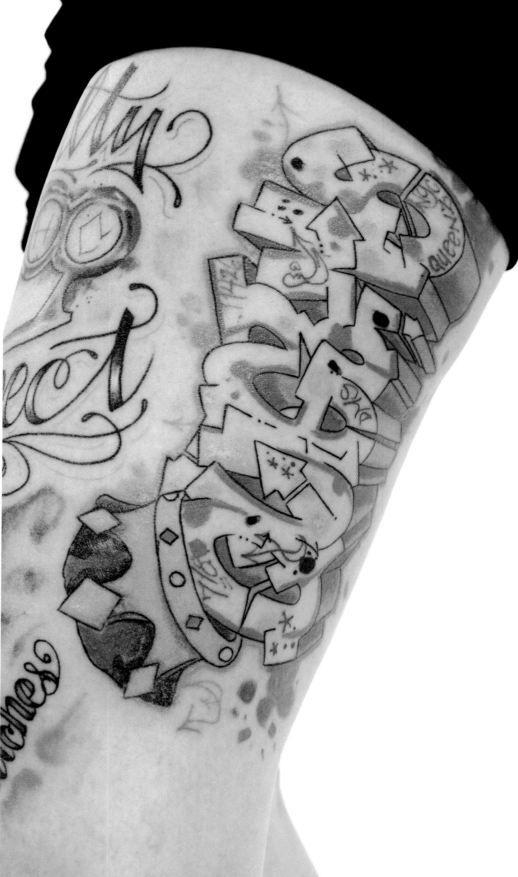

◁ This nearly fluorescent thigh ink offers a glimpse of a woman's personal philosophy and shows off her pride in her NYC hometown.

Subject: Bella / Artist: AJ and Vindeft

▽ Her belly tattoo displays a more whimsical message with its familiar Halloween refrain.

Subject: Bella / Artist: Joe Black

"My upper left leg is dedicated to hardcore; that's my life, so I wanted to do a whole piece for that, to represent where I'm from, Queens, and what I live for."

--Bella

> **"There is no 'underground' community, no dark den of drunken sailors initiating themselves into manhood via cheap, ill-conceived exercises in bodily perforation; it's just a group of people who delight in using their bodies as billboards."**
>
> —Joanne McCubrey, "Walking Art Tattoos"

▲ Eight fingers offer the perfect canvas for message tattoos, including, "Torn Soul," "Stay Away," "Pure Evil," and the self-evident "Knuckles."

Subjects: Spider, Bella, and Nikki Sparks

◄ These three proudly show off their dramatic body art statements.

Subjects: Bella, Spider, and Nikki Sparks

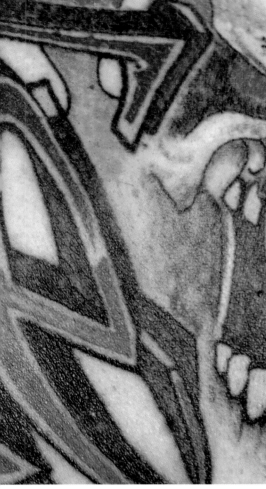

◄ This subject and his son wear matching tattoos—their surname across their backs.
Subject: Michael Conte / Artist: Patrick Levins

▼ These tattoos symbolize a mother's love. "The swallows are for my twin son and daughter. Each banner holds their name and it is on the side they were on in my womb."
Subject: Laura DiBenedetto, World Wide Gypsy Queen President / Artist: Israel

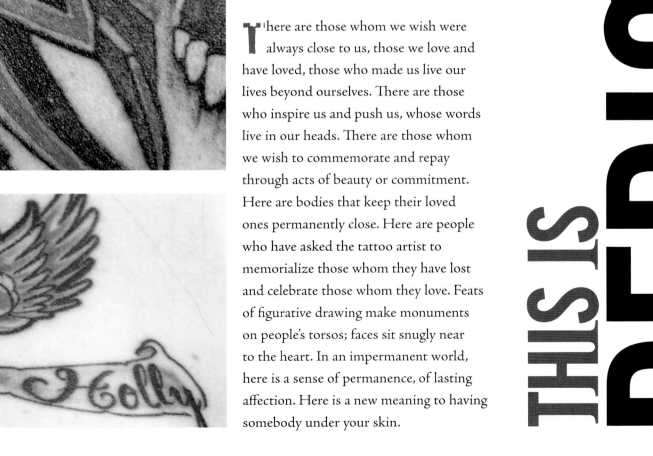

THIS IS DEDICATED

There are those whom we wish were always close to us, those we love and have loved, those who made us live our lives beyond ourselves. There are those who inspire us and push us, whose words live in our heads. There are those whom we wish to commemorate and repay through acts of beauty or commitment. Here are bodies that keep their loved ones permanently close. Here are people who have asked the tattoo artist to memorialize those whom they have lost and celebrate those whom they love. Feats of figurative drawing make monuments on people's torsos; faces sit snugly near to the heart. In an impermanent world, here is a sense of permanence, of lasting affection. Here is a new meaning to having somebody under your skin.

◄ A baby's handprints delicately etched on a mother's shoulder becomes a permanent record of a precious new life.

Subject: Hillary Cwick and Asher Schwartz / Artist: Jay

▶ Feathered wings of gray and black with carefully placed highlights of blue and red adorn the subject's back, perhaps reminding her of the better angels of our nature.

Subject: Hillary Cwick

"Usually all my tattoos came at good times. A tattoo is something permanent when you've made a self-discovery, or something you've come to a conclusion about. "

--Angelina Jolie, actor

A common sign in tattoo parlors is the old saying "Think Before You Ink," and that is certainly an appropriate warning for people thinking about tattooing names of girlfriends, boyfriends, wives, or husbands on their bodies. How many of them sat down in the tattoo chair absolutely sure that their object of affection was worth the ink? How many of them came to later regret that expression of undying passion for the lover or spouse who turned into an "ex"? A far safer dedication is also one of the most common: a memorial to Mom and Dad. While boyfriends and girlfriends come and go, our parents are with us forever.

▲ "Mom" and "Dad" may be common subjects for tattoos, but rarely are the sentiments so beautifully expressed in ink.
Subject: Sara Purr

◀ The subject's upper back reveals a Geisha framed by exotic butterfly wings.
Subject: Sara Purr

"Beauty is skin deep. A tattoo goes all the way to the bone. "

—Vince Hemingson, tattoo historian

◁ Another loving testimonial to Mom, worked with elegant swashes and deep red roses.
Subject: Pamela Francis

▷ Of her collection of body art, the subject says it's a "work in progress. I've added bits and pieces over the past few years."
Subject: Pamela Francis / Chop, Chop Shop Tattoos

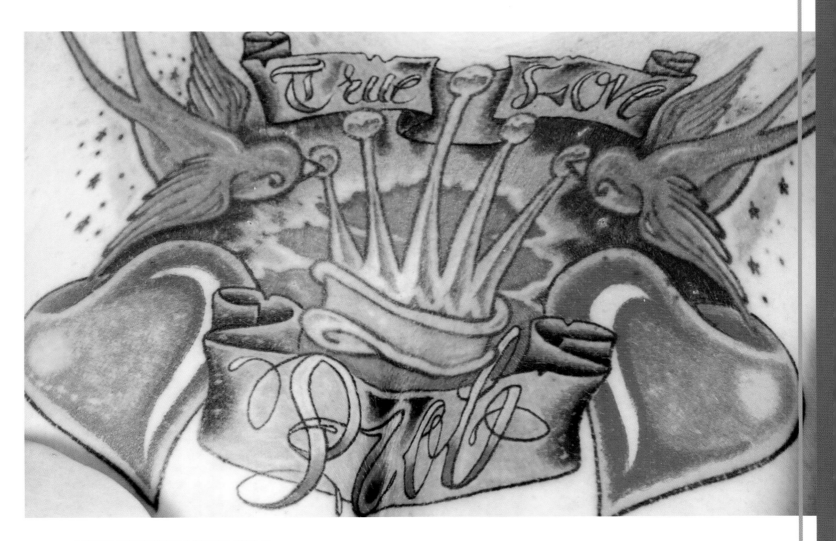

▲ The "True Love" tattoo on her upper chest is striking, with its vivid colors and twin hearts. The richness of the blues, shading from cerulean to cobalt stands up to the bold purples that blend from lavender to grape.

Subject: Pamela Francis / Chop, Chop Shop Tattoo

◀◀ A magical underwater scene complete with a lush koi immediately draws the viewer in. "I always wanted a large tattoo," the female subject explains. "And I love the Asian-inspired designs. Not meaningful, just beautiful."

Subject: Pamela Francis / Chop, Chop Shop Tattoos

◀ This diamond-eyed skull tattoo, located on the subject's left foot, is "half of a complete set representing my husband and I. Sort of death 'til do us part."

Subject: Pamela Francis / Chop, Chop Shop Tattoo

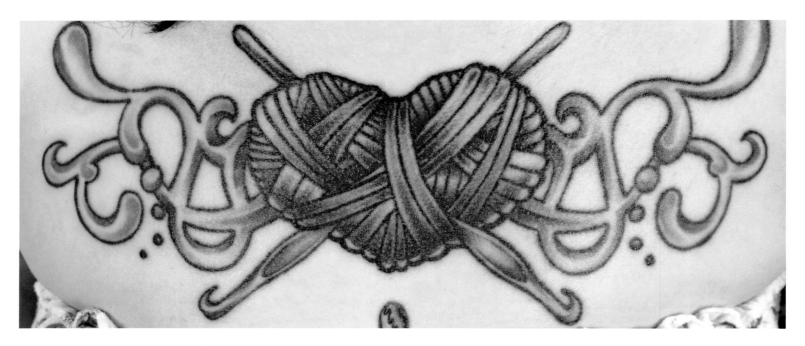

"My grandfather passed away this past November, and he drove a truck his entire life. The tattoo was the least I could do for him after all of the things he had done for everybody else."

--Mandi Starcher

▷ Not your typical tattoo, a purple yarn heart with crossed crochet hooks makes a homey, domestic statement. Above, a close-up of the heart shows intricate shading and skillful highlighting.

Subjects: Mandi Starcher and Rylee

◁ The image on the subject's inner left arm was inspired by her love of her grandfather.

Subject: Mandi Starcher / Artist: JR Tubbs

Nothing is more natural than wanting to commemorate a time of growth or a life-altering encounter. This could explain why many servicemen (and women) return from military duty bearing tattoos. They might want to show pride in their branches of service—the U.S. Marine bulldog, an RAF soaring falcon, or a navy anchor, for instance; memorialize a particular battle or action; or simply remind themselves of the sense of unshakeable brotherhood and camaraderie that those in combat share. And is it any wonder that service members stationed in Asia take advantage of skilled local practitioners and come home wearing exotic body art?

Whatever their motivation, military men and women take pride in these tattoos, which represent their service to flag and country.

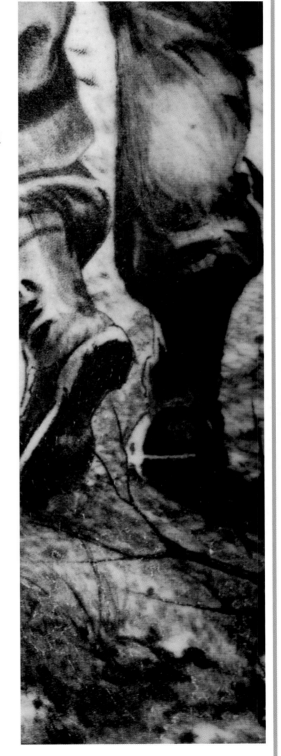

◀ This striking full-back tattoo conveys devotion to duty, as two medics aid a wounded comrade. The stark, photographic realism of the image underscores the urgency and poignancy of the scene.
Subject: Radoslaw Pieslak / Artist: Radek

▶ A close-up shows the tattoo artist's mastery of light and shadow.
Subject: Radoslaw Pieslak / Artist: Radek

"An everlasting gem that you will take into your grave."

--Line from a traditional
Polynesian song about tattooing

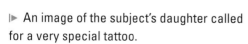 An image of the subject's daughter called for a very special tattoo.

*Subject: Alex Alien, Alid, Marquez, and Dafne Zoe /
Artist: Alex Alien, Aztec Roots Tattoo*

▶▶ Dad displays the shoulder portrait, which he says shows "the love for my daughter." She seems to approve the likeness.

*Subject: Dafne Zoe / Artist: Alex Alien,
Aztec Roots Tattoo*

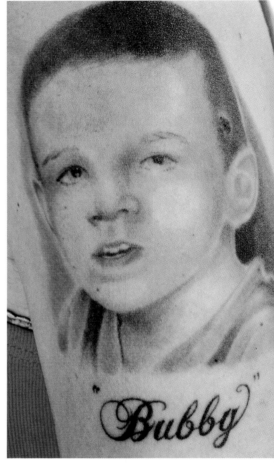

"My husband, Frank, always puts so much of his heart into each tattoo. Being his 'living canvas' and the mother of his children gives me more joy than words could ever express."

--Kristal Frank

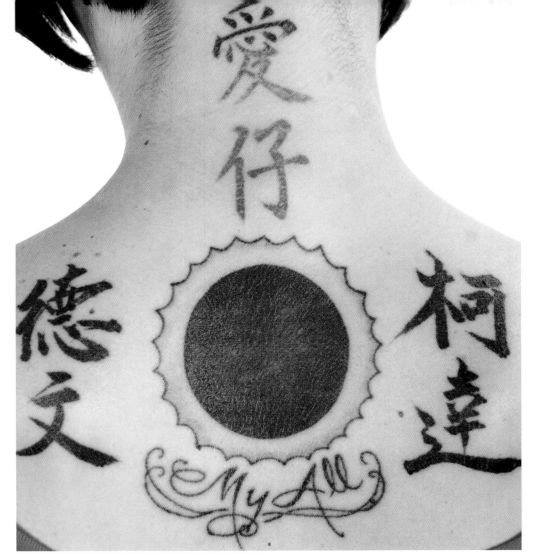

◀◀◀ Opposite page, left: this stunning portrait of a Native American woman, full of rich colors and amazing detail, graces the subject's right arm.

Subject: Kristal Frank / Artist: Walter "Sausage" Frank

◀◀ Opposite page, right: a realistic rendering of her son Devon is inked on her left arm.

Subject: Kristal Frank / Artist: Terry "Wookie" Hoffman

◀ A simple sun and the words "My All" grace the subject's back. Of her other tattoos, she says, "My tattoos all represent my three sons, Devon, Kodah, and Keeghan."

Subject: Kristal Frank / Artist: Walter "Sausage" Frank

▽ Strategically placed jewel studs decorate this butterfly, the centerpiece of a belly tattoo.

Subject: Kristal Frank / Artist: Walter "Sausage" Frank

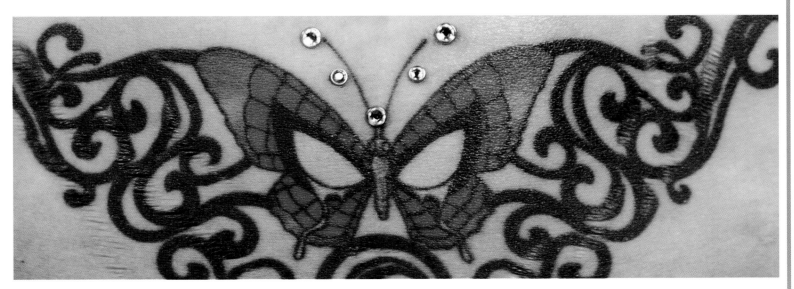

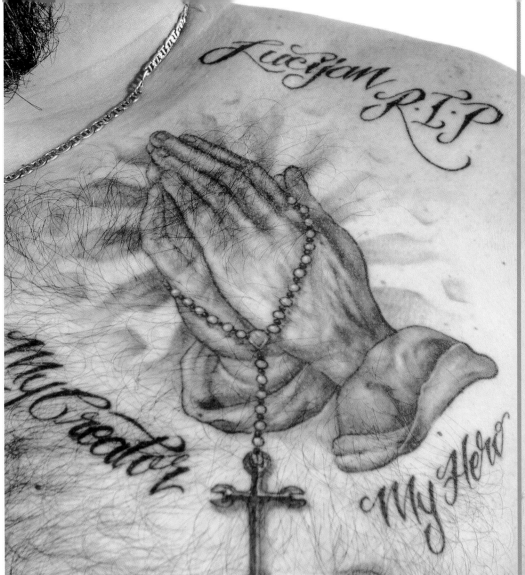

▲ An ink interpretation of Albrecht Dürer's famous *Praying Hands* holding a crucifix is the centerpiece of a memorial tattoo for a departed loved one.
Subject: Ziccy / Artist: Ian Shaffer

◄│◄ This father and daughter pair has opted for strong black tattoos, rather than bright colors, to express themselves. He shows off a female shaman on his side, while she displays a winged heart at her waist.
Subjects: Ziccy and Nicole "Nixy" Zic / Artist: Ian Shaffer

◄ This tattoo of the archangel Michael defeating Satan is graphic and stirring, a prime example of the effective use of monochromatic color. Note the one kick of blood red at the devil's severed neck.
Subject: Ziccy / Artist: Michelle Haspel

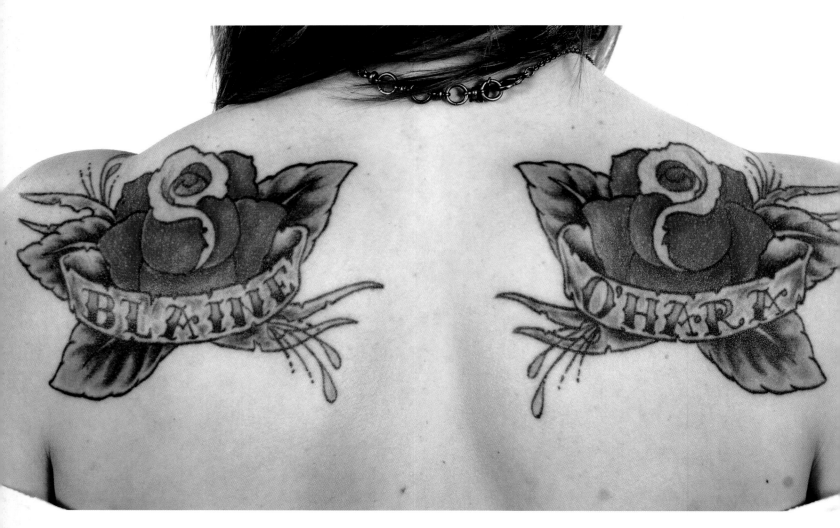

▲ Matching shoulder tattoos of carmine roses contain two names that are meaningful to the female subject.
Subject: loo / Artist: Chris Stumpf, Timeless Tatz

◀ A skeleton key is a popular motif, symbolizing secrets, knowledge, or maybe the key to someone's heart.
Subject: loo / Artist: Chris Stumpf, Timeless Tatz

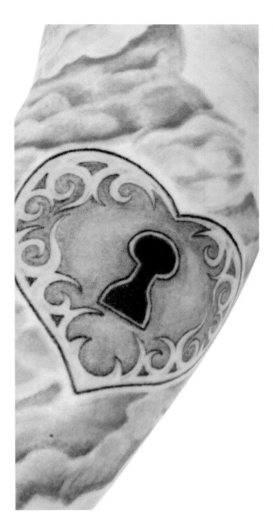

▲ A simple heart awaits a key to unlock it.
Subject: loo / Artist: Chris Stumpf, Timeless Tatz

▷ This is a beautiful example of impressionistic nonlinear tattoo art. The woman shares her own philosophy behind the image: "Nothing lasts forever . . . sunsets, youth, etc. Live each moment as it happens."
Subject: loo / Artist: Chris Stumpf, Timeless Tatz

▲ The entire chest is a testament to family, featuring "Mom," "Dad," and "Zachary" tattoos.
Subject: Mike Jone$

◀ The subject describes the brilliant skull butterfly on his throat as "tough but kinda cute." The traditional and carefully rendered image of Our Lady of Sorrows on his right arm contrasts with the version of the madonna on his abdomen, which has taken a quirky turn. Rather than the heart, the madonna herself is impaled with swords, like a figure from the Tarot.
Subject: Mike Jone$ / Artists: Steve Monie; Tattoos by Phil

▶ A companion piece to right, his left arm bears a detailed image of the Sacred Heart of Jesus.
Subject: Mike Jone$

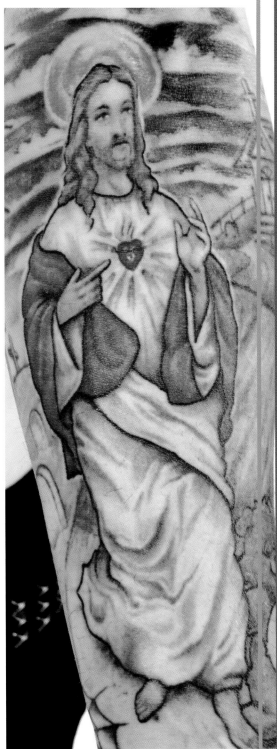

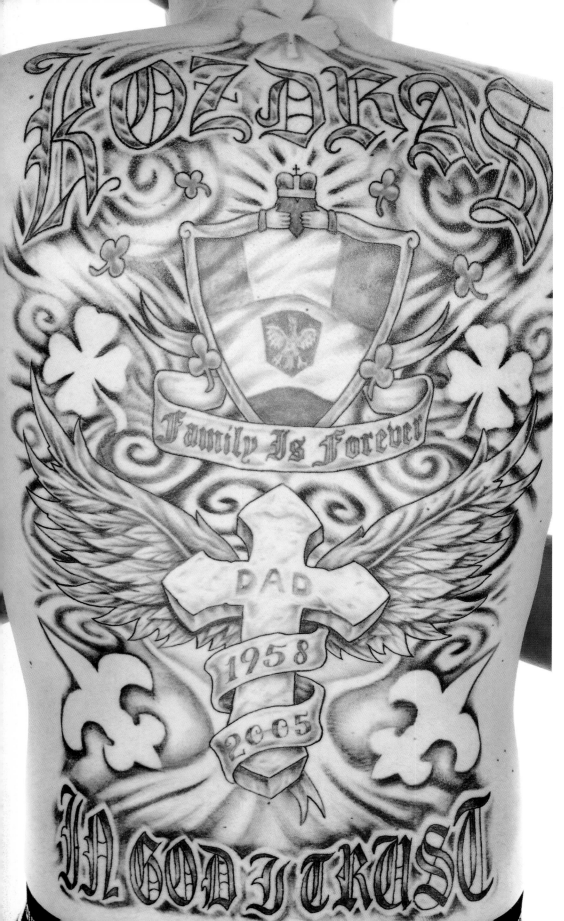

"The parrot's banners, 'Be good—If you can't be good, be careful,' it's something my grandmother used to say to me."

—Jenny B. Good

◄ The inspiration behind this dramatic full-back tattoo—which features a winged cross, shamrocks, fleur de lis, and a crest displaying the Irish and Polish flags—was "Family, Father, Passing Away."
Subject: Kyle Izozoras / Artist: Steve Monie

▶ This realistic tattoo of two parrots on a cherry tree branch expresses a warning that the subject's grandmother offered her.
Subject: Jenny B. Good / Artist: Kevin LeBlanc, White Lotus Tattoo

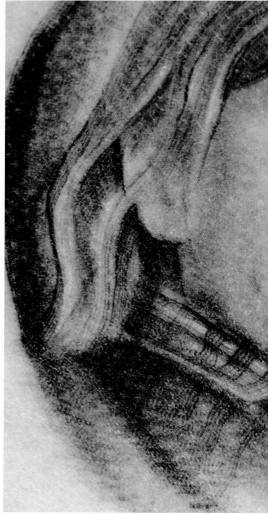

▲ A soft-focus portrait of a young girl displays an unusual stippled inking effect.

Subject: Nakia Lawton / Artist: Ink Slingers

◄ A portrait tattoo can be a true art form in the right hands. This elegant lady is dedicated to the female subject's mentor. "Rachel Telles . . . inspires me with my art and is one of my best friends. The Victorian lady was more for her to express herself through her art. It inspires me as an apprentice to strive to reach her level."

Subject: Shannaan / Artist: Rachel Telles

▶ This serene beauty has a madonna-like feel, posed against a cross amid a cascade of roses. This elegant tattoo evokes the feel of an Art Nouveau poster.

Subject: Karen Herb / Artist: Christopher Depinto

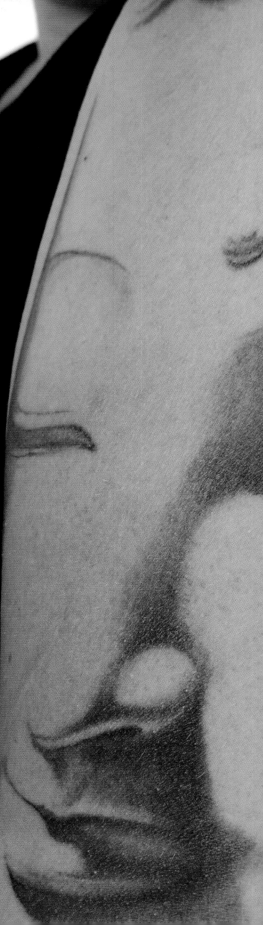

> **"My idea of a good picture is one that's in focus and of a famous person."**
>
> —Andy Warhol

▷ On her left arm, the subject shows off the serene, mysterious face of the Buddha.
Subject: Carly "Underscore"

▷▷ On her right arm is an homage to Camille Rose Garcia, whose "art is amazing and daring. I took different pieces from her books and created a great tattoo."
Subject: Carly "Underscore" / Artist: Justin (Jersey)

▽ Of this vivid portrait of pop-art icon Andy Warhol, the female subject confesses, "he's my own idol in the art world."
Subject: Carly "Underscore" / Artist: Aaron Is

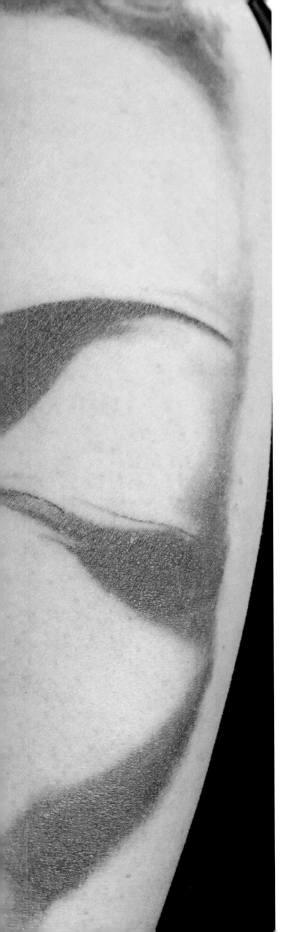

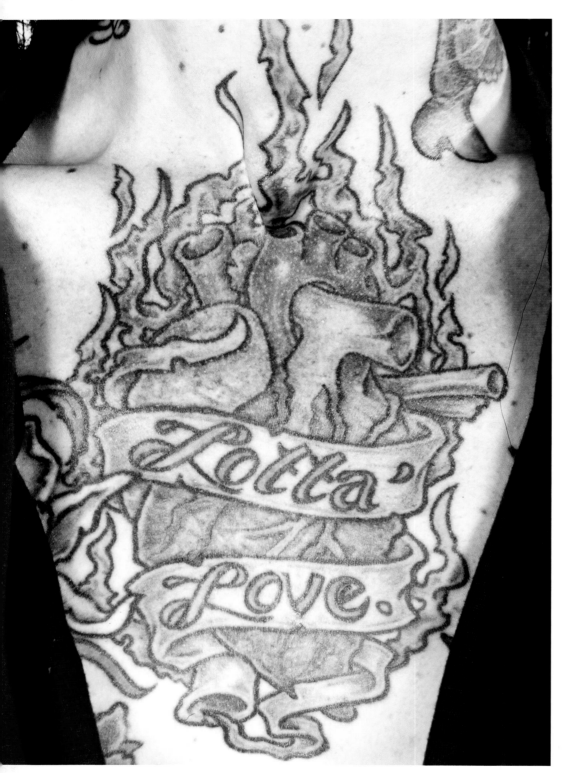

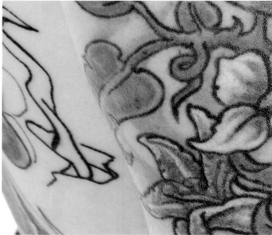

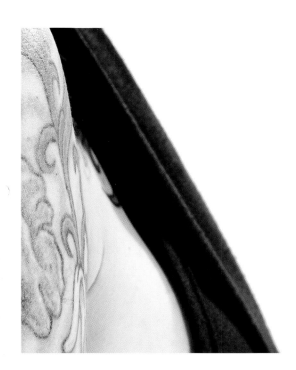

"Grandfather was raised in the depression and said, 'We ain't got a lotta money, but we got a whole lotta love.' He raised me, and it's a memorial to him."

--Nikki Sparks

◄ Far left, this chest tattoo is a memorial to the subject's grandfather, who brought her up. Left, irises and toadstools add a touch of spring.
Subject: Nikki Sparks / Artist: Greg Hess

▶ Of the rib tattoo of a candle hanging on a string, which was inspired by a past relationship, she explains, "No one holds a candle to you."
Subject: Nikki Sparks / Artist: Greg Hess

▷ This unusual tattoo with science fiction overtones runs right across the back of the subject's two clenched hands.

Subject: Anthony Enochs

▷▷ This photogenic couple displays their impressive upper body tattoos, while their smiling baby looks on—and maybe contemplates his own future ink.

Subject: Anthony Enochs, Erin McNish, and Evers Enochs

▽ More irony, as the sentiment *pur vida*, or "pure life," is juxtaposed with straight razors, brass knuckles, and twining, bloody thorns.

Subject: Anthony Enochs

▷ This subject asked each of his family members to pick a flower. He proudly showed off the finished art at a family wedding.
Subject: Matt McGarvey / Artist: Troy Timpel
Photograph by Troy Timpel

CREDITS & ACKNOWLEDGMENTS

All photography by Jonathan Conklin, unless otherwise noted.

The publisher and authors wish to thank H. Lee, the book's designer, for jumping in head first on one of her first assignments, not only wrangling subjects but also coming up with a brilliant design; Suzanne Lander, ace editor, organizer, and wonder woman, who made the tattoo shoot happen and, with her usual charm, convinced so many people to smile for the camera; and Jonathan Conklin, photographer, for shooting so many images so quickly and still making each one a work of art.

We also sincerely thank the many, many subjects who willingly bared their skin to show off some amazing ink. This book is really all about them and their tattoos. We have made our best effort to credit each one as accurately as we could.

Special thanks to Troy Timpel (check out tattooedkingpin.com), tattoo artist and organizer of the Philadelphia Tattoo Arts Convention. Troy graciously gave us room to shoot. Without his generous help, we would have never had such a beautiful—and authentic—book.

Herbert Puchta and Jeff Stranks with Meredith Levy

English in Mind

* **Workbook Starter**

CAMBRIDGE
UNIVERSITY PRESS

CAMBRIDGE UNIVERSITY PRESS
Cambridge, New York, Melbourne, Madrid, Cape Town, Singapore, São Paulo

Cambridge University Press
The Edinburgh Building, Cambridge CB2 8RU, UK

www.cambridge.org
Information on this title: www.cambridge.org/9780521750417

First published 2004
7th printing 2007

Printed in Italy by Legoprint S.p.A.

A catalogue record for this publication is available from the British Library

ISBN 978-0-521-75041-7 Workbook with Audio CD / CD-ROM
ISBN 978-0-521-75038-7 Student's Book
ISBN 978-0-521-75042-4 Teacher's Book
ISBN 978-0-521-75043-1 Teacher's Resource Pack
ISBN 978-0-521-75044-8 Class Cassettes
ISBN 978-0-521-54503-7 Class Audio CDs

Contents

1 I know!

1 Remember and check

a Write the names under the pictures.

Amy   Alex   Rob   Lucy

1 _____   2 _____   3 _____   4 _____

b Write the words. Then check with the dialogue on page 5 of the Student's Book.

is   Hello   ~~Rob~~   name's   I'm   your

Rob: Hi! I'm ___*Rob*___ . What's ¹ _____ name?
Amy: ² _____ Amy, and this ³ _____ Lucy.
Alex: ⁴ _____ . My ⁵ _____ Alex.

2 Vocabulary

International words

a 🔊 Listen and write the numbers 1–10.

b 🔊 Listen again and write the words. Then check with the list on page 8 of the Student's Book.

 a

 b

_____

 c
7
_____
taxi

 d

_____

 e

_____

 f
2
_____
hamburger

 g

_____

 h

_____

 i

_____

 j

_____

Classroom objects

c What are the words?
Write them on the picture.

np e   abdro   lepnic   ~~wwdion~~   tnokeoob   kdse   rchia   orod

1 _window_

3 _____

2 _____

5 _____

4 _____

6 _____

7 _____

8 _____

3 Grammar

Plurals

a Look at these examples for writing plurals.

1	door	2	doors
1	phone	2	phones
1	hobby	2	hobbies
1	watch	2	watches

Complete the table.

Singular	Plural
1 hotel	_hotels_
2 page	_____
3 notebook	_____
4 sandwich	_____
5 city	_____
6 taxi	_____
7 nationality	_____

b Write the numbers and the plural form of the words.

cassette   child   woman   ~~computer~~   person   man

1 _2 computers_

2 _____

3 _____

4 _____

5 _____

6 _____

a or an?

c Write *a* or *an*.

1 _a_ good team

2 _____ small museum

3 _____ interesting book

4 _____ big television

5 _____ cheap pencil

6 _____ expensive hotel

7 _____ old city

8 _____ boring video

4 Vocabulary

Adjectives

Look at the pictures. If the adjective is correct, write ✓. If the adjective is wrong, write the correct adjective.

small
1 a ~~big~~ restaurant

2 an expensive pen ✓

3 a new computer

4 an interesting book

5 a bad team

6 a big hamburger

7 an old car

8 a good hotel

5 Pronunciation

Word stress

🔊 Listen and write the words in the lists. Listen again, check and repeat.

> ~~hotel~~ ~~cheap~~ ~~hamburger~~ football
> people expensive board new
> video boring museum phone

1 syllable	2 syllables	3 syllables
cheap	*hotel*	*hamburger*

6 Spelling

The alphabet

(a) 🔊 Listen to the spelling. Write the letters. What is the sentence?

Lu

(b) 🔊 Listen and write the words.

1 Name: *Kevin*
  City:

2 Name: *Julie*
  City:

7 Vocabulary

Numbers 0–20

(a) Write the answers.

1 nine + nine = *eighteen*
2 four + seven =
3 two + twelve =
4 one + eight =
5 three + two =
6 twelve + eight =
7 ten + seven =
8 four + eight =

Numbers 20–100

b Write the next two numbers.

1	ten	thirty	fifty	*seventy* _____
2	four	eight	sixteen	_____ _____
3	forty-one	fifty-two	sixty-three	_____ _____
4	eighty-four	eighty-one	seventy-eight	_____ _____
5	twenty-nine	thirty-three	thirty-seven	_____ _____

c 🔊 Listen and (circle) the numbers you hear.

1 ⑬ 30
2 15 50
3 17 70
4 14 40
5 16 60
6 18 80

8 Everyday English

Complete the dialogues with the words in the box.

> I can help you   that's right   Thanks   the answer
> ~~OK~~   How do you say   I don't know   don't understand

1 Kim: The homework is on page 12. _OK_ ?
   James: Yes, great. ¹ _____ , Kim.

2 Ben: I ² _____ these words.
   Mike: No problem. ³ _____ .
   Ben: Thanks!

3 Teacher: What's ⁴ _____ , Kate?
   Kate: Sorry, ⁵ _____ .

4 Teacher: ⁶ _____ 'Ciao' in English?
   Tony: 'Hi'.
   Teacher: Yes, ⁷ _____ .

9 Study help

Using a dictionary

a Look at the pairs. Underline the word that is first in a dictionary.

1 restaurant   sandwich
2 taxi   English
3 cinema   city
4 phone   museum
5 hamburger   teacher
6 video   hotel
7 pizza   excellent
8 cheap   good

b Put the words in alphabetical order. Write them in the list.

1	*cheap*	9	_____
2	*cinema*	10	_____
3	*city*	11	_____
4	_____	12	_____
5	_____	13	_____
6	_____	14	_____
7	_____	15	_____
8	_____	16	_____

Skills in mind

10 Listen

🔊 Listen and write the numbers 1–6 in the boxes.

a

b

c

Thank you!

Thank you!

d

e

1

f

11 Read

Read the message. Mark the sentences *T* (true) or *F* (false).

Sarah

Problems! I don't know how to find the restaurant — can you help me? And what's the name of the cinema? Please phone me on 06529 61174, OK?

You can listen to my new CD. It's on my desk and it's great!

Paul

1   The message is from Paul.   [T]

2   Paul is in a restaurant.   [   ]

3   He knows the name of the cinema. [   ]

4   His phone number is 06529 61174. [   ]

5   Paul's CD is old.   [   ]

6   It's an excellent CD.   [   ]

Unit check

1 Fill in the spaces

Complete the sentences with the words in the box.

| phone | Thanks | I | What's | ~~computer~~ | I'm | page | don't | help | your |

1 It's a good _____computer_____ game.

2 A: Hi! I'm Claudio. What's [1]_____ name?

B: [2]_____ Joanne, and this is my friend Louise.

3 A: [3]_____ the answer?

B: Sorry, I [4]_____ know.

4 A: What's your [5]_____ number?

B: It's 813028.

5 A: [6]_____ don't understand.

B: No problem. I can [7]_____ you.

A: [8]_____ , Amy.

6 Look at the picture on [9]_____ 28.

9

2 Choose the correct answers

(Circle) the correct answers, a, b or c.

1 I _____ the answer.

a help   b (know)   c OK

2 Look at the three _____ .

a men   b man   c person

3 What's your phone _____ ?

a name   b notebook   c number

4 79 = _____

a seven nine   b ninety-seven   c seventy-nine

5 Twenty-three + eighteen = _____

a thirty-one   b forty-one   c fifty

6 He's a great football _____ .

a man   b player   c team

7 It's an _____ restaurant.

a big   b expensive   c good

8 A: Is it a new desk?

B: No, it's _____ .

a bad   b small   c old

9 A: Is it a good book?

B: Yes, it's _____ .

a interesting   b cheap   c boring

8

3 Correct the mistakes

In each sentence there is a mistake. <u>Underline</u> the mistake and write the correct sentence.

1 Eleven + two = <u>threeteen</u>   _Eleven + two = thirteen_ _____

2 It's a expensive CD. _____

3 The two woman are Sally and Caroline. _____

4 Four + twelve = sixty _____

5 What's you name? _____

6 It's a new cinemas. _____

7 He's an interesting people. _____

8 Forty-nine + seven = fivety-six _____

9 The homework is in page 35. _____

8

How did you do?

Total: **25**

| 😊 | Very good 20 – 25 | 😐 | OK 14 – 19 | 😞 | Review Unit 1 again 0 – 13 |

2 She isn't American

1 Grammar

The verb *be* (singular)

a Match the sentences with the pictures. Write numbers 1–9 in the boxes.

b Look at the <u>underlined</u> words. Write the short form, with *'m, 's* or *'re*.

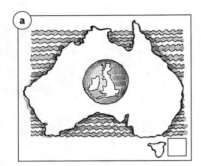

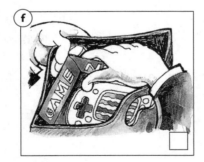

1   It <u>is</u> a boring film.
   _It's_

2   She <u>is</u> an excellent singer.
   ....

3   <u>You are</u> a great teacher.
   ....

4   It <u>is</u> a new computer game.
   ....

5   <u>Richard is</u> from New York.
   ....

6   <u>Australia is</u> a big country.
   ....

7   <u>I am</u> Carla. <u>What is</u> your name?
   ....

c Complete the dialogues.

1   A: Is Serena Williams a film star?
    B: No, ..._she's_..... a tennis player.

2   A: Leonardo DiCaprio is an English actor, I think.
    B: No, ... from the USA.

3   A: Is this video good?
    B: Yes, ... great!

4   A: I think .... from Italy.
    B: No, I'm not. I'm American.

5   A: What's *porta* in English?
    B: .... a door.

d Write the negative forms in the table.

Positive	Negative – full form	Negative – short form
1 I am	_I am not_	_I'm not_
2 You are	....	....
3 He is	....	....
4 She is	....	....
5 It is	....	....

e Write positive or negative sentences.

1 he / a singer	2 she / British	3 it / Japanese	4 she / the winner
He isn't a singer.	*She's British.*		

5 it / boring	6 you / a film star	7 it / expensive	8 you / a bad dog

f Put the words in order to make questions.

1 you OK Are ?
  Are you OK?

2 British she Is ?

3 Istanbul you Are from ?

4 right I Am ?

5 big a Is it city ?

6 Brad Pitt good a actor Is ?

g Write questions. Then listen, check and repeat.

1 She's American.
  Is she American?

2 You're from Japan.

3 He's a good footballer.

4 It's a cheap restaurant.

5 I'm the winner!

6 Broadway's in New York.

7 The hotel's expensive.

8 Maria's from Spain.

9 You're a singer.

10 The answer's on page 5.

2 Vocabulary

Countries

a Write the countries on the map.

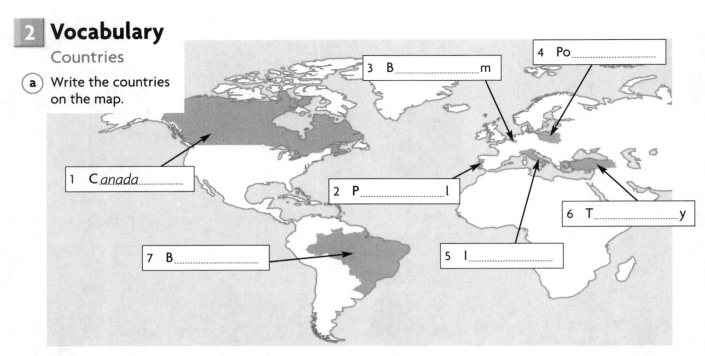

3 B_____m

4 Po_____

1 C _anada_____

2 P_____l

6 T_____y

5 I_____

7 B_____

Nationalities

b Find seven more nationalities in the puzzle.

I	T	A	A	L	L	B	A	R	H	T
T	U	R	M	I	S	R	U	S	S	I
A	R	C	E	F	T	I	O	I	A	N
L	L	I	R	A	T	T	A	L	S	Q
I	D	P	I	S	W	I	S	S	T	B
A	H	O	C	W	I	S	T	P	V	E
N	S	L	A	A	S	H	R	A	I	L
I	P	I	N	S	T	A	G	L	O	G
A	U	S	T	R	A	L	I	A	N	I
N	X	H	T	U	R	K	I	S	H	A
A	M	E	X	T	R	S	P	F	E	N

3 Pronunciation

🔊 Listen and <u>underline</u> the word you hear.

1 Poland   <u>Polish</u>
2 Australia   Australian
3 Russia   Russian
4 Germany   German
5 Turkey   Turkish
6 Canada   Canadian

c Where are they from? Write two sentences about each person.

1 _He's from Brazil._   2 _____
   He's Brazilian.   _____

3 _____   4 _____
   _____   _____

5 _____   6 _____
   _____   _____

4 Grammar

wh- question words

a Match the questions and answers.

1	Who's she?	a	Yes, thanks.
2	Are you American?	b	I don't know.
3	Is Oxford a big city?	c	No, it's small.
4	Are you OK?	d	Yes, she's great!
5	Where are you from?	e	No, I'm Australian.
6	Is she a good teacher?	f	Turkey.

b Complete the sentences. Use *Who*, *Where*, *What* or *How*.

1 I don't know her. _____ is she?

2 _____'s your phone number?

3 _____ are you from?

4 _____'s the name of the hotel?

5 A: _____'s Sydney?

   B: It's in Australia.

6 A: _____'s that girl?

   B: My friend Sally.

7 _____ old is she?

8 A: _____'s this?

   B: It's my vocabulary notebook.

5 Culture in mind

Complete the sentences.

1 It's in _____ *Australia* _____ .

2 He's _____ .

3 _____ from Argentina.

4 It's a _____ city.

5 I'm _____ .

6 She _____ in Germany

6 Study help

Vocabulary

a For every unit, write new words in your Vocabulary notebook. Write them in groups. For example:

Classroom things	Classroom verbs
desk	listen
board	read
pen	_____
_____	_____
_____	_____
_____	_____
_____	

Write these words in the lists.

> pencil   write   look at   chair   notebook   say   ask   table

b Look at the words in Unit 2. Write all the words you can find in these lists.

Countries	Nationalities	Jobs
Italy	Italian	film star
Spain	_____	_____
China	_____	_____
_____	_____	_____

Skills in mind

7 Read

Read the text. Then mark the statements *T* (true) or *F* (false).

I'm Helen. I'm fourteen and I'm British. My home is in Wells. It's an old city, but it isn't very big. My address is 32 Castle Road and my phone number is 01749 652013.

My best friend is Michael. He's from Ireland and his father is French. Michael is fifteen, so he isn't in my class at school. He isn't a very good football player, but I think he's a great singer. He's a good friend and he helps me with my homework.

1	The girl's name is Helen.	T
2	She's from Britain.	
3	Wells is a new city.	
4	It's a small city.	
5	Michael is Helen's friend.	
6	He's a French boy.	
7	He isn't in Helen's class.	
8	He's an excellent footballer.	

Reading tip

New words

What happens if you don't know a word in a reading text?

- You can understand the text even if you don't know all the words.

- Look at the word. Is it similar to a word in your language?

- Look at the other words in the sentence, and think about the new word. Can you guess the meaning?

8 Write

Complete the interview with Helen. Write one word in each space.

Interviewer: Where _____ _____ from?

Helen: _____ from _____ . It's a city in England.

Interviewer: _____ _____ a big city?

Helen: _____ , it _____ .

Interviewer: _____ your _____ ?

Helen: It's 32 Castle Road.

Interviewer: I know Michael's your _____ _____ . Is _____ Irish?

Helen: Yes, _____ _____ .

Interviewer: _____ old _____ he?

Helen: _____ _____ .

Unit check

1 Fill in the spaces

Complete the dialogues with the words in the box.

| Is | Polish | actor | from | Who's | teacher | ~~What's~~ | is | Belgium | isn't |

1 A: Hello. _____*What's*_____ your name?

   B: I'm Dieter and I'm from ¹ _____ . This ² _____ my friend Sonia.

   A: Is she ³ _____ Russia?

   B: No, she ⁴ _____ . She's ⁵ _____ .

2 A: ⁶ _____ this?

   B: He's Luc Duval.

   A: ⁷ _____ he an ⁸ _____ ?

   B: No, he's a ⁹ _____ .

`9`

2 Choose the correct answers

Circle the correct answers, a, b or c.

1 I think he's great! He's my _____ .
   a (hero) b singer c winner

2 She's a famous film _____ .
   a player b star c model

3 Ricardo's nationality is _____ .
   a Switzerland b Spain c Swiss

4 How old _____ ?
   a she is b she's c is she

5 _____ is a big country.
   a Canada b French c Russian

6 This tennis player _____ Australian.
   a are b aren't c isn't

7 _____ are you from?
   a What b Where c How

8 Is _____ a Japanese flag?
   a he b she c it

9 _____ your address?
   a What's b Who's c Where's

`8`

3 Correct the mistakes

In each sentence there is a mistake with the verb *be*, countries and nationalities.
Underline the mistake and write the correct sentence.

1 My friend is Germany. _*My friend is German.*_ _____

2 Are you Italyan? _____

3 I not a good singer. _____

4 What your address? _____

5 You isn't an actor. _____

6 Im from Poland. _____

7 Is he a China footballer? _____

8 Maria is from Spain? _____

9 What this is in English? _____

`8`

How did you do?

Total: `25`

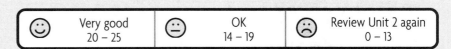

| :) | Very good 20 – 25 | :\| | OK 14 – 19 | :(| Review Unit 2 again 0 – 13 |

3 We're a new band

Check with the dialogue on page 20 of the Student's Book.

1 Remember and check

Match the two parts of the sentences, and write the name of the speaker, *Zoë* or *Nick*. Check with the dialogue on page 20 of the Student's Book.

1	___Zoë___ : How old	a the show.
2	_____ : Are you all from	b 17.
3	_____ : You're very	c new band.
4	_____ : We're a	d are you?
5	_____ : Welcome to	e popular in Cambridge.
6	_____ : I'm	f Cambridge?

2 Grammar

The verb *be* (singular and plural)

a Complete the sentences.

1 ____I'm____ a tennis player.

2 _____ my favourite singer.

3 I think _____ Australian.

4 What's this in English? / _____ a notebook.

5 _____ from Germany.

6 _____ the winners.

7 _____ fantastic!

8 _____ boring.

b Write true sentences with the verb *be*.

1 Mel Gibson / American   *Mel Gibson isn't American. He's Australian.*

2 Madonna / singer   *Madonna is a singer.*

3 Tokyo / city in China   _____

4 My favourite restaurant / expensive   _____

5 I / British   _____

6 Ferrari cars / cheap   _____

7 Ben Afleck / sports star   _____

8 We / in Rome   _____

c Match the questions with the answers.

1 Is he German?
2 Are they a Brazilian band?
3 Is this CD expensive?
4 Are you and John football players?
5 Are you from Poland?
6 Are Ann and Sophie good singers?
7 Am I a good tennis player?
8 Is she your friend?

a No, she isn't. I think she's boring.
b No, it isn't. It's quite cheap.
c Yes, I think you are.
d Yes, he is. He's from Hamburg.
e No, they aren't. They're from Spain.
f No, I'm not. I'm Russian.
g Yes, we are. We're in the school team.
h Yes, they are. They're great.

d Write the questions.

1 Maria / from Milan?   *Is Maria from Milan?*
2 Ken and Sandy / American?
3 I / a good singer?
4 Where / you from, Sarah?
5 the film / interesting?
6 you and Robert / football players?
7 Ricky Martin / popular in Belgium?
8 Julie and I / good actors?
9 Who / you?
10 What / your phone number?

e Read the questions and write true answers.

1 Are you a teacher?   *No, I'm not. I'm a student.*
2 Are you a good singer?
3 Are you from New York?
4 Are you and your friends in a band?
5 Are CDs expensive in your country?
6 Is your mother a tennis player?
7 Is your teacher British?
8 Is your school very big?

I like ...

f Complete the dialogue.

Kate: Do *you like* sports?

Ben: Yes, I ¹ _____ . I ² _____
football and ³ _____ . But I ⁴ _____
_____ volleyball.

Kate: ⁵ _____ you _____ golf?

Ben: ⁶ _____ , I _____ .
It's boring!

3 Vocabulary

Positive and negative adjectives

a) Circle the correct word.

1 I don't like pizza. I think it's *awful / wonderful*.
2 I like this video. It's *boring / fantastic*.
3 Enrique Iglesias is my favourite singer. He's *terrible / excellent*.
4 I don't want to listen to REM. I think they're *great / terrible*.

b) Use the words in the box to write about the pictures.

I like	I think it's	great	terrible	wonderful
I really like	I think they're	awful	excellent	boring
I don't like		fantastic	interesting	

Example

I don't like computer games. I think they're boring.

1 _____
2 _____
3 _____
4 _____
5 _____
6 _____

4 Grammar

Object pronouns

Complete the sentences with object pronouns.

1 I don't like _____ . She isn't very interesting.
2 Paul's a good singer. Listen to _____ .
3 Dogs are great. I like _____ a lot.
4 Bye! See _____ on Friday!
5 Look! A picture of my favourite band! I want _____ !
6 I like James, but he doesn't like _____ .

5 Pronunciation
/ɪ/ and /iː/

a 🔊 Listen to the <u>underlined</u> sounds. Write the words in the lists. Then listen again, check and repeat.

~~s<u>ee</u>~~   ~~th<u>i</u>nk~~   s<u>i</u>nger   pl<u>ea</u>se   f<u>i</u>lm
r<u>ea</u>d   mus<u>eu</u>m   c<u>i</u>nema   C<u>D</u>   b<u>i</u>g
p<u>eo</u>ple   w<u>o</u>men

is /ɪ/	three /iː/
think	*see*
‑‑‑‑‑‑‑‑	‑‑‑‑‑‑‑‑
‑‑‑‑‑‑‑‑	‑‑‑‑‑‑‑‑
‑‑‑‑‑‑‑‑	‑‑‑‑‑‑‑‑
‑‑‑‑‑‑‑‑	‑‑‑‑‑‑‑‑

b 🔊 Listen and repeat.

1 Three big museums.
2 We think he's Swiss.
3 Fifteen CDs, please.
4 The Italian singer is the winner.

6 Everyday English

Complete the dialogues. Use words from box A and box B.

A
want   really   Guess   Let's

B
go together   what   to go   excited

Mark: ¹ .... ? 4Tune are on TV on Tuesday!

Chris: I know. Isn't it fantastic? I'm
² .... !

Dave: The new cinema is open on Saturday.

Sue: Oh, great! I ³ .... What about you?

Dave: Yes, me too. ⁴ ....

7 Study help
Pronunciation

Mark the stress on new words in your Vocabulary notebook like this:

● <u>underline</u> the stressed sound
fan<u>ta</u>stic   <u>wo</u>nderful   <u>fa</u>vourite

● use the sign '. This is the sign in a dictionary.
fan'tastic   'wonderful   'favourite

a Write the sign ' to show the stress in these words.

1 popular   5 computer
2 American   6 concert
3 Japanese   7 seventeen
4 terrible

b Write adjectives from Unit 3 in this list. Mark the stress.

<u>Adjectives</u>

fan'tastic   ....

....

....

Skills in mind

8 Read and listen

a 🔊 Look at this girl's Internet homepage. Listen and complete the text. Write one word in each space.

Judy Dahrendorf

Hi! Welcome to my homepage

My ___name___ is Judy Dahrendorf. I live in Santa Cruz in California and I really like pop [1] _____ . Can you guess who my [2] _____ pop stars are? Yes, you're right: they're the 'Backstreet Boys'

Here are four things I want to tell you about them:

♥ There are five people in the
[3] _____ :
A.J. McLean, Howie Dorough, Nick Carter, Kevin Richardson and Brian Littrell.

♥ My favourite Backstreet Boy
[4] _____
A.J. McLean. I think he's
[5] _____ ! And
he's [6] _____
singer!

♥ My favourite BSB song is
I'll never break your heart.
All my friends say their favourite is *Quit playing games with my heart.* (I think it's [7] _____ good, but it isn't my favourite.)

♥ The Backstreet Boys are
all [8] _____ .
Brian is from Kentucky, and the other four are
[9] _____ Florida.

Click here and listen to me!

★ ★ ★ ★ ★

Do you [10] _____ my homepage? I hope so. And I hope you like the BSB too!

Listening tip

Before you listen

- Look at the pictures with the text. What is the topic of the text?

- Read the text before you listen.

- Try to guess the missing words. Write your ideas in pencil in the text.

- What <u>type</u> of word is it? Is it the name of a thing or a person? Is it a verb (*is/are /go/like/listen ...*)? Is it an adjective (*popular/cheap/wonderful ...*)?

b Read the text again. Mark the sentences *T* (true) or *F* (false).

1 Judy is Australian. — [F]

2 The Backstreet Boys are Judy's favourite band. — [ ]

3 There are five people in the band. — [ ]

4 Judy really likes the song *I'll never break your heart*. — [ ]

5 Judy thinks *Quit playing games with my heart* is a terrible song. — [ ]

6 The Backstreet Boys are all from Kentucky. — [ ]

Unit check

1 Fill in the spaces

Complete the sentences with the words in the box.

| wonderful | are | she's | together | ~~band~~ | aren't | we're | from | them | film |

Mick, Keith and Carla are in a ___band___ . Carla's [1] _____ Australia and
[2] _____ the singer. The other two [3] _____ from Canada. People don't know
[4] _____ in my country, so they [5] _____ very popular here. But I think their music
is [6] _____ . They're in a new [7] _____ now. Elizabeth and I want to see it
[8] _____ , and [9] _____ really excited.

9

2 Choose the correct answers

(Circle) the correct answers, a, b or c.

1 Cathy's really _____ about the concert.
   a fantastic   b popular   c (excited)

2 A: I want a sandwich. _____
   B: No, thanks. I'm OK.
   a Guess what?   b What about you?   c Let's go.

3 We don't like this CD. It's _____ .
   a favourite   b awful   c wonderful

4 Jan and Petra _____ from Germany.
   a is   b isn't   c aren't

5 A: Is she a good singer?
   B: Yes, we really like _____ .
   a us   b her   c him

6 _____ Brazilian?
   a You are   b Are you   c Do you

7 Paris _____ the capital of Italy.
   a not   b isn't   c aren't

8 A: Do you like classical music?
   B: Yes, I _____ .
   a do   b is   c am

9 Listen to the words and repeat
   _____ .
   a it   b him   c them

8

3 Correct the mistakes

In each sentence there is a mistake with the verbs *be* and *like* and with object pronouns.
Underline the mistake and write the correct sentence.

1 This <u>are</u> my favourite music.   *This is my favourite music.*

2 I think he an actor. _____

3 The pencils isn't expensive. _____

4 John and Philip are from London? _____

5 No, they not good friends. _____

6 This film is great. I like him a lot. _____

7 You like this band? _____

8 Jim loves hamburgers, but I don't like. _____

9 Are rap music popular in your country? _____

8

How did you do?

Total: **25**

| ☺ | Very good 20 – 25 | ☹ | OK 14 – 19 | ☹ | Review Unit 3 again 0 – 13 |

(4) She likes Harry Potter

1 Remember and check

Match the two parts of the sentences. Then check with the text on page 26 of the Student's Book.

1 J.K. Rowling   a Scotland.
2 Millions of people read   b a computer.
3 She lives in   c famous.
4 She's very   d is a writer.
5 She writes on   e cartoons.
6 She really likes   f her books.

2 Grammar

Present simple – positive and negative

(a) Find 11 more verbs in the word snake. Write them under the pictures.

learnreadworkliveplayspeakstopwatchwritestudyunderstandlisten

1 ....   2 ....   3 ....

4 ....   5 *learn* ....   6 ....

7 ....   8 ....   9 ....

10 ....   11 ....   12 ....

(b) Complete the sentences with the verb + *s*, *es* or *ies*.

1 She ...*likes*... the film. (like)
2 James .... TV after school. (watch)
3 Sarah .... to the cinema on Saturdays. (go)
4 He .... German. (speak)
5 My father .... to classical music. (listen)
6 School .... at 3.30. (finish)
7 My friend .... in a shop. (work)
8 Lisa .... Music at school. (study)

c Complete the sentences. Use the correct form of the verbs in the box.

speak   watch   ~~listen~~   understand   write   live   play

1 I _____*listen*_____ to pop music on the radio.
2 J.K. Rowling _____ books about Harry Potter.
3 My cousins _____ a lot of films.
4 We _____ volleyball at school.
5 My aunt _____ four languages.
6 You _____ in a big house!
7 I _____ the question, but I don't know the answer.

d Look at the pictures and write sentences.

1
¡Hola! ✓
Bonjour! ✗

2 ✗   ✓

3 ✓   ✗

4 ✓   ✗

5 ✗   ✓

1 Caroline / speak   *Caroline speaks Spanish but she doesn't speak French.*
2 Sam / like   _____
3 Tony and Jill / watch   _____

4 We / play   _____
5 Julie / listen   _____

Present simple – questions and short answers

e Complete the sentences with *Do* or *Does*.
1 __*Do*__ you like sport?
2 _____ Marcel live in Paris?
3 _____ your mother listen to music?
4 _____ Peter and Jack sometimes go to the cinema?
5 _____ you play computer games at home?
6 _____ we know the answer to this question?
7 _____ your uncle have a mobile phone?

f Write the questions. Then write true answers.
1 you / watch TV before school?
   Do you watch TV before school?
   Yes, I do.   or   *No, I don't.*
2 you / always finish your homework?
   _____
3 your best friend / like football?
   _____
4 you and your friends / play volleyball?
   _____
5 your teacher / speak English?
   _____
6 your friends / understand Russian?
   _____

3 Pronunciation

/s/, /z/ and /ɪz/

🔊 Listen and write the underlined sound: /s/, /z/ or /ɪz/. Then listen again, check and repeat.

1 She likes it here.   /s/
2 Does Anna learn music?   ....
3 Sam watches films.   ....
4 She writes a lot of letters.   ....
5 He lives in London.   ....
6 The class finishes soon.   ....
7 Paul speaks Italian.   ....

4 Vocabulary and grammar

Family and possessive 's

a Look at the family tree and complete the sentences.

1 Rosa is Maria's _mother_ .
2 Barbara is Maria's ....
3 Maria's .... are Steve and John.
4 Steve's .... is Patricia.
5 Rosa is Barbara's ....
6 David is .... uncle.
7 Sally's .... are Maria's grandparents.
8 Matt is .... father.
9 .... sister is Sally.

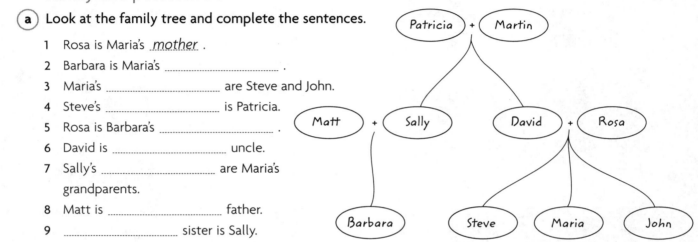

b Draw your family tree. In the boxes, write the family words and the people's names.

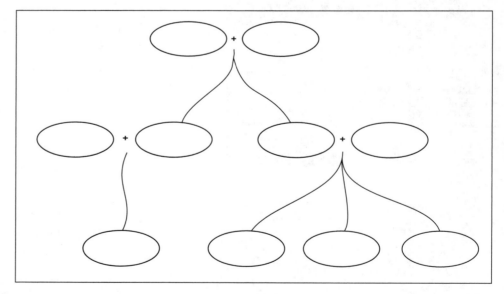

c Write five sentences about your family.

Example

My father's name is David and my mother's name is Rosa.
Steve and John are my brothers and Barbara is ...

....
....
....

5 Grammar

Possessive adjectives

<u>Underline</u> the correct words.

1 I play games on *my* / *I* / *me* computer.
2 No problem! We can help you with *you* / *your* / *our* homework.
3 Dave lives in England, but *his* / *her* / *their* grandparents live in France.
4 Amy watches *he* / *she* / *her* favourite football team on TV.
5 My friends and I like *me* / *their* / *our* new teacher.
6 The classroom is big, but *its* / *his* / *their* windows are small.
7 My aunt and uncle go shopping in town, but *his* / *her* / *their* children don't go.

6 Culture in mind

What are the words? Write them under the pictures.
Then check with the text on page 30 of the Student's Book.

eusho rac shawdeshir posh	
stophila shangwi hanmice	

1 ....

2 ....

3 ....

4 ....

5 ....

6 ....

7 Study help

Vocabulary

In your Vocabulary notebook, write words together. For example:

go   to the cinema   **speak**   a language
          for a walk   French
          shopping   to my friend

Write words that go with these verbs.

<u>Verbs</u>

work   *in a shop* ....

play   ....

watch   ....

write   ....

read   ....

listen to   ....

Skills in mind

8 Listen

🔊 Listen to Alice talking about her friend Rebecca. Write ✓ or ✗ in the boxes.

London ✓

family

Rebecca and Alice

9 Write

Write sentences about Mateo.

Mateo is 15. He lives in Rome.
....
....
....
....
....
....

Writing tip

Don't always repeat names in your writing – use pronouns. For example:

          He
Mateo is 15. ~~Mateo~~ lives in Rome.

               his
Mateo's sister is Sonia and ~~Mateo's~~ brother is ...

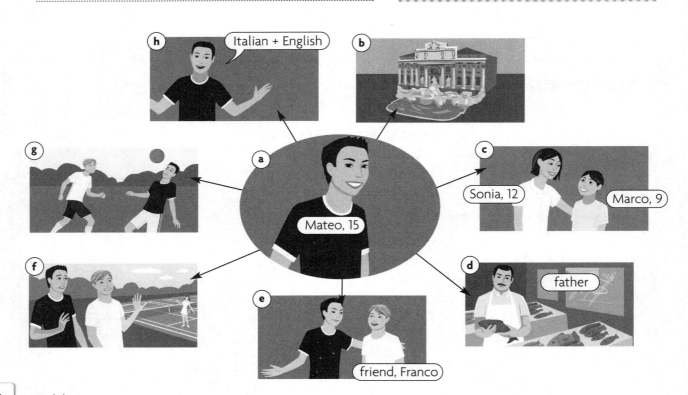

h Italian + English

b

g

a Mateo, 15

c Sonia, 12   Marco, 9

d father

e friend, Franco

f

Unit check

1 Fill in the spaces

Complete the sentences with the words in the box.

| learn | doesn't | have | live | ~~her~~ | their | volleyball | don't | Tara's | speaks |

Alison Short and _her_ sister Tara [1] _____ in Cambridge with [2] _____ parents. Mr Short [3] _____ work, but Mrs Short is a teacher at [4] _____ school. The two sisters [5] _____ music, and Alison [6] _____ French and Italian. They play [7] _____ together, but they [8] _____ fights because they [9] _____ like the same music.

9

2 Choose the correct answers

(Circle) the correct answers, a, b or c.

1 I've got five brothers and _____ .
  a (sisters) b grandmothers c fathers

2 Your mother's brother is your _____ .
  a cousin b uncle c aunt

3 Dave goes for a walk with _____ dog.
  a he b his c him

4 We have 28 people in _____ class.
  a our b their c my

5 My cousins _____ football.
  a like b likes c do like

6 Maria _____ in Portugal.
  a live b lives c don't live

7 _____ speak English?
  a You are b Are you c Do you

8 A: Do they work in this town?
  B: No, _____ .
  a they aren't b they do c they don't

9 Does _____ cartoons on TV?
  a she watches b you watch c Peter watch

8

3 Correct the mistakes

In each sentence there is a mistake with the present simple and possessive forms. Underline the mistake and write the correct sentence.

1 We goes to the same school. _We go to the same school._

2 Her father speak's Japanese. _____

3 Sally and Frank learns French at school. _____

4 Richards sister plays tennis. _____

5 My cousin doesn't works in a factory. _____

6 Do you like me bicycle? _____

7 We not understand this question. _____

8 Your father listens to pop music? _____

9 Yes, he is my friend uncle. _____

8

How did you do?

Total: **25**

| ☺ | Very good 20 – 25 | ☹ | OK 14 – 19 | ☹ | Review Unit 4 again 0 – 13 |

5 Where's the café?

1 Remember and check

Fill in the crossword. Check with the text on page 36 of the Student's Book.

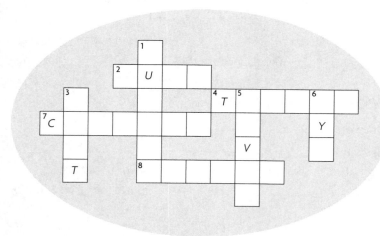

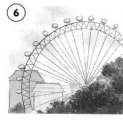

.... card

London ....

2 Vocabulary

Numbers 100+

a 🔊 Listen and ⟨circle⟩ the numbers you hear.

1	⟨139⟩	193	5	740	714
2	318	380	6	1,000	10,000
3	561	651	7	2,924	2,524
4	807	870			

b 🔊 Listen and write the numbers you hear. Then write the answer in words.

1 12 + *30* = *forty-two*
2 50 + ... = ...
3 11 + ... = ...
4 110 + ... = ...
5 266 + ... = ...
6 309 + ... = ...

3 Pronunciation

/θ/ and /ð/

🔊 Listen to the sentences. Are the *th* sounds /θ/ (*three*) or /ð/ (*mother*)? Tick (✓) the correct box. Then listen again, check and repeat.

		/θ/	/ð/
1	I think he's thirty.	☐	☐
2	That's their father.	☐	☐
3	They buy clothes together.	☐	☐
4	Thanks for the birthday party.	☐	☐

Grammar

there's / there are

a Complete the sentences with *'s* or *are*.

1 There _____ a good restaurant in this town.

2 There _____ over nine million people in London.

3 There _____ interesting clothes in this shop.

4 In London there _____ a river called the Thames.

5 There _____ an expensive cinema in the city centre.

6 There _____ six children in their family.

b Look at the picture and complete the text. Use *there's*, *there isn't*, *there are* or *there aren't*.

> *There are* only about 3,000 people in my town. It's very small, so ¹ _____ a lot to do. ² _____ about 12 shops and ³ _____ a good market here on Fridays, but ⁴ _____ any supermarkets. ⁵ _____ a cinema but that's OK – ⁶ _____ a good collection of videos at the video shop. ⁷ _____ two schools in the town and ⁸ _____ an excellent restaurant called the Black Horse. ⁹ _____ any trains here because ¹⁰ _____ a station.

5 **Vocabulary**

Places in a town

a Match the words with the pictures. Write 1–8 in the boxes.

1 library
2 bank
3 railway station
4 café
5 newsagent
6 chemist
7 bookshop
8 post office

(b) Write the questions. Use *Is there a* or *Are there any*. Then write true answers.

1. good cafés / in your town?
   Are there any good cafés in your town?
   Yes, there are. or *No, there aren't.*

2. big post office / in your town?

   ----

3. bookshops / near your school?

   ----

4. good library / in your school?

   ----

5. railway station / near your home?

   ----

6. newsagents / in your street?

   ----

6 Grammar

Positive imperatives

Write the sentences from the box under the pictures.

> Turn left.   Turn right.   Go home.   Sit down.
> Listen to me.   ~~Look!~~

1. ----------------------------   2. ----------------------------

3. ----------------------------   4. *Look!* ----------

5. ----------------------------   6. ----------------------------

7 Vocabulary

Directions

(a) Look at the pictures and complete the sentences.

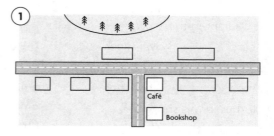

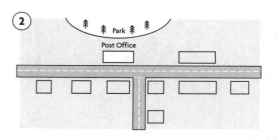

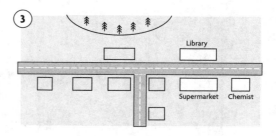

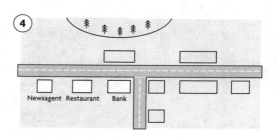

1. The café is *next to the bookshop* .
2. The park is _____ .
3. The supermarket is _____
   _____ .
   The chemist is _____
   _____ .
4. The bank is on _____
   _____ .
   The restaurant is _____
   the _____
   and the _____ .

b Where does the tourist want to go? Look at the map and complete the dialogue. Start at the station.

Tourist: Excuse me, where's the
.... ,
please?

Woman: Go down Station Road and turn right. The .... is on the right between the post office and the newsagent.

Tourist: Thanks. And is there a .... near here?

Woman: Yes, there is. Turn right into East Street. The .... is on the left opposite the bank.

Tourist: Thank you very much.

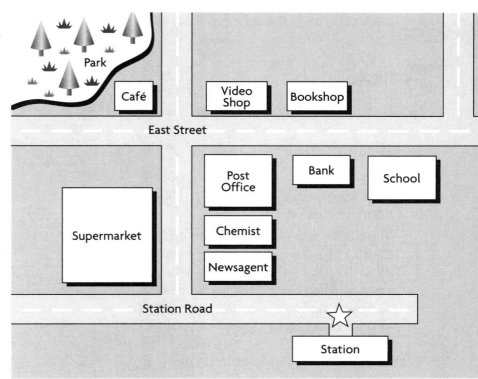

c Look at the map again. Give directions from the school to the café.

Tourist: Excuse me, is there a café near here?

You: Yes, ¹..................................... . Go ²..................................... and turn ³..................................... . The café is ⁴..................................... .

8 Everyday English

Complete the dialogues. Use words from box A and box B.

A	
Wait	Are you
You're	I have

B	
sure	no idea
welcome	a minute

1 Tania: There's a supermarket on the corner of New Street.

   Brian: .... ? I don't think there are any shops near here.

2 Magda: Excuse me, is this your book?

   Man: Oh, yes! Thank you very much.

   Magda: ....

3 Pietro: Come on! Let's go!

   Sandra: .... I want to write a message for Mum.

4 Leo: Where are we?

   Jane: .... I don't know this place.

9 Study help

Vocabulary

Sometimes it's a good idea to draw pictures or diagrams in your Vocabulary notebook. Draw pictures to show the meaning of these prepositions:

~~on~~ in behind opposite between
near next to under

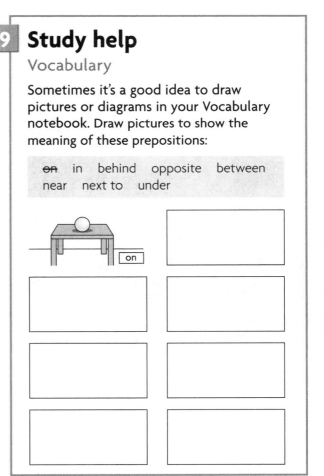

Skills in mind

10 Read

a Read the text and complete the table.

Paul lives in a town called Katoomba in Australia. It's in the Blue Mountains, 110 km from Sydney, and there are about 18,000 people in the town.

There isn't a museum in Katoomba, but there's a library and an excellent cinema called The Edge. There are also lots of shops. Paul's parents often go shopping at the Coles supermarket and they buy their newspapers at Dixon's. Paul likes bicycles, and his favourite shop is Cycletech. His brother George sells books at a bookshop called Elizabeth's. Paul goes to Katoomba High School and his little sister goes to Katoomba North Public School.

Katoomba is very popular with tourists, so there are lots of hotels in the town. Tourists often come from Sydney by train – the trip takes two hours.

Reading tip
Completing a table

Exercise 10a asks you to find information in the text and put it in a table.

● First, read the text.

● Now look at the table. Read the two headings and think about the words under them.

● Read the text again and find the names of shops. They all start with a capital letter. But be careful! *Sydney, Blue Mountains* and *Katoomba* have capital letters – but they're names of places, not shops.

Name	Type of business/shop
1 The Edge	.... *cinema* ....
2 Coles	....
3	newsagent
4	bicycle shop
5 Elizabeth's	....

b Read the questions and write short answers.

1 Is Sydney very near Katoomba?
  No, it isn't. ....

2 Are there twenty thousand people in Katoomba?
  ....

3 Do people watch films at The Edge?
  ....

4 Is there a museum in the town?
  ....

5 Do people buy clothes at Elizabeth's?
  ....

6 Is Paul's sister a student at his school?
  ....

7 Are there lots of tourists in Katoomba?
  ....

8 Is there a railway station in the town?
  ....

11 Write

Write a short text about a town that you like in your country or in a different country. Think about these questions:

● Is there a river / a beach?

● Is there a cinema? Are there any cafés and restaurants? Is there a station?

● What shops are there?

● What's your favourite place in town?

Unit check

1 Fill in the spaces

Complete the sentences with the words in the box.

| opposite | there's | ~~centre~~ | market | are | takes | newsagent | aren't | underground | between |

Martin lives in the city _centre_ and there [1] _____ lots of shops in his street. His house is [2] _____ a chemist and a [3] _____ . There's an [4] _____ station [5] _____ the house and Martin [6] _____ the tube to school. There [7] _____ any big supermarkets, but that's no problem — [8] _____ a very good [9] _____ in the street every day.

| | 9 |

2 Choose the correct answers

(Circle) the correct answers, a, b or c.

1 Change your money at the _____ .
  a (bank) b market c university

2 You can buy magazines at a _____ .
  a library b chemist c newsagent

3 100,000 = _____
  a a million b a thousand hundred
  c a hundred thousand

4 The post office is _____ the corner.
  a on b in c in front

5 I want to buy a _____ card.
  a railway b train c travel

6 Go straight on and _____ left.
  a start b turn c send

7 I think there's _____ river in this town.
  a any b a c the

8 There _____ any good clothes in this shop.
  a are b aren't c isn't

9 A: Is the railway station near here?
  B: _____
  a I have no idea. b You're welcome.
  c No, there isn't.

| | 8 |

3 Correct the mistakes

In each sentence there is a mistake with *there is/are*, imperatives and prepositions of place. Underline the mistake and write the correct sentence.

1 <u>There's</u> 28 students in my class. _There are 28 students in my class._

2 Excuse me, there's a library near here? _____

3 There aren't a cheap CDs in this shop. _____

4 Is there a garden on front of the house? _____

5 Go to the post office and buys a stamp. _____

6 Is there any good bookshops in this town? _____

7 Go straight on and turn to left. _____

8 The café's next the post office. _____

9 There isn't any factories near the river. _____

| | 8 |

How did you do?

Total: | 25 |

| ☺ | Very good 20 – 25 | ☺ | OK 14 – 19 | ☹ | Review Unit 5 again 0 – 13 |

(6) They've got brown eyes

1 Remember and check

Think about Sally the chimpanzee and <u>underline</u> the correct words. Then check with the text on page 42 of the Student's Book.

1 Sally is *four / fourteen* years old.
2 She's got *blue / brown* eyes.
3 *She's got / She hasn't got* a big family.
4 She *likes / doesn't like* bananas.
5 She lives in a *park / forest*.
6 She isn't *intelligent / stupid*.

2 Grammar

Why ...? Because ...

(a) Match the questions and answers.

1 Why do people like football?
2 Why isn't the library open?
3 Why do you like these shoes?
4 Why are you happy today?

a Because it's my birthday.
b Because they're fashionable.
c Because it's an exciting game.
d Because it's Sunday today.

has / have got

(b) Complete the sentences with *has / have got*. Use short forms where possible.

1 You *'ve got* a fantastic DVD player!
2 Mr and Mrs Martin _____ a house near the river.
3 Sue _____ a new bicycle.
4 I _____ a very big family.
5 We _____ an excellent computer at home.

6 This town _____ two cinemas and a museum.
7 My brother _____ an interesting collection of stamps.
8 Chimpanzees _____ four fingers on each hand.

(c) Look at the table and write sentences about Jessie and her brother Tom. Use the correct form of *have got*.

Jessie   Tom

	Jessie	Tom
a bicycle	✗	✓
a mobile phone	✓	✗
a CD player	✗	✓
brown hair	✓	✗
a big family	✗	✗
brown eyes	✓	✓
a computer	✓	✗

1 Jessie / bicycle
   Jessie hasn't got a bicycle.
2 Tom / mobile phone
   _____
3 Jessie and Tom / big family
   _____
4 Tom / CD player
   _____
5 Jessie / brown hair
   _____
6 Jessie and Tom / brown eyes
   _____
7 Tom / computer
   _____
8 Jessie / computer
   _____

d Complete the questions. Then look at the pictures and write short answers.

 ①  ② ③  ④  ⑤ ⑥

1 A: ___*Have*___ you ___*got*___ a bicycle?

  B: ___*Yes, I have.*___

2 A: _____ Andy _____ a computer?

  B: _____ .

3 A: _____ you _____ a DVD player?

  B: _____ .

4 A: _____ Jane _____ a big nose?

  B: _____ .

5 A: _____ your parents _____ a car?

  B: _____ .

6 A: _____ Steve _____ a big family?

  B: _____ .

e Write four true sentences with the correct form of *have got* (positive or negative). Choose words from box A and box B.

A
I   My parents   My sister   My best friend
My friends   My English teacher   My aunt

B
an old car   brown hair   a nice smile
blue eyes   long fingers   fashionable clothes

----

3 # Vocabulary

Colours

a Fill in the puzzle with the names of the colours (1–6).
What is the other colour (7)?

 ① 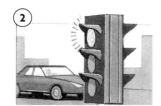 ②

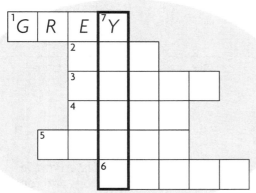

¹G	R	E	⁷Y

③

④  ⑤  ⑥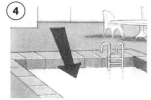

Parts of the body

b) Find 11 more parts of the body in the puzzle. Write the words under the pictures.

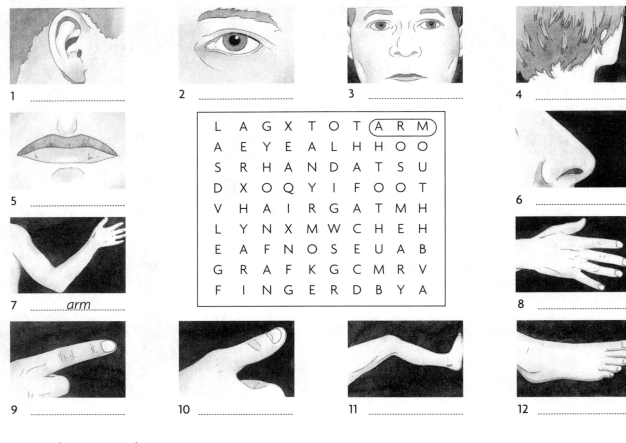

1 _____

2 _____

3 _____

4 _____

5 _____

6 _____

7 *arm*

8 _____

9 _____

10 _____

11 _____

12 _____

```
L  A  G  X  T  O  T (A  R  M)
A  E  Y  E  A  L  H  H  O  O
S  R  H  A  N  D  A  T  S  U
D  X  O  Q  Y  I  F  O  O  T
V  H  A  I  R  G  A  T  M  H
L  Y  N  X  M  W  C  H  E  H
E  A  F  N  O  S  E  U  A  B
G  R  A  F  K  G  C  M  R  V
F  I  N  G  E  R  D  B  Y  A
```

Describing people

c) Complete the descriptions with the words in the box. Then draw the two people's faces.

| green | nose | wavy | blond | good-looking |
| smile | eyes | | | |

Janet has got straight ¹ _____ hair and blue ² _____ . She's got a small ³ _____ and a happy ⁴ _____ .

I think Chris is very ⁵ _____ . He's got a long straight nose and his eyes are ⁶ _____ .
He's got ⁷ _____ black hair.

Janet ☐   Chris ☐

Giving personal information

d) Match the questions and answers.

1 What's your surname?   a   C-L-A-R-K.
2 How do you spell that, please? b   Yes, I have. It's 07976 648712.
3 What's your first name?   c   I'm 15.
4 How old are you?   d   Clark.
5 What's your address?   e   01367 995024.
6 What's your telephone number?   f   Diana.
7 Have you got a mobile number?   g   16 Felton Street, Dover.

e) 🔊 Listen to the questions and reply with true information.

4 Pronunciation

/v/

🔊 Listen and repeat.

1 They've got wavy hair.
2 We've got twelve TVs.
3 Travel cards aren't very expensive.
4 He gives five interviews every day.
5 Vivien drives to the university.

5 Culture in mind

Find and label these pets in the picture.

~~dog~~ cat budgie hamster guinea pig
rabbit snake spider lizard

5 ....
4 ....
6 ....
3 ....
2 _dog_
7 ....
1 ....
9 ....
8 ....

6 Study help

Vocabulary

In your Vocabulary notebook, write adjectives with their opposites. For example:

| big | small |
| awful | wonderful |

Find opposites in the box and write them together in the lists.

interesting ~~long~~ cheap intelligent curly dark boring straight stupid fair expensive ~~short~~

Adjectives for hair		Other adjectives	
long	_short_	....	....
....	....	....	....
....	....	....	....

Skills in mind

7 Listen

🔊 Joe is talking about his sister's boyfriend. Listen and write the information in the table.

1	First name:	*Gilles*
2	Nationality:	
3	City:	*Geneva*
4	Language:	
5	Age:	
6	Colour of eyes:	
7	Colour of hair:	

Listening tip

Listen to the spelling of *Gilles* in the recording. The speaker says 'double L,' like this:

G - I - **double-L** - E - S

It's the same with telephone numbers.
For example: 0188 35669: oh one **double-eight**, three five **double-six** nine.

8 Read

a Read the letter. Which picture shows David and his family?

Dear Pietro

I'm David Ling, and I'm your new penfriend. I'm 15 and I live in Vancouver, a city in Canada. I've got short black hair and brown eyes.

My mother and father are from Hong Kong and we speak English and Chinese at home. My father works in a bank in the city centre and my mother works in a restaurant. My sister doesn't live at home, because she's got a job in a library in San Francisco. She's 22. My brother Jack is at university in Vancouver and he studies Computer Science.

Please write and tell me about you and your family.

All the best,

David

b Correct these sentences.

1 David's fourteen. *No, he isn't. He's fifteen.*
2 He's got long hair. ....
3 His parents are from Canada. ....
4 His mother hasn't got a job. ....
5 His sister lives in a library. ....
6 Jack works in a computer shop. ....

Unit check

1 Fill in the spaces

Complete the sentences with the words in the box.

> clothes   eyes   fair   ~~are~~   wears   he's   isn't   haven't   good-looking   wavy

Paul and Harry ___are___ my brothers. Harry looks like Dad. He [1] _____ very tall
and [2] _____ got blond [3] _____ hair. He wears dark [4] _____ and
he thinks he's very [5] _____ . Paul and I are also quite short, but we [6] _____ got
[7] _____ hair – our hair is brown. We've got blue [8] _____ and Paul
[9] _____ glasses.

9

2 Choose the correct answers

(Circle) the correct answers, a, b or c.

1 You've got long arms and _____ .
   a foot   b mouths   c (legs)

2 Julie's eyes are _____ .
   a brown   b blond   c pink

3 I think your brother's very _____ .
   a curly   b wavy   c good-looking

4 She's got short _____ hair.
   a long   b straight   c medium-length

5 Rabbits have got big _____ .
   a nose   b ears   c faces

6 My first name is Helen and my
   _____ is Johnson.
   a surname   b age   c address

7 A lot of people _____ pets at
   home.
   a got   b have got   c has got

8 A: Has Denise got a mobile phone?
   B: Yes, she _____ .
   a got   b has   c does

9 Alan _____ glasses.
   a doesn't get   b doesn't got   c hasn't got

8

3 Correct the mistakes

In each sentence there is a mistake with *have/has got* and with questions about personal information.
Underline the mistake and write the correct sentence.

1 I <u>got</u> a sister and two brothers. *I've got a sister and two brothers.*

2 My friend have got a guinea pig. _____

3 Does she get wavy hair? _____

4 Where's your address? _____

5 Tony and Joe has got blue eyes. _____

6 Karen haven't got a computer. _____

7 Why do you spell your surname, please? _____

8 Are you got a mobile number? _____

9 No, I don't got a little brother. _____

8

How did you do?

Total: [25]

| 😊 | Very good 20 – 25 | 😐 | OK 14 – 19 | 😞 | Review Unit 6 again 0 – 13 |

7 This is delicious!

1 Remember and check

Match the two parts of the words, and then write the words under the pictures.

1 grass ⟍   gator
2 kanga   ⟍ hopper
3 rattle   ail
4 alli   roo
5 sn   snake

a ....   b ....   c ....

d ....   e ....

2 Vocabulary

Food

a 🔊 Listen and write the numbers 2–15.

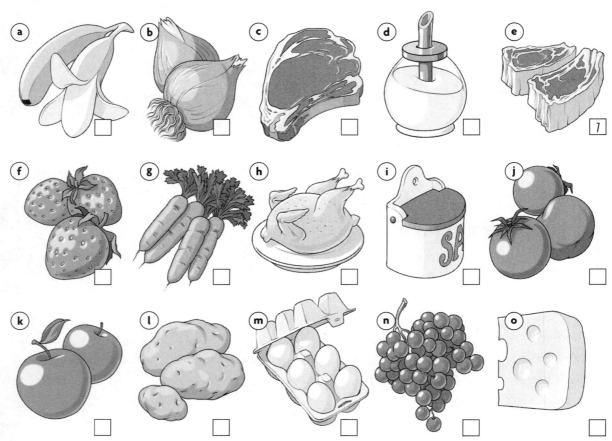

b Look at the pictures again. Write the names of the things in the table. Give each list a heading.

....	....	.... Meat	.... Groceries ....
...... bananas	...... onions	....	...... sugar ......
....	....	....	....
....	....	....	....
....	....	....	....

Grammar

Countable and uncountable nouns

a Write the words in the correct lists.

~~banana~~ ~~rice~~ onion carrot cheese
salt apple sugar

Countable	Uncountable
banana	*rice*

b Look at these word pairs. Which word is countable and which is uncountable? Write *C* or *U*.

1 fruit _____*U*_____ orange _____*C*_____
2 sandwich _____ bread _____
3 beef _____ burger _____
4 coffee _____ café _____
5 shop _____ food _____
6 singer _____ music _____
7 shampoo _____ book _____

c Complete the sentences with *a*, *an* or *some*.

1 I want to buy ___*some*___ shampoo at the chemist.
2 Let's go to the supermarket and get _____ food.
3 I'd like _____ orange, please.
4 I've got _____ sandwich and _____ fruit.
5 We need _____ rice and _____ onions.
6 It isn't _____ newsagent – it's _____ bookshop.
7 He wants _____ cheese and _____ apple.

d Write the words under the pictures with *a*, *an* or *some*.

1   *a lettuce*

2   _____

3   _____

4   _____

5   _____

6   _____

7   _____

8   _____

this / that / these / those

e Complete the sentences with *this*, *that*, *these* or *those*.

1 There are some great CDs in .... shop.

2 Mum! Look at .... snails!

3 .... apple's really good!

4 Wow! .... players are really good!

5 .... book's very expensive.

6 Boy: What's .... ?
Dad: It's a kangaroo.

I'd like / Would you like … ?

f <u>Underline</u> the correct words in the dialogue.

Woman: Good morning. [1] *Can I help you? / Would you like?*

Man: Yes, [2] *I like / I'd like* three kilos of potatoes, please.

Woman: Right. [3] *Do you like / Would you like* anything else?

Man: Yes, [4] *I'd like / You'd like* some bananas – a kilo, please.

Woman: Fine. That's £1.25, please. [5] *Do you like / Would you like* a bag?

Man: Yes, please.

g Jane is in a restaurant. Put the waiter's words in the correct order, and then write Jane's answers.

Waiter: to ready you Are order ?
1 ....

Jane: (yes / roast chicken)
2 ....

Waiter: vegetables like or you salad Would ?
3 ....

Jane: (vegetables)
4 ....

Waiter: drink like would to What you ?
5 ....

Jane: (orange juice)
6 ....

Waiter: like you else Would anything ?
7 ....

Jane: (no)
8 ....

4 Pronunciation

/w/

a) 🔊 Listen and repeat.

1 The S<u>w</u>iss waiter's got wavy hair.
2 We want some white wine.
3 William's got a wonderful dishwasher.
4 Would you like some water with your sandwich?

b) 🔊 In these sentences, there are three words with a 'silent' *w*. <u>Underline</u> them, then listen, check and repeat.

1 Which ans<u>w</u>er is correct?
2 What's <u>w</u>rong with you?
3 <u>W</u>ho's the winner?
4 Where does Wendy write letters?

5 Everyday English

Complete the dialogues. Use words from box A and box B.

A	B
Do you I'm	really hungry
What's	wrong think so

1 **Paola:** .... Is there any food in the house?

   Fiona: Yes, of course. Have some bread and cheese.

2 **George:** If we leave now, we can catch the 10 o'clock train.

   John: .... ? It's 9.50 now.

3 **Rachel:** Oh no!

   Tim: .... , Rachel?

   Rachel: I've got a problem with my mobile. I can't get a connection.

6 Study help

Grammar and vocabulary

a) Put countable and uncountable nouns together in lists, for example:

a/an	banana	some	cheese
	egg		rice
	....		....
	....		....
	....		....

Add these words to the two lists.

> potato   water   meat   lettuce
> mayonnaise   mushroom

b) In your Vocabulary notebook, write all the words you know for food and drink in the lists in Exercise 6a.

c) A good dictionary gives symbols for countable and uncountable nouns. Look at these examples.

> **garlic** /'gaːlɪk/ *noun* [U] a vegetable like a small onion
> **biscuit** /'bɪskɪt/ *noun* [C] a thin flat cake that is usually dry

Skills in mind

7 Listen

(a) 🔊 Listen to a conversation between Martin and his mother. What food have they got at home, and what haven't they got? Write ✓ or ✗.

1	chicken	✓
2	beef	
3	cheese	
4	lettuce	
5	tomatoes	
6	mayonnaise	

(b) What sandwich does Martin decide to have?

....

8 Write

(a) Martin and Harry are having a party at Harry's house on Saturday. Read Martin's email about food at the party.

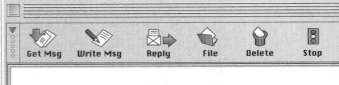

To:	**harry.davis@freelink.co.uk**
From:	**martin.jones@hotspot.com**
Subject:	**party food**

Hi Harry

I want to make some food for our party. These are my ideas:

- **home–made pizza OR lasagne**
- **sandwiches OR salad**
- **fruit salad**

What do you think? What food have you got at home? What do we need to buy? Let me know, OK? I can go to the supermarket tomorrow.

Martin

(b) Imagine you are Harry. Write an email in reply to Martin and answer his questions about food.

Hi Martin
I like your ideas for party food. Let's have …
At home I've got … I've also got …
I want you to buy …

Unit check

1 Fill in the spaces

Complete the sentences with the words in the box.

| vegetables | ~~beef~~ | dessert | sandwiches | meat | fruit | an | some | meal | have |

We always have roast __beef__ or lamb for lunch on Sunday and it's my favourite [1] _____ .
We eat the [2] _____ with potatoes and other [3] _____ , and then we have some
[4] _____ or ice cream for [5] _____ . On school days I don't [6] _____
a big lunch. I make some [7] _____ in the morning, and I eat them at lunchtime with
[8] _____ orange or [9] _____ grapes.

9

2 Choose the correct answers

(Circle) the correct answers, a, b or c.

1 A: I'm starving!
   B: _____
   a What's wrong?   b (Have a sandwich.)
   c Do you think so?

2 Are you _____ to order?
   a ready   b hungry   c lovely

3 A: Have you got any vegetables?
   B: Yes, we've got some mushrooms and some
   _____ .
   a oranges   b onions   c grapes

4 Does Tom want _____ apple?
   a a   b an   c some

5 I want a _____ for the salad.
   a salt   b mushroom   c lettuce

6 A: _____ you like some cheese?
   B: Yes, please.
   a Would   b Do   c Have

7 I'd like some _____ , please.
   a rice   b strawberry   c chip

8 Do you know _____ woman in
   the white car?
   a this   b that   c these

9 These tomatoes are OK, but _____
   bananas don't look fresh.
   a this   b that   c those

8

3 Correct the mistakes

In each sentence there is a mistake with countable/uncountable nouns, *I'd like / Would you like*
and *this/that/these/those*. Underline the mistake and write the correct sentence.

1 She has <u>some</u> apple at lunchtime. *She has an apple at lunchtime.*

2 I like a kilo of tomatoes, please. _____

3 They have some waters with their meal. _____

4 I want to buy a fruit at the market. _____

5 Mum wants some egg from the shop. _____

6 Come and look at this lovely strawberries! _____

7 I don't eat a lot of sugars. _____

8 You like some cheese before the dessert? _____

9 I love this car over there. _____

8

How did you do?

Total: [ ] 25

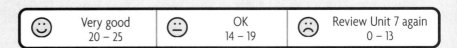

| ☺ | Very good 20 – 25 | ☹ | OK 14 – 19 | ☹ | Review Unit 7 again 0 – 13 |

8 I sometimes watch soaps

1 Remember and check

Think back to the text about Joshua and Judy. <u>Underline</u> the correct words.
Then check with the text on page 54 of the Student's Book.

1. Joshua and Judy both live <u>*on a farm*</u> / *in a city.*
2. Joshua wears *black / white* clothes.
3. He goes *dancing / shopping* with his parents.
4. His father *drives / doesn't drive* a car.

5. Judy's home is in *Australia / the USA.*
6. She studies *at home / in the nearest town.*
7. She *watches / doesn't watch* a lot of television.
8. She *often / hardly ever* sees her teacher.

2 Vocabulary

The days of the week

a Find the days of the week.
Write them in the correct order.

ednwdsaye   yundas   iyfard   ustdeay   trusaayd   ~~ondmya~~   ytuhrsad

Weekdays: ___*Monday*___ _____ _____ _____ _____

Weekend: _____ _____

b Answer the questions about Karen's week.

Mon   Tues   Wed   Thur   Fri   Sat   Sun

1. When does Karen go shopping?
   _____*On Friday.*_____
2. When does Karen watch her favourite TV programme?
   _____
3. When does she play volleyball?
   _____
4. When does she see her grandmother?
   _____
5. When does she have a music lesson?
   _____

6. When does she study in the library?
   _____
7. When does she go to the cinema?
   _____

c Write four sentences about things you do on different days.
1. _____
2. _____
3. _____
4. _____

3 Grammar

Adverbs of frequency

a) Put the adverbs in the correct order. | never always often hardly ever usually sometimes |

```
├──────────┼──────────┼──────────┼──────────┼──────────┼──────────┤
1 _____  2 _____  3 _____  4 _____  5 _____  6 _never___
```

b) Put the adverbs in the correct place in the sentence.

1 Susan wears black shoes. (usually)
   Susan usually wears black shoes.

2 Robert plays football with his friends. (often)
   ....

3 Tony and Philip are on the school bus. (never)
   ....

4 Beth listens to classical music. (hardly ever)
   ....

5 We have pizzas on Friday. (always)
   ....

6 The music is fantastic on this programme. (usually)
   ....

7 My parents help me with my homework. (sometimes)
   ....

c) How often do you do these things? Write true sentences. Use adverbs from Exercise 3a.

| go swimming on Sunday | have a burger at lunchtime | go to bed before ten o'clock | listen to the radio in bed | watch TV before school |

Example: *I sometimes go swimming on Sunday.*

1 .... 3 ....

2 .... 4 ....

                                          5 ....

d) Look at the information about Alex. Write sentences about him.

	Mon	Tues	Wed	Thur	Fri	Sat	Sun
have an English lesson		✓		✓		✓	
play football						✓	✓
write letters							✓
walk to school	✓	✓	✓	✓	✓		

1 *Alex has an English lesson three times a week.*

2 *He* ....

3 ....

4 ....

e Write sentences with frequency expressions (for example, *twice a day*, *every morning*).

1

Matthew

2

Julie

3

Danny

4

Denise

5

Greg

1   *Matthew catches a train twice a day.*
2   ....
3   ....
4   ....
5   ....

4 Vocabulary

TV programmes

newssoapoperachatshowcomedycartoongameshowdocumentarysportsprogramme

a Find seven more kinds of TV programmes in the word snake.

b Read about some programmes on TV tonight. Write the types of programmes.

1   Tonight, Mike Figgis talks to two great film stars.
    .... *chat show* ....

2   We've got Italian football, and skiing from Switzerland. ....

3   The latest information from around the world, with Sue Baxter. ....

4   Tonight – *The Simpsons*.
    ....

5   In tonight's programme, Mary sees Bill with Amanda – and she isn't happy about it!
    ....

6   Lots of laughs and smiles with the popular Benny Hall. ....

7   The prize tonight: £10,000!!
    ....

8   This week: Life in Japan.
    ....

5 Pronunciation

Compound nouns

a 🔊 Add the words in the box to make new nouns. Listen and check.

work	berry	hopper	friend	day
snake	~~fast~~	time		

1   break *fast* ....
2   week ....
3   lunch ....
4   home ....
5   straw ....
6   grass ....
7   rattle ....
8   girl ....

b 🔊 Where is the stress in each word? Listen again and repeat.

6 Vocabulary

What's the time?

a Look at the pictures and write the times in list 1–7. Then match them with the other expressions in list a–g.

(1) (2) (3) 0650 (4) 07:10 (5) (6) 07:35

1 *It's seven thirty.*   a It's twenty-five to eight.

2 *It's* _____   b It's half past seven.

3 _____   c It's ten past seven.

4 _____   d It's quarter to eight.

5 _____   e It's ten to seven.

6 _____   f It's quarter past six.

b 🔊 Listen and write the times in number form. Then listen again and check your answers.

1 *11.55*   2 _____   3 _____   4 _____   5 _____   6 _____

7 Culture in mind

Complete the summary about Jane Taylor. Use the words in the box. Then check with the text on page 58 of the Student's Book.

| sometimes   hardly   ever   hours   north   programmes   lives   doesn't |

Jane is 16 and she ¹ _____ in the ² _____ of England. She watches five or six
³ _____ of TV a week. Her favourite ⁴ _____ are soap operas, and she
⁵ _____ watches chat shows and films. She ⁶ _____ like sports programmes
and she ⁷ _____ watches news programmes.

8 Study help

Grammar

a Learn the parts of speech. Look at the sentence. Where are the <u>underlined</u> words in the lists?

Sam <u>often</u> <u>wears</u> <u>white</u> <u>shoes</u>.

Nouns	Verbs	Adjectives	Adverbs
shoes	*wears*	*white*	*often*

b Look at the words in the box and add them to the lists.

| black   never   buys   sandwiches   sometimes   coffee
always   delicious   has   expensive   clothes   makes |

c Make new sentences with the four parts of speech. There are lots of possible answers!

Sam _____

Jill _____

Jack _____

Rosa _____

_____

Skills in mind

9 Read

(a) Read the text and choose the best title.

1 Television in a British family
2 Soap operas on British TV
3 Football programmes in Britain

(b) Read the text again and answer the questions.

Reading tip
Choosing a title for a text

In Exercise 9a, all the words in the three titles are in the text. But two of these aren't good titles because they go with only one small part of the text.

● Read the text from beginning to end before you decide about the title.

● Don't only look for words – think about general ideas.

● Remember, the title is for the *whole* text.

TELEVISION is very important in a lot of British homes. On average, people spend about 23 hours a week in front of the TV. The nation's favourite programmes are soaps, but game shows, 'reality TV' shows, dramas and comedies are also popular. We talked to one family, the Parkers from Leeds, about how often they watch TV.

Mr Simon Parker (42) isn't typical. He doesn't watch a lot of TV, but he usually looks at the news and he sometimes watches a football match on Saturday. The two children love TV. Jamie (12) watches every day, usually for about three hours a day. His favourite programmes are cartoons and comedies. His sister Kim (16) watches three different soaps every week. 'I really love soaps, and chat shows are good too,' she says. Mrs Elizabeth Parker (38) likes watching TV at the weekend, when there's a good film on. 'I love old films,' she says. 'And I often watch documentaries too.'

Like a lot of British families, the Parkers have two televisions in their home, and the members of the family watch different things at different times. Do they watch anything together? 'Yes,' says Jamie. 'Football matches when England's playing!'

1 How often do British people watch TV?   *About 23 hours a week.*
2 Does Mr Parker watch game shows?
3 Which kinds of programmes does Jamie like?
4 Does he watch TV seven days a week?
5 What is Kim's favourite kind of programme?
6 When does Mrs Parker watch films?
7 What do the family watch together?

10 Listen

(a) 🔊 Listen to an interview about TV. How often does the woman watch TV?

(b) 🔊 Listen again and tick (✓) the correct adverb.

		never	hardly ever	sometimes	usually
1	comedies				✓
2	documentaries				
3	soaps				
4	the news				

Unit check

1 Fill in the spaces

Complete the sentences with the words in the box.

> on   at   every   usually   do   comes   news   ~~weekdays~~   days   soap

On _____weekdays_____ I leave school ¹ _____ 3.45 in the afternoon. I ² _____ walk home with my friend Diane, but ³ _____ Wednesday I have a swimming lesson at the sports centre. Diane often ⁴ _____ round to my place and we watch our favourite ⁵ _____ – it's on at 5.30, five ⁶ _____ a week. We also watch the ⁷ _____ at 6 o'clock. I ⁸ _____ my homework after dinner ⁹ _____ evening, so I don't watch a lot of TV.

▢ 9

2 Choose the correct answers

(Circle) the correct answers, a, b or c.

1 We can get a lot of information from _____ .
   a (documentaries) b comedies   c soap operas

2 People try to win money on _____ .
   a chat shows   b game shows
   c sports programmes

3 Quarter past four is _____ .
   a 4.15   b 4.30   c 4.45

4 _____ the time?
   a When's   b What's   c Where's

5 10.40 is _____ .
   a forty past ten   b twenty to eleven
   c twenty past eleven

6 The day before Thursday is _____ .
   a Wednesday   b Friday   c Monday

7 Sandra isn't at home. She _____ goes shopping on Saturday.
   a never   b hardly ever   c always

8 I check my email three times _____ day.
   a the   b a   c of the

9 _____ do you watch soap operas?
   a Which   b How many   c How often

▢ 8

3 Correct the mistakes

In each sentence there is a mistake with the present simple and adverbs of frequency. Underline the mistake and write the correct sentence.

1 We hardly ever <u>watches</u> cartoons. *We hardly ever watch cartoons.* _____

2 I have lunch at 1 o'clock every days. _____

3 Students don't go to school in the weekend. _____

4 We watch always the news on TV. _____

5 They play tennis two times a month. _____

6 Does your mother go sometimes to the market? _____

7 Patrick doesn't never help his parents at home. _____

8 George and Sam usually are in bed before 11 o'clock. _____

9 Carla has a music lesson one a week. _____

▢ 8

How did you do?

Total: ▢ 25

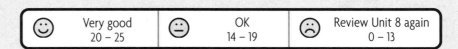

| ☺ | Very good 20 – 25 | ☺ | OK 14 – 19 | ☹ | Review Unit 8 again 0 – 13 |

9 Don't close the door!

1 Remember and check

🔊 Can you complete the dialogue between Anna and Martin? Complete the sentences. Then listen and check.

Anna: All right, all right. Hang on a minute. I'm coming. Oh, it's you! What do you ¹ _____ ?

Martin: Don't close the ² _____ , Anna. I just want to ³ _____ to you.

Anna: Oh Martin. Go away! Leave me alone!

Martin: Anna, don't shout, please. Look – you're ⁴ _____ . I know that.

Anna: Angry? Of course I'm angry! Go ⁵ _____ . I don't want to talk to you!

Martin: I know. But please, ⁶ _____ this letter.

Anna: All right. ⁷ _____ it to me. Now leave me ⁸ _____ .

2 Grammar

Imperatives

a Complete the dialogues with the verbs in the box.

> be   laugh   shout   cry

1 **A:** What's the matter, Cynthia?
   B: It's awful here. I miss my friends at home.
   A: I know you're unhappy. But please don't _____ .

2 **A:** That's the new boy, Klaus. He's from Germany.
   B: His English is really funny!
   A: Don't _____ at his English. You don't speak German!

3 **A:** Hi, Mum! I'm home!
   B: Shhh! Don't _____ ! Your dad's asleep!

4 **A:** I want to take a photo of you in front of the museum.
   B: Oh no! I hate photos of myself!
   A: Don't _____ stupid! Come on!

b Read the text. Complete the sentences with the verbs in the box.

> Ask   ~~Listen~~   Don't eat   Go   Listen
> Write   Don't tell   Talk   Don't sit

Advice for teens

When you or your friends are in trouble …

We all have good and bad days. When you have a problem, here are some things you can do:

- _Listen_ to music and try to relax.
- ¹ _____ the problem on a piece of paper. Then make a list of things you can do and put them in order.
- ² _____ a lot of food – it doesn't make you feel better.
- ³ _____ in the house.
- ⁴ _____ for a walk – exercise is good for you.
- ⁵ _____ to a friend about your problem.

What can you do when a friend has a problem? Here are some ideas:

- ⁶ _____ to your friend – don't speak a lot.
- ⁷ _____ questions. Help your friend to talk openly.
- Your friend's problem is private. ⁸ _____ other people about it.

c Write sentences. Use the positive or negative form of the verbs in the box.

look at ~~eat~~ go open switch on talk

1 *Eat your vegetables.*
2 *Don't*
3
4
5
6

3 Pronunciation

Linking sounds

🔊 In these sentences, underline the word *don't* when you think the *t* is silent. Then listen, check and repeat.

1 I <u>don't</u> know why she isn't here.
2 Don't leave now.
3 Don't eat all the chocolate!
4 Please don't ask a lot of questions.
5 I don't understand why he's so angry.
6 Stop the music. I don't like it.
7 Don't open the box.
8 I don't think it's a good idea.

4 Vocabulary

How do you feel?

a In the puzzle, find seven more words to describe feelings. Write the words under the pictures.

A	E	X	C	I	T	E	D	W	W
A	R	W	O	R	R	I	E	D	O
S	R	U	N	S	A	D	P	J	R
C	F	F	F	H	H	A	I	S	B
A	G	I	U	A	F	N	P	A	O
R	N	Z	S	P	J	G	L	H	R
E	E	T	E	P	N	R	Q	A	E
D	X	C	D	Y	G	Y	W	P	D

1 ....

2 ....

3 ....

4 _excited_

5 ....

6 ....

7 ....

8 ....

b Underline the correct words.

1 Look! There's a snake! I'm *angry / scared*.
2 This lesson's awful. We're *bored / scared*.
3 Our teacher smiles a lot. She's always *happy / unhappy*.
4 I don't know what to do. I'm *happy / confused*.
5 It's my little sister's birthday tomorrow. She's really *excited / angry*.
6 My father's got a problem. He's *worried / happy*.
7 Lee hasn't got any friends here. He's *excited / unhappy*.
8 I haven't got my homework with me. The teacher's *angry / confused*.

c Listen to the five speakers. Match them with the feelings and the reasons why they feel this way. Then write sentences.

Speaker	Feeling	Why?
1	confused	There's a problem with the computer.
2	worried	She's the winner of a trip to the USA.
3	bored	It's late and her daughter isn't home.
4	angry	He hasn't got anything to do.
5	excited	The homework is difficult.

1 _Speaker 1 is bored because he hasn't got anything to do._ ....

2 _Speaker 2_ ....

3 ....

4 ....

5 ....

d Look at these examples.

We're **interested** in these books.   (describes a person's feeling)

These **books** are **interesting**.   (describes something that produces a feeling)

Complete the dialogues. Choose adjectives from the box.

> confused/confusing   excited/exciting   worried/worrying   bored/boring

1 A: This film's _____ .

   B: I think so too. Let's switch off the TV.

2 A: My grandmother is in hospital.

   B: Oh no! Really?

   A: Yes, we're all very _____ about her.

3 A: What's the answer to question 3? I don't understand it.

   B: I have no idea. I think the question's very _____ .

4 A: Why is the dog so _____ ?

   B: Because she knows Leo's coming. He always takes her for a walk in the afternoon.

5 Everyday English

Complete the dialogues. Use words from box A and box B.

A	B
What's she she's	misses fine the matter

1 Luke: Hi, Danny. How's your aunt? Is she OK?

   Danny: Yes, thanks, _____ .

2 Martina: You don't look very happy, Sandro. _____ ?

   Sandro: Oh, I'm worried about my cat. I can't find him anywhere.

3 Irena: I've got an email from Petra here.

   Jan: Oh, really? How is she? How does she like Australia?

   Irena: She says she loves Sydney, but _____ her family and friends.

6 Study help

Vocabulary

In your Vocabulary notebook write examples to help you learn how to use new words. For example:

excited   (I feel <u>excited</u> before a big party.)

bored   (I feel <u>bored</u> when I watch golf on TV.)

Think of your own example sentences for these adjectives:

excited   (_____)

scared   (_____)

bored   (_____)

worried   (_____)

happy   (_____)

Skills in mind

7 Read

Read Jennifer's letter to a magazine. Mark the statements *T* (true) or *F* (false).

Claire's
PROBLEM PAGE

DEAR CLAIRE,

I'm fourteen and I'm really unhappy. Please help me!

My mum, my brother and I have moved from London to San Diego in California. My mum is a computer programmer and she's got a new job at the university here. We live in a new house, and I go to a new school. It's a nice place — but everything is new for me! New teachers, new students in my class, new school work! I really miss my old friends from London. I even miss my teachers there!

And I'm worried about my school work — sometimes I'm confused because it's different from the work at my old school.

I feel very alone — but what can I do? Please don't tell me to talk to my mum. She works eight hours a day and she's always tired. She never has time for me. And my brother? He's only ten, so he can't help me.

San Diego is a nice city, but there are so many things I miss! Please tell me what to do.

Yours,

Jennifer

1 Jennifer isn't happy and she needs some help. ☐

2 She and her family live in London. ☐

3 Her mother works in a computer shop. ☐

4 Jennifer doesn't miss her old friends. ☐

5 She has problems with her studies at school. ☐

6 Jennifer's mother doesn't talk to her about her problems. ☐

7 Jennifer often talks to her brother. ☐

> ## Writing tip
>
> *Planning your writing*
>
> Before you write to Jennifer, make notes about the things you want to say to her. Organise your ideas under these headings:
>
> **General ideas   Friends   School work**
>
> Keeping old friends
>
> Making new friends

8 Write

Imagine you are Claire. Write an answer to Jennifer — tell her what to do!

Dear Jennifer

I'm sorry you're feeling sad and I understand your problem. Here are some ideas. ...

Unit check

1 Fill in the spaces

Complete the dialogue with the words in the box.

| matter listen ~~you~~ help angry happy worried don't fine boyfriend |

Rosa: Are __you__ OK, Lynn? You don't look very [1] _____ .

Lynn: Oh, I'm [2] _____ .

Rosa: Come on. What's the [3] _____ ?

Lynn: Oh, I'm [4] _____ with Janet Martin. She's saying bad things about my
[5] _____ .

Rosa: Lynn, don't [6] _____ to her. She's stupid.

Lynn: Yes, I guess you're right.

Rosa: Look, [7] _____ think about her. Come round to my place and [8] _____ me with my English. I'm [9] _____ about the test tomorrow.

Lynn: OK, let's go.

| 9 |

2 Choose the correct answers

(Circle) the correct answers, a, b or c.

1 I think this music is _____ .
   a (boring) b bored c unhappy

2 Is this word right or wrong? I'm _____ .
   a confused b excited c scared

3 Tom's _____ because his pet budgie is dead.
   a angry b worried c sad

4 Switch _____ the television, please.
   a in b on c up

5 Laura's a happy person. She smiles and _____ a lot.
   a shouts b cries c laughs

6 Go _____ ! I'm trying to listen to the radio.
   a over b away c straight on

7 My sister's unhappy because she _____ her friends.
   a forgets b visits c misses

8 Please leave me _____ .
   a alone b around c about

9 I don't want to talk to you. _____ me again.
   a Call b Contact c Don't contact

| 8 |

3 Correct the mistakes

In each sentence there is a mistake with imperatives and talking about feelings.
Underline the mistake and write the correct sentence.

1 I like this film – it's <u>excited</u>. *I like this film – it's exciting.* _____

2 Come in and you close the door. _____

3 Not park in front of the post office, please. _____

4 I'm worried for my test tomorrow. _____

5 What the matter? _____

6 Hang up a minute! I'm coming. _____

7 How you feeling today? _____

8 It's OK. Be not scared. _____

9 We're boring – there's nothing to do. _____

| 8 |

How did you do?

Total: | 25 |

| ☺ | Very good 20 – 25 | ☹ | OK 14 – 19 | ☹ | Review Unit 9 again 0 – 13 |

10 We can't lose

1 Remember and check

Complete the summary of the text about Rick Hoyt. Use the verbs in the box. Then check with the text on page 70 of the Student's Book.

swim   uses   ride   pulls   take part   works   sits   pushes

Rick Hoyt has got cerebral palsy, but he ¹ ....
in a university and he ² .... a computer to
communicate. Rick and his father also ³ ....
in triathlons together. Rick can't run, so his father
⁴ .... him in a wheelchair. He can't
⁵ .... , so his father ⁶ .... him
through the water in a boat. And he can't ⁷ ....
a bike, so he ⁸ .... in a seat on the front of his
father's bike.

2 Grammar

can/can't (ability)

a Look at the pictures. Write a sentence for each picture.

1   *She can drive.*   2   3   ....

4   5   6   ....

b Write questions for the activities in Exercise 2a. Start with *Can you ...?*
Then write true answers (*Yes, I can / No, I can't*).

1   *Can you drive?* ....
....

2   ....
....

3   ....
....

4   ....
....

5   ....
....

6   ....
....

	(stand on head)	(walk on hands)	(ride a horse)	(juggle)
Sylvia	✓	✗	✗	✗
Paul	✓	✓	✗	✓
George	✓	✗	✓	✓
Eva	✗	✓	✗	✗

1 A: _Can_____ George walk on his hands?
   B: _No___ , he _can't_____ .

2 Sylvia _____ stand on her head, but she _____
   _____ on her hands.

3 Paul and George _____ juggle.

4 Sylvia, Paul and Eva _____ _____ a horse.

5 A: _____ Sylvia and Eva juggle?
   B: _____ , they _____ .

6 A: _____ Paul and Sylvia walk on their hands?
   B: Paul _____ , but Sylvia _____ .

d Make true sentences. Use your own ideas.

1 I can't _____ , but I _____ .
2 I can _____ , but I can't _____ .
3 My parents can _____ , but they can't _____ .
4 My best friend can _____ , but he/she _____ .
5 A chimpanzee can't _____ , but it can _____ .
6 Young children can _____ , but they can't _____ .

---

3 **Pronunciation**

can/can't

a 🔊 Listen to the questions and answers. Underline the words that are stressed.

1 Can you <u>read</u>?   <u>Yes</u>, I <u>can</u>.
2 Can they write?   Yes, they can.
3 Can she play the guitar?   Yes, she can.

🔊 Listen again. This time, listen to the pronunciation of *can*. Is it the same in the questions and the answers?

b 🔊 Read these sentences. <u>Underline</u> the words that you think are stressed. Then listen, check and repeat.

1 I can dance, but I can't sing.
2 He can read, but he can't write.
3 Can she play the piano?
4 Can you speak Spanish?

4 Vocabulary

Sports

a Look at the pictures and complete the sentences.

1 John _plays_ _volleyball_ with his friends.
2 People _____ here in the winter.
3 We _____ _____ once a week.
4 Can James _____ a _____ ?
5 Kate _____ in the park.
6 People sometimes _____ in this river.
7 Can you _____ ?
8 We often _____ _____ after school.

b Look at these lists. Complete them with more sports.

go + ...ing	play + name of game	do
go skiing	play tennis	do sport
go riding	_____	_____
_____	_____	
_____	_____	

5 Grammar

like / don't like -ing

a Look at the information about the people. Write sentences about them using these verbs:

= like

= love

= not like

= hate

	Joanna	Kevin	Brian and Louise

1 Joanna _likes skiing. She loves swimming, but she doesn't like rollerblading. She hates playing football._

2 Kevin _____

3 Brian and Louise _____

b Write similar sentences about you, your best friend and people in your family.

1 I ....
....

2 My best friend ....
....

3 My ....
....

4 My ....
....

6 Culture in mind

a Match the names of the sports with the pictures. Write the numbers 1–6 in the boxes.

1 rugby   2 tennis   3 netball   4 football   5 hockey   6 cricket

a **b** **c** **d** **e** **f**

b Who does which sports? Write the sports from Exercise 6a under the names. (Some go under both names.) Then check with the text on page 74 of the Student's Book.

Miriam

Jack

7 Study help
Pronunciation

a For help with pronunciation, group words under their sounds. For example:

/æ/	/ɑː/	/eɪ/
sad	park	race
match	basketball	holiday
....	....	....
....	....	....
....	....	....

Add these words from Units 9 and 10 to the lists.

part   camel   rollerblade   strange   grass   gymnastics   laugh   fantastic   late

b Look for words in Units 9 and 10 to write under these sounds. If you aren't sure of the pronunciation, check in your dictionary.

/ɪ/	/iː/	/ɒ/	/əʊ/
swim	team	hop	open
finish	wheelchair	problem	photo
....	....	....	....
....	....	....	....
....	....	....	....
....	....	....	....

Skills in mind

8 Listen

🔊 Listen and choose the correct picture. (Circle) A, B or C.

1 What sports does Tom do?

 (A)   B   C

2 What can Cristina do?

 A   B   C

3 What does Matt do in the winter?

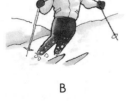

 A   B   C

4 What can Pete do?

 A   B   C

9 Listen and write

(a) 🔊 Listen to an interview with Mark Cavalcanti. Complete the information in the box.

(b) Use the information in the box to write a paragraph about Mark.

Listening tip
Choosing the correct picture

- Before you listen, read the questions. What information do they ask for?

- Study the pictures. Look for the differences between them.

- Now listen. You hear the recordings twice.

Name: *Mark Cavalcanti*

Age: [1] _____

Language(s): [2] _____

Nationality: [3] _____

His main sport:
4 _____

His other sports:
5 _____
6 _____

People in his family:
Helen (mother)
Anna [7] (_____)
Their sporting interests:
Helen: [8] _____
Anna: [9] _____

Unit check

1 Fill in the spaces

Complete the sentences with the words in the box.

| team | can | swim | doesn't | loves | races | ~~sport~~ | free | guitar | hockey |

Jackie is very good at __*sport*__ . She can play ¹ _____ and she's in the basketball
² _____ at school. She can also ³ _____ well and she often wins ⁴ _____
on sports days. Her brother Tim does different things in his ⁵ _____ time. He ⁶ _____
juggle and walk on his hands and he ⁷ _____ playing the ⁸ _____ , but he
⁹ _____ like doing sport.

[ ] 9

2 Choose the correct answers

(Circle) the correct answers, a, b or c.

1 I _____ mushrooms. I think they're awful.
   a like b love c (hate)

2 _____ is my favourite sport.
   a Rugby b Singing c Juggling

3 We often go _____ in winter.
   a netball b skiing c football

4 John _____ gymnastics twice a week
   after school.
   a goes b plays c does

5 They want to take part _____ the
   triathlon.
   a with b for c in

6 I _____ swim, but not very well.
   a can b can't c like

7 Barbara doesn't like team games, but she likes
   _____ .
   a rollerblading b hockey c volleyball

8 Can you _____ a bike?
   a ride b run c go

9 I _____ 20 minutes to walk
   to school.
   a have b take c do

[ ] 8

3 Correct the mistakes

In each sentence there is a mistake with *can/can't* and with verbs of liking + *-ing*.
<u>Underline</u> the mistake and write the correct sentence.

1 Graham <u>cant</u> play football today. *Graham can't play football today.* _____

2 Maria can she use a computer? _____

3 We love watch sports programmes on TV. _____

4 Sorry, I can come to your party on Saturday. _____

5 My brother likes basketball and snowboard. _____

6 Can your friends swimming? _____

7 Nick not likes running, so he never plays tennis. _____

8 Do you can play the violin? _____

9 I hate play hockey in the rain. _____

[ ] 8

How did you do?

Total: [25]

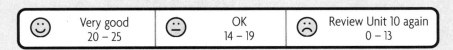

| ☺ | Very good 20 – 25 | ☻ | OK 14 – 19 | ☹ | Review Unit 10 again 0 – 13 |

11 Reading on the roof!

1 Remember and check

Can you remember the conversation between Kate and Ben? Mark the sentences *T* (true) or *F* (false). Then check with the dialogue on page 76 of the Student's Book.

1 Kate is having a holiday on a boat. ☐

2 At the moment, she's sitting in the dining room. ☐

3 Her parents are playing cards. ☐

4 Her mother is taking photos. ☐

5 Jamie is looking after his little brother. ☐

6 Ben's having a great time. ☐

2 Grammar

Present continuous

a Write the verbs in the *-ing* form and put them in the lists. Think about the spelling.

~~come~~ ~~sit~~ ~~watch~~ play swim write shop do use eat have run

+ *ing*	*e* + *ing*	double letter + *ing*
watching	_coming_	_sitting_
....	....	....
....	....	....

b Complete the answers. Use the present continuous form of verbs from Exercise 2a.

1 **Max:** Where's James?

Peggy: He's in his room. _He's reading_ a book.

2 **Norma:** Is Barbara at home?

Cynthia: No, sorry. She's in town. _____ at the supermarket.

3 **Chris:** Where are Mum and Dad?

Peter: They're in the living room. _____ a video.

4 **Caroline:** Do you want to go for a walk?

Richard: No, not right now. _____ some postcards.

5 **Monica:** I can't see Nick and Petra.

Phil: They're over there. _____ on that seat under the tree.

6 **Dad:** Tony and Frank, where are you?

Tony: We're up here. _____ our homework.

7 **Dad:** Is Mum at home?

Kate: Yes, she's in the bathroom. _____ a shower.

c Look at the picture. Correct these false statements.

1 Anne and Peter are playing cards.
Peter isn't playing cards. He's reading.

2 George and Alice are eating fish.
....

3 Dorothy is talking to George.
....

4 Maria and Bill are listening to music.
....

5 Pat is dancing.
....

6 Martin, Wendy and Lisa are playing the guitar.
....

d Make present continuous questions. Then write the short answers.

1 Mum and Dad / sit in the garden?
Are Mum and Dad sitting in the garden?
✓ Yes, they are.

2 you / watch the news?
....
✗..

3 Helen / do her homework?
....
✓..

4 Ken and Neill / play tennis?
....
✗..

5 Joe / use the computer?
....
✗..

e Write true answers. Use the present continuous.

1 Where are you sitting at the moment?
....

2 What are you doing?
....

3 What are you using?
....

4 Are you sitting alone in the room?
....

5 Are you wearing glasses?
....

6 What are other people doing?
....
....
....

Present continuous and present simple

(f) **Look at these examples. Then underline the correct words in the sentences.**

Janet often **goes** to the market on Saturday, but this morning she**'s playing** basketball.

I**'m having** pizza for lunch today, but I usually **have** sandwiches.

1 My sister *talks* / *is talking* to Sophie on the phone. *They sometimes* <u>talk</u> / *They're sometimes talking* for over an hour!

2 *I read* / *I'm reading* a lot. At the moment *I read* / *I'm reading* a book about Russia.

3 A: Are Philip and Greg at home?

   B: No, *they play* / *they're playing* tennis. *They play* / *They're playing* three times a week.

4 A: Where's Eva?

   B: *She visits* / *She's visiting* her aunt and uncle. *She often stays* / *She's often staying* with them at the weekend.

5 A: How does your brother get to work?

   B: *He catches* / *He's catching* a train. But he *doesn't work* / *isn't working* this week – he's on holiday.

🔊 **Listen and repeat.**

1 Harry's hobby is horse-riding.
2 I'm hardly ever hungry at home.
3 He's unhappy about his hair.
4 How often does Helen help you?
5 Hanna's having a hamburger at the Hilton Hotel.

4 **Vocabulary**

House and furniture

(a) **Fill in the crossword.**

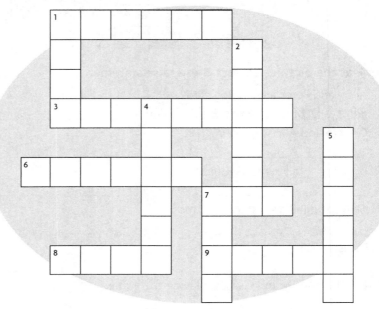

Across   **Down**

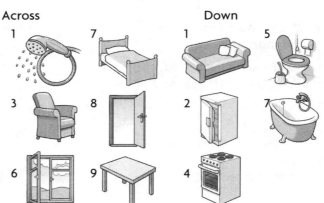

(b) **Write the names of the rooms.**

1 My family watches TV in this room. ....

2 We wash and have a shower in this room. ....

3 I sleep in this room. ....

4 There's a cooker and a fridge in this room. ....

5 The front door opens into this small room. ....

Prepositions

(c) 🔊 Listen and complete the text with the prepositions. Then draw the missing things in the picture of the room (table, window, computer, pictures, door).

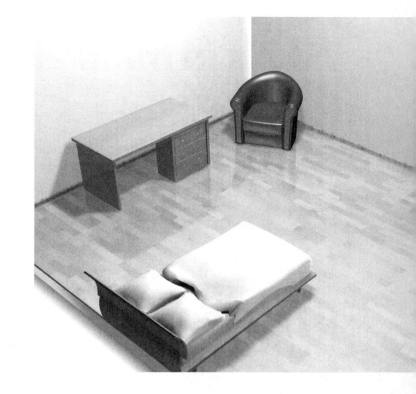

on	~~in~~	near	between	next to	under

I've got a bed and a desk _____in_____ my room.
There's a small table [1] _____ the
bed. The desk is [2] _____ the
window and I've got my computer
[3] _____ the desk. There's a small
armchair in the corner of the room. On the wall
[4] _____ the desk and the armchair
I've got three pictures of my favourite pop stars.
The door is [5] _____ the armchair.

5 Everyday English

Complete the phone conversation. Use words from box A and box B.

A
I'm   Come round   See
What are you

B
up to   you   on my way
to my place

Liz: Hi, Robbie. [1] _____ ?

Robbie: Nothing much, really. I'm just reading the newspaper.

Liz: [2] _____ . Adam and Liz are here and they're making lasagne.

Robbie: Great! [3] _____ .

Liz: [4] _____ .

Robbie: Bye.

6 Study help

A good way to remember words is to draw a spidergram.
Complete this spidergram.

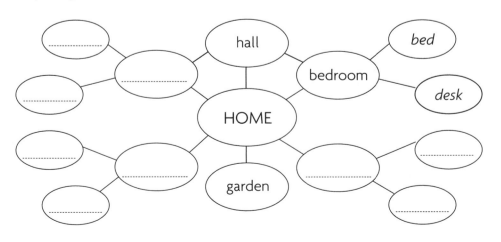

Skills in mind

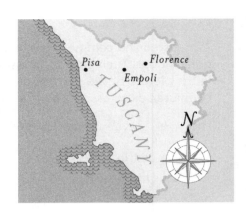

7 Read and listen

(a) Sue is on a school trip in Italy. Read her postcard to her parents. In the table, write ✓ (good) or ✗ (not good) under 'Sue'.

12th April

Dear Mum and Dad,

I'm writing this in Florence. The city's lovely, but it's raining at the moment. We're staying in a hotel, but the rooms aren't very nice – they're too small and dark. I'm not doing very well with my Italian, but I'm trying! The food's delicious and we're all having a good time.

Lots of love,

Sue

Mr and Mrs Castle
32 Bridge Road
CAMBRIDGE
CB1 3FJ
Inghilterra

		Sue (Florence)	Emma (Empoli)
1	Hotel	....	✓
2	Speaking the language	....	....
3	Food	....	....
4	Weather	....	....
5	Having a good time?	....	....

(b) 🔊 Emma is also on the school trip. It's three days later and they're in Empoli. Listen to Emma talking to her father. In the table, write ✓ (good) or ✗ (not good) under 'Emma'.

8 Write

Imagine you're a tourist on holiday in your town. Write a postcard to your parents or to a friend. Use the topics from the table on this page.

Writing tip
Writing a postcard

- Start with *Dear* .... ,

- Here are some endings you can use.

  All the best,
  Love,
  Lots of love,
  Love from

Unit check

1 Fill in the spaces

Complete the sentences with the words in the box.

| in | is | aren't | are | finishing | reading | ~~sitting~~ | they're | living | bedroom |

At the moment, Jill's ___*sitting*___ in front of the computer in her [1] _____ . She's
[2] _____ her homework and her cat Sammy [3] _____ sleeping on her bed. Her two
brothers [4] _____ watching a cricket match in the [5] _____ room and her sister is
[6] _____ a book [7] _____ the garden. Their parents [8] _____ here because
[9] _____ visiting some friends this afternoon.

⬜ **9**

2 Choose the correct answers

Ⓒircle the correct answers, a, b or c.

1 Dad's in the _____ . He's having a
   shower.
   a (bathroom) b kitchen c dining room

2 There's a new _____ in the kitchen.
   a bed b sofa c cooker

3 Put the milk in the _____ , please.
   a fridge b bath c toilet

4 Helen is in Poland. She's _____
   a great time.
   a doing b having c making

5 Don't switch off the TV. Jack and I
   _____ watching this film.
   a am b is c are

6 Listen! Susan _____ the violin.
   a play b plays c 's playing

7 _____ the computer at the
   moment?
   a Are you use b You're using
   c Are you using

8 What _____ today?
   a 's the weather like b does the weather
   like c 's the weather liking

9 A: Meet me at the sports centre in ten
       minutes.
   B: Right. I'm _____ my way.
   a in b on c at

⬜ **8**

3 Correct the mistakes

In each sentence there is a mistake with the present continuous. <u>Underline</u> the mistake
and write the correct sentence.

1 Right now Tina <u>play</u> cards with Andrew. *Right now Tina's playing cards with Andrew.* _____

2 The weather is good and we stay in a nice hotel. _____

3 What's happening? Is our team wining? _____

4 No, they not playing well today. _____

5 I not wear my glasses at the moment. _____

6 What Kate is doing? _____

7 She's rideing her new bike. _____

8 Don't make a noise – your grandfather sleeps. _____

9 This shop is always selling delicious ice cream. _____

⬜ **8**

How did you do?

Total: ⬜ **25**

| ☺ | Very good 20 – 25 | ☺ | OK 14 – 19 | ☹ | Review Unit 11 again 0 – 13 |

12 Can I try them on?

1 Remember and check

Complete the sentences with the words in the box. Then check with the text on page 82 of the Student's Book.

> colourful   balloons   clothes   dance   carnival   national holiday
> festivals   parade

1 St Patrick's Day, Mardi Gras and Thanksgiving are .... in the USA.
2 St Patrick's Day is the .... of Ireland. People wear green ....
3 On Thanksgiving Day, there is a big .... in the streets of New York and other cities. You can see big .... of famous cartoon characters.
4 Mardi Gras is a two-week party, similar to a .... People sing and .... in the streets and they wear .... clothes.

2 Vocabulary

Months of the year and seasons

a Fill in the puzzle with months of the year (1–9). What's the other month (10)?

b Which two months aren't in the puzzle?
....

c Answer the questions.
1 What month is your birthday?
....
2 What month is your mother's birthday?
....
3 Name a month when you don't go to school. ....
4 Which months are cold in your country?
....
5 Which is your favourite month?
....
Why? ....
....

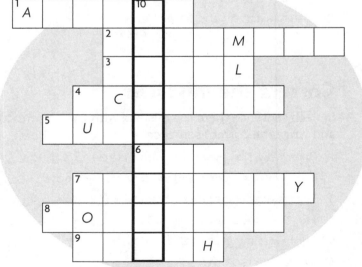

d Write the names of the seasons (J = January, etc.).

1 J + F + M   = ...
2 A + M + J   = ...
3 J + A + S   = ...
4 O + N + D   = ...

e What do you do in the four seasons? Write a sentence for each season. For example:

In winter I play hockey and I sometimes go skiing.
....
....
....
....

3 Grammar

Prepositions

Complete the paragraph with *in*, *on* or *at*.

In my country, the school year begins [1] _____ February. My school day starts [2] _____ 8.40, so I get up [3] _____ 7 o'clock. That's fine when the weather's nice, but it isn't so good [4] _____ winter. There are usually seven lessons a day, but [5] _____ Wednesday we always have sport in the afternoon. School finishes at 3.45, but [6] _____ Thursday I stay until 5 o'clock to practise netball with the junior team. We have our long holiday [7] _____ summer – it begins [8] _____ December and I usually go away with my family for two weeks [9] _____ January.

4 Vocabulary

Clothes

(a) Put the letters in the correct order to make words for clothes. Write the words on the pictures.

| osehs | serds | tkejac | risht | anjes | peumjr |
| riantser | ~~opt~~ | srutores | cossk | frasc | hitTrs |

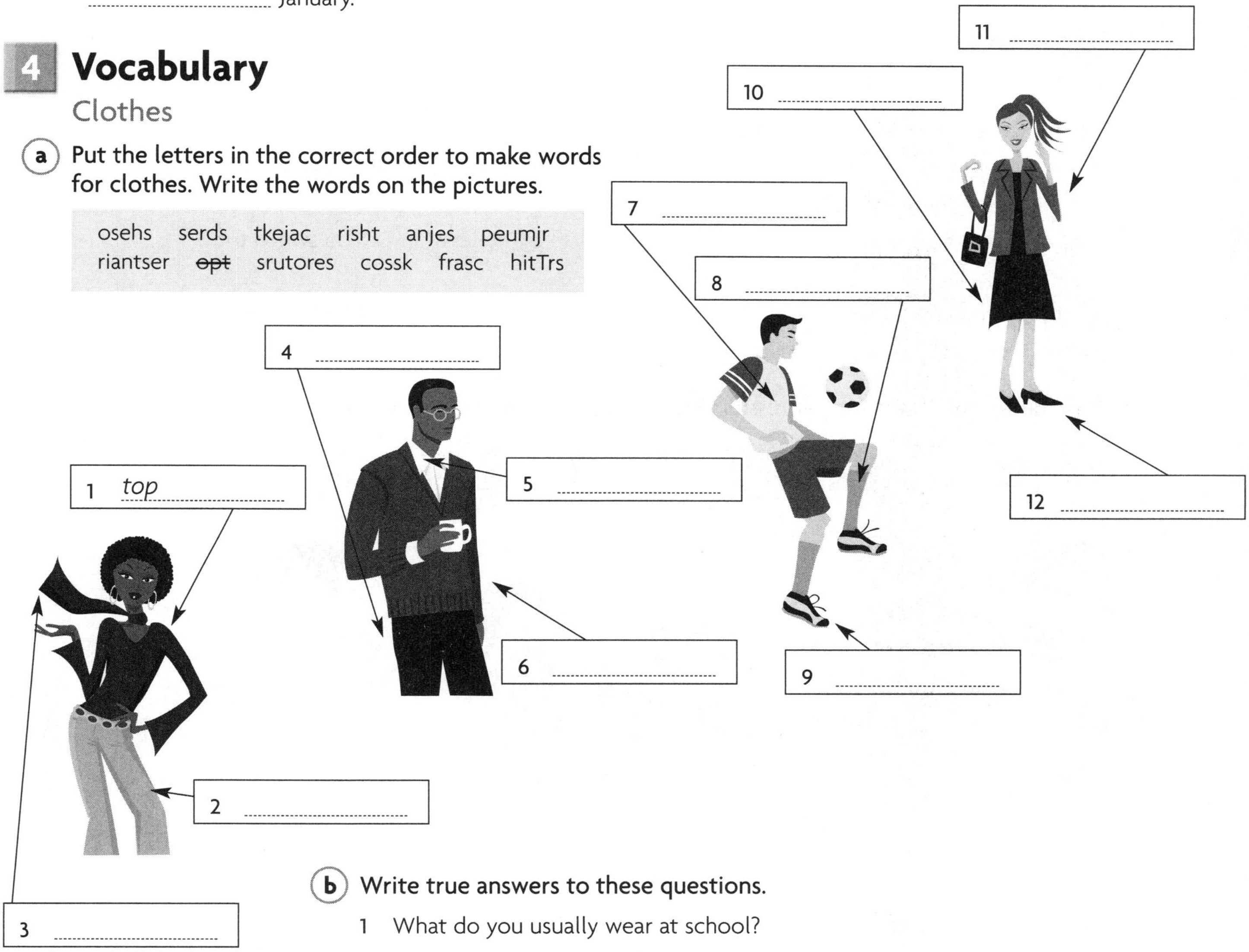

11 _____

10 _____

7 _____

8 _____

4 _____

1 *top*

5 _____

12 _____

6 _____

9 _____

2 _____

3 _____

(b) Write true answers to these questions.

1 What do you usually wear at school?

_____

2 What are your favourite clothes?

_____

3 What clothes do you hate wearing?

_____

4 What does your best friend usually wear?

_____

5 Where do you buy your clothes?

_____

Pronunciation

/æ/ and /e/

(a) 🔊 Listen to the word pairs and repeat.

	/æ/			/e/	
1	sad	☐	said	☐
2	bad	☐	bed	☐
3	man	☐	men	☐
4	dad	☐	dead	☐
5	sat	☐	set	☐

(b) 🔊 Listen to the sentences. Tick (✓) the word you hear in the lists in Exercise 5a.

(c) 🔊 Now listen to these sentences and repeat.

1 Annie is Alan's best friend.
2 I'm helping Joanna in December and January.
3 Emma's jacket is black and yellow.
4 How many magazines is Danny sending?

6 Grammar

Asking for permission

(a) Put the words in order to make questions.

1 window close I the Can ?
   Can I close the window?

2 have Can a I banana ?
   ....

3 I use computer your Can ?
   ....

4 play I football Can with you ?
   ....

5 I television Can on switch the ?
   ....

6 to toilet go the Can I please ?
   ....

(b) Write questions asking for permission. Then complete the answers with the words in the box.

> They're really expensive.   I'm using it.   What's the problem?   Here you are.
> ~~What size?~~   We've got visitors.

1 try on / trainers?
   A: *Can I try on those trainers?*
   B: Yes, of course. *What size?*

2 borrow / dictionary?
   A: ....
   B: Sorry, not right now.

3 come round / your place?
   A: ....
   B: No, sorry. I'm busy.

4 see / homework?
   A: ....
   B: Yes, OK.

5 wear / sunglasses?
   A: ....
   B: No, you can't.

6 talk to you?
   A: ....
   B: Yes, of course.

one/ones

c Complete the sentences with *one* or *ones*.

1 Mum, my jeans are really old. Can I have some new .... ?

2 Can I see the shirt in the window, please – the blue .... ?

3 A: I love TV game shows.
   B: Me too! Which .... is your favourite?

4 A: I like your ski jacket.
   B: Thanks. It's a new .... It's nice, isn't it?

5 A: I'd like two kilos of apples, please.
   B: Certainly. Would you like these green .... ?
   A: No, the red .... , please.

6 A: Those two people are from Russia.
   B: Which .... ?
   A: The .... in the corner, next to John and Linda.

7 Culture in mind

Match the words with the definitions.

1 enjoy   a someone who plays recorded music for people to listen or dance to

2 huge   b something that is popular

3 costumes   c machines for playing music

4 sound systems d traditional music from the Caribbean

5 DJ   e very big

6 attraction   f like

7 stalls   g special clothes

8 calypso   h small shops in the street or at a market

8 Study help

Punctuation

a Which of these need a capital letter at the beginning of the word? Tick (✓) the boxes.

1 names of places ☐   5 seasons ☐

2 names of people ☐   6 adjectives for colours ☐

3 days of the week ☐   7 nationalities ☐

4 months ☐

b Which words need to start with a capital letter? Correct them.

  B
  ~~b~~ritain friday dave autumn japanese yellow august spring tuesday april

To help you remember, you can write the capital letter in a different colour in your Vocabulary notebook.

Skills in mind

9 Listen

Listen to Nadia talking to a woman in a clothes shop. Circle the correct answers, a, b or c.

1	the thing Nadia wants	a	dress	b	shirt	c	jumper
2	colour	a	black	b	yellow	c	green
3	price	a	£54	b	£45	c	£49
4	Nadia's size	a	10	b	12	c	16
5	the thing she tries on	a	top	b	trousers	c	jeans

10 Read

Read the text. Write words for colours on the pictures.

1 ____blue____

2 _____

3 _____

4 _____

5 _____

6 _____

7 _____
_____

Clothes in London

People in Britain wear all kinds of clothes – London is one of the world's centres for fashion. But some people wear special clothes when they are at work. Here are some examples.

In London you sometimes see British policemen with tall blue hats or helmets – they're the traditional British 'bobbies'. But these days, police officers in Britain usually wear black and white hats. They also wear black trousers and shoes, and white shirts.

In front of Buckingham Palace you can see the soldiers who guard the Palace and the Queen. They're called Coldstream Guards, and they wear their famous uniform of red jacket, black trousers and shoes, and a big black hat. (The hat is called a busby.) The guards are also famous because they stand very still and never smile or talk!

In the business centre of London, you no longer see the traditional 'city gent' with his dark clothes and black bowler hat. Now, men who work in the city wear shirts and ties of different colours – but favourite colours are still grey or dark blue for trousers and jackets.

Reading tip

Reading for specific information

Exercise 10 asks you to find information about the photos in the text.

● There are four photos. Find the part of the text that tells you about each one.

● Look for key words in the text. In this exercise, the key words are clothes and colours.

Unit check

1 Fill in the spaces

Complete the sentences with the words in the box.

| at   in   festival   huge   clothes   enjoy   ~~party~~   trousers   costume   parade |

I've got a photo here of me and my friends at Carlo's carnival ___party___. Everyone's wearing crazy
1 _____ . Carlo's wearing a strange red 2 _____ , and Fiona has got short black
3 _____ and a 4 _____ hat. The carnival is 5 _____ April every year
and it's a big 6 _____ in my town. There's a 7 _____ in the streets – it starts
8 _____ 7 o'clock and lasts all evening. We all really 9 _____ it.

☐ 9

2 Choose the correct answers

(Circle) the correct answers, a, b or c.

1   We don't wear scarves and _____
    in hot weather.
    a T-shirts   b (jumpers)   c jeans

2   He's wearing a white shirt and a black
    _____ .
    a socks   b trousers   c hat

3   I wear _____ when I go running.
    a trainers   b dress   c shirt

4   The month after March is _____ .
    a February   b April   c June

5   _____ I look at your magazine,
    please?
    a Am   b Can   c Do

6   A: Which shoes do you like?
    B: I like the red _____ .
    a once   b one   c ones

7   Meet me _____ half past eleven.
    a at   b in   c on

8   _____ is my favourite season.
    a July   b Autumn   c August

9   A: I can't help you at the moment. Sorry.
    B: _____ .
    a Just a moment   b Here you are
    c Never mind

☐ 8

3 Correct the mistakes

In each sentence there is a mistake with prepositions or with expressions for asking permission.
Underline the mistake and write the correct sentence.

1   I catch the bus 7.45 every morning.   *I catch the bus at 7.45 every morning.*

2   Dan's birthday is on February. _____

3   I can use your phone? _____

4   Of corse you can. _____

5   Our garden is beautiful at spring. _____

6   Can I borow your jacket? _____

7   Sorry, you can. I want to wear it today. _____

8   Can I try up this dress, please? _____

9   We always go shopping the Saturday. _____

☐ 8

How did you do?

Total: ☐ 25

| ☺ Very good 20 – 25 | ☺ OK 14 – 19 | ☹ Review Unit 12 again 0 – 13 |

(13) He was only 40

1 Remember and check

Match the questions and answers about John Lennon. Then check with the text on page 92 of the Student's Book.

1 Where was John in the afternoon on 8 December?
2 Who was with him?
3 Where were they in the evening?
4 Who was at the door?
5 How many shots were there?
6 What were Chapman's words?

a In front of their apartment.
b Mark Chapman.
c 'I shot John Lennon.'
d Five.
e At a recording studio.
f His wife, Yoko Ono.

2 Grammar

Past simple: *was/wasn't / were/weren't*

(a) Complete the texts about these famous actors.
Use *was* or *were*.

Marilyn Monroe ¹ _____ an American film star.
Her real name ² _____ Norma Jean Baker. She
³ _____ a beautiful woman and her films
⁴ _____ very popular. People all around the
world ⁵ _____ very sad when she died in 1962.

Laurel and Hardy ⁶ _____ comedy actors. Stan Laurel
⁷ _____ from England. When he ⁸ _____
a teenager, he and Charlie Chaplin ⁹ _____ in the
same English acting group. Oliver Hardy ¹⁰ _____
American. All their films together ¹¹ _____ in black
and white, and they ¹² _____ very funny.

(b) Correct the statements about the people in Exercise 2a.

1 Marilyn Monroe was French.
   No, she wasn't. She was American.

2 She was a pop star.
   _____

3 People were happy when she died.
   _____

4 Laurel and Hardy's films were documentaries.
   _____

5 Laurel's first name was Oliver.
   _____

6 Their films were in colour.
   _____

c Look at the pictures and the times. Write past simple questions and short answers.

1 Joe / the station / 4 o'clock?
   A: *Was Joe at the station at 4 o'clock?*
   B: *No, he wasn't.*

2 Jane and Diana / the park / 2.30?
   A: ....
   B: ....

3 Julia / her bedroom / 9 o'clock?
   A: ....
   B: ....

4 Paul and Carol / the supermarket / 10.15?
   A: ....
   B: ....

5 Anna / the bookshop / 5.30?
   A: ....
   B: ....

6 Matt / the kitchen / 1 o'clock?
   A: ....
   B: ....

3 Vocabulary

Time expressions

a Complete the sentences with *last* or *yesterday*.

1 The bus was late .... afternoon.
2 My aunt and uncle were in Madrid .... week.
3 All my friends were at Karen's birthday party .... weekend.
4 The library wasn't open .... evening.
5 There was a good film on TV .... night.

b Write true answers to these questions.

1 Where were you at 8.15 yesterday morning?
   ....

2 Where were you at 5 pm last Friday?
   ....

3 Were you in bed at 10 o'clock last night?
   ....

4 Were you and your friends at school yesterday?
   ....

5 Was your friend at your place last weekend?
   ....

6 What day was your birthday last year?
   ....

4 Remember and check

Complete this part of the conversation from Exercise 5 of the Student's Book.
Use *was*, *wasn't*, *were* or *weren't*. Then listen and check.

Mother: Oh, I love that song.

Tom: I think I know it. Is it John Lennon?

Mother: That's right. He ¹ .... my favourite.
I remember the day he was shot. I ² .... really
sad.

Tom: When ³ .... that, Mum?

Mother: 1980. December 1980. He ⁴ .... very old –
he ⁵ .... only 40.

Tom: What ⁶ .... the name of that band he was
in? Before he was shot?

Mother: Oh, Tom – the Beatles!

Tom: Oh yes, right. Of course. ⁷ .... they from
London?

Mother: No they ⁸ .... ! They ⁹ ....
from Liverpool.

5 Pronunciation

was/wasn't and *were/weren't*

(a) Listen and repeat. Underline the words
that are stressed.

1 Were they in <u>London</u>? <u>Yes</u>, they <u>were</u>.
2 Were they happy? No, they weren't.
3 Were the girls at home? Yes, they were.
4 Was he an actor? Yes, he was.
5 Was she worried? No, she wasn't.
6 Was Dave at school? No, he wasn't.

(b) <u>Underline</u> the words that you think
are stressed. Then listen again, check and
repeat.

1 Helen was in hospital on Wednesday.
2 Our parents were at the library yesterday.
3 When were you in Paris?
4 What was your address?

6 Vocabulary

Ordinal numbers and dates

(a) Complete the table.

4	four	4th	fourth
12	twelve	....	....
....	....	....	second
....	....	....	fifteenth
3	....	....	....
1	....	....	....
50	....	50th	....
22	twenty-two	....	....
31	....	....	....

(b) Answer the questions.

1 What's the sixth month of the year?

----

2 What's the ninth month?

----

3 What's the last day of the school week?

----

4 What's the second day of the weekend?

----

5 What's your first lesson on Wednesday?

(c) Write sentences. Write the dates as we say them.

1 Sheila's birthday / May 17
Sheila's birthday is on the seventeenth of May.

2 Our national holiday / 3 July

----

3 Christmas Day / 25 December

----

4 New Year's Day / 1 January

----

5 The festival / 9 October

----

6 My party / 30 August / last year

----

7 Everyday English

Complete the dialogues. Use words from box A and box B.

A	B
Oh	be joking
Can I have	down
You must	a look
Calm	brilliant

1 **Nick:** I've got a new computer magazine. It's quite good.

Jenny: Yeah? [1] _____ ?

Nick: Yes, OK. It's over there on the table.

2 **Alison:** Mum's making lasagne for dinner tonight.

Chris: [2] _____ ! That's my favourite meal.

3 **Greg:** Jules, can I borrow some money?

Jules: How much do you need?

Greg: £40.

Jules: [3] _____ ! I've only got about £10 in my wallet.

4 **Paula:** I'm so angry! My computer isn't working properly. I hate the stupid thing! How can I finish my homework now?

Andy: [4] _____ , Paula. I'm sure it isn't a big problem.

8 Study help

Revision

To revise words, it's a good idea to make vocabulary cards.

- Write a word on one side of the card and a translation or picture on the other side. Use the cards to test yourself, or ask another person to test you.

- Put vocabulary cards up around your room – on the walls, on the door, on your furniture. If you see the words often, they are easier to remember.

Think of some words that are important or difficult in Unit 13. Write them on these cards. Put the word on side A and the translation on side B.

Side A	Side B
wallet	

Skills in mind

Listen

Listen to the dates. Write the numbers 1–6.

a 03/03/2001 ☐   d 30/07/1995 ☐
b 25/11/1980 ☐   e 11/12/2004 ☐
c 31/08/1999 ☐   f 13/09/1959 ☐

10 **Read**

Read the text and answer the questions.

Charlie Chaplin

Charlie Chaplin (1889–1977) was a very famous film star. He was from a poor home in South London, and he was already a comedy actor in the theatre when he was a teenager.

He went to the USA in 1910, and in 1914 he was in his first Hollywood film. In those days, the film industry was very young. Chaplin's early comedies were in black and white and they were 'silent' – there were no words or music.

Chaplin's favourite character was 'the tramp' – a little man with big trousers, an old black hat and a sad face. This was Chaplin's character in his famous comedy films – for example *The Kid* (1920), *The Gold Rush* (1924) and *City Lights* (1931). *Modern Times* (1936) was his first 'talking' film, and in *The Great Dictator* he was the director and music writer as well as the star.

Chaplin decided to leave the USA in 1952 and his new home was in Switzerland. He died there on Christmas Day at the age of 88.

1 What nationality was Charlie Chaplin?
  British. --

2 What city was he from?
  ----

3 When was he first in America?
  ----

4 Where was he in 1914?
  ----

5 Why were early films called 'silent films'?
  ----

6 When was *The Kid* first in the cinemas?
  ----

7 What was Chaplin's first film with words?
  ----

8 Where was Chaplin when he died?

Reading tip

Answering questions

Make sure you know what the questions are asking. Study the question words.

- If the question asks *When ...?*, the answer is a date or a time.

- If it asks *Where ...?*, the answer is a place.

- If it asks *Why ...?*, the answer is a reason (*Because ...*).

Unit check

1 Fill in the spaces

Complete the sentences with the words in the box.

| was   were   wasn't   weren't   afternoon   ~~yesterday~~   fifth   way   first   recording |

Richard Deane is a piano player and a music teacher. At 10.00 _____*yesterday*_____ morning his
¹_____ music student was at the door, and there ²_____ two others at 11.00 and
12.30. Richard ³_____ hungry, but there ⁴_____ time for lunch – at 1.45 he was on
his ⁵_____ to North London in a taxi. At 2 o'clock in the ⁶_____ he and his band
were in the ⁷_____ studio. But at the end of the day they ⁸_____ very happy –
their first four songs were OK, but the ⁹_____ one wasn't very good.

9

2 Choose the correct answers

(Circle) the correct answers, a, b or c.

1 22/05 is the _____ of May.
   a twenty-two   b (twenty-second)
   c twentieth-two
2 Her birthday is _____ 16th March.
   a in   b on   c at
3 Kate was in Portugal _____ 2002.
   a in   b on   c at
4 Today is my father's _____ birthday.
   a forty   b fourteenth   c fortieth
5 Jack's cousins _____ in England
   last year.
   a are   b were   c was

6 I _____ angry with you last
   week.
   a wasn't   b were   c weren't
7 _____ there a lot of children
   at the beach?
   a Is   b Were   c Was
8 Where _____ at 4 o'clock
   yesterday?
   a you were   b you was   c were you
9 I was ill _____ afternoon.
   a last   b yesterday   c before

8

3 Correct the mistakes

In each sentence there is a mistake with *was/were* and time expressions. <u>Underline</u> the mistake
and write the correct sentence.

1 My friend <u>is</u> at my place yesterday. *My friend was at my place yesterday.*_____
2 Anne's brothers was in Paris last weekend. _____
3 Tom and I wasn't here yesterday morning. _____
4 Where you were last Saturday? _____
5 There was about 50 people at the party. _____
6 When were Sara in Canada? _____
7 I was in bed at 10.30 yesterday in the night. _____
8 They were at school on Friday? _____
9 Was James in the bookshop last afternoon? _____

8

How did you do?

Total: **25**

| ☺ | Very good
20 – 25 | ☺ | OK
14 – 19 | ☹ | Review Unit 13 again
0 – 13 |

14 She didn't listen

1 Remember and check

Complete the summary of the text about Florence Nightingale. Use the adjectives in the box. Then check with the text on page 98 of the Student's Book.

> different   dirty   famous   angry   clean
> terrible   hungry

Lots of people in England were ¹ .... about the ² .... conditions in the hospitals in the Crimea. When Florence Nightingale arrived at Scutari, there were no beds or toilets. The soldiers' clothes were ³ .... , and they were ⁴ .... because there wasn't much food.

Six months later, conditions in the Scutari hospital were ⁵ .... The hospital was ⁶ .... and the soldiers were in comfortable beds. Soon Florence Nightingale was ⁷ .... all over the world.

2 Grammar

Past simple – regular verbs

a) Complete the table.

Verb	Past simple
1 work	*worked*
2 visit	....
3 hate	....
4 study	....
5 die	....
6 try	....
7 travel	....
8 arrive	....

b) Complete the dialogues. Use five more of the past simple verbs in Exercise 2a.

1 **Dad:** Was the film good?

   Tony: No. I ___*hated*___ it.

2 **Monica:** Peter! You're here!

   Peter: Yes, I .... at five o'clock this morning.

3 **Dave:** Was Florence Nightingale in America?

   Peggy: I don't think so. But she .... quite a lot of countries in Europe.

4 **Tom:** What were you up to last night?

   Fiona: Nothing much. I .... for the English test at home.

5 **Lee:** Were you at home last summer?

   Chris: No, we .... to China and Japan.

6 **Martin:** Sandra looks sad. Do you know why?

   Jane: Yes, her uncle .... last week.

c Write positive and negative sentences. Use the past simple.

1 (stay) Last summer, Julia *stayed in Paris.*
   She didn't stay in Rome.

2 (play) Last night, Ben and Adam _____

3 (work) In 2002, Alan _____

4 (phone) Yesterday, I _____

5 (dance, watch) On Friday, we _____

6 (park) On Saturday, Mum _____

d Complete the sentences. Use the negative form of the verbs in the box.

> phone   close   ~~enjoy~~   switch on
> have   play

1 I _*didn't enjoy*_ the party because I didn't know any people there.
2 Danny _____ a jumper, so he borrowed one from Robert.
3 We were worried when you _____ us.
4 I didn't get your message because I _____ my computer yesterday.
5 It wasn't a very good match – the team _____ well.
6 The shops opened at 8.30 am and they _____ until 9.00 pm.

3 **Pronunciation**
-ed endings

a 🔊 Write the verbs in the lists. Then listen and check.

> ~~liked~~   ~~hated~~   travelled   called
> started   landed   watched
> wanted

/t/ or /d/	/ɪd/
liked	*hated*
_____	_____
_____	_____
_____	_____

b 🔊 Listen and repeat. Make sure you say /ɪd/ for the *ed* sound.

1 They visit**ed** a museum.
2 They land**ed** on the moon.
3 The concert end**ed** at 11 o'clock.
4 We wait**ed** at the station.

c 🔊 Listen and repeat. Is the *ed* sound /t/ or /d/? Write /t/ or /d/ in the spaces.

1 We watch**ed** a film.   /t/
2 He liv**ed** in Barcelona.   _____
3 We help**ed** Annie with her homework.   _____
4 They laugh**ed** at me.   _____
5 Sally stay**ed** in a hotel.   _____
6 We open**ed** our books.   _____

4 Grammar

Past simple – questions

a Write true answers.

1 Did you enjoy your breakfast this morning?

....

....

2 Did you cycle to school?

....

....

3 When did you arrive at school?

....

....

4 When did your English lesson start?

....

....

5 How many lessons did you have yesterday?

....

....

6 Did you finish your homework yesterday?

....

....

7 What did you and your family watch on TV last night?

....

....

b Complete the questions. Use the past simple.

1 Tracey: What .... for lunch? (have)

Nick: I had a pizza.

Tracey: .... it? (like)

Nick: Yes, it was delicious.

2 Lee: My grandfather lived in that house. But he's dead now.

Bob: When .... ? (die)

Lee: In 2001.

3 John: What .... last Sunday? (do)

Debbie: We visited my aunt.

4 Susan: Rosa and Ken were in America for ten years.

Kevin: .... in New York? (live)

Angie: No, they didn't. They lived in Chicago.

c Read the information and complete the dialogue.

Holiday to Barcelona
Arrival: 28/07
Hotel Metropol

Angela: Mike! (have / good holiday?)
Did you have a good holiday? ....

Mike: (yes / great time) [1] ....

....

Angela: (Where / go?) [2] ....

.... ?

Mike: (travel) [3] ....

....

Angela: (When / get there?) [4] ....

.... ?

Mike: (arrive) [5] ....

....

Angela: (stay / with friends?) [6] ....

.... ?

Mike: [7] ....

....

5 Vocabulary

Verb and noun pairs

a Complete the sentences with the correct form of *have, play* or *go*.

1 Kevin and Tony _are playing_ tennis this afternoon.

2 Do you want to .... to Eva's party?

3 My cousin .... the piano.

4 Can I .... an ice cream?

5 I like .... lunch at this café.

b Here are some more expressions with *have, play* and *go to*. Can you match the nouns in the box with the verbs?

the guitar   the bank   a good time   a meal   the shops
a fight   tennis   hockey   university   a wash   basketball
town   a swim   the toilet   the violin

have	play	go to
....	....	....
....	....	....
....	....	....
....	....	....
....	....	....

6 Culture in mind

Match the two parts of the sentences. Check your answers with the text on page 102 of the Student's Book.

1 Steve Biko was born
2 He and other students
3 He was often
4 He died
5 Apartheid didn't end until
6 Nelson Mandela

a in a prison hospital.
b 1991.
c worked against apartheid.
d in 1946.
e was the first black South African president.
f in prison.

7 Study help

Spelling and pronunciation

a To remember the spelling rules for past simple verbs, you can group them like this in your Vocabulary notebook.

+ ed	+ d	y̶ + ied	double letter
start – started	love – loved	study – studied	shop – shopped
....	....	....	....
....	....	....	....

Add these words to the lists.

marry   answer   dance   stop   play   cry   travel   practise

b You can also group past simple verbs to show their pronunciation.

/t/	/d/	/ɪd/
helped	loved	started
....	....	....
....	....	....
....	....	....

Add the past simple form of these words to the lists.

hate   travel   want   ask   enjoy   watch   end   look   die

Skills in mind

8 Listen

🔊 Tony is on holiday in England with his father. Listen to his conversation with Sandro. Look at the pictures and circle the correct answer, a, b or c.

1 When did they arrive in London?

Sunday	**Monday**	**Tuesday**
A	Ⓑ	C

2 What time did the plane land?

A   B   C

3 Where did they stay on Tuesday?

A   B   C

4 What *didn't* they do in London?

A   B   C

5 How did they get to Cambridge?

A   B   C

9 Write

Write a reply to Carla's email. Tell her about the information you heard in Exercise 8.

> **Hi**
>
> **This is just a short message – I'm wondering if you've got any news from Tony. He phoned me yesterday from England, but I wasn't home. Did he ring you or Sandro? Have you got any news from him? I really miss him!**
>
> **Love**
>
> **Carla**

Unit check

1 Fill in the spaces

Complete the sentences with the words in the box.

| were   on   didn't   in   ~~born~~   stopped   studied   died   hospital   nurse |

My grandmother was _____born_____ in Germany [1] _____ 18 February 1944. Her family moved
to Italy [2] _____ 1960. She [3] _____ at the university in Milan and later she became
a [4] _____ . She worked in a big [5] _____ in Bologna for four years, but after she was
married she [6] _____ working. She and my grandfather had five children. They [7] _____
have a lot of money, but they [8] _____ very happy together. Grandma [9] _____ in 2003
— she was only 59. We still miss her a lot.

| | 9 |

2 Choose the correct answers

Circle the correct answers, a, b or c.

1 I'd like to _____ an ice cream.
   a practise   b play   c (have)

2 Mum goes to _____ every morning.
   a work   b a bath   c a coffee

3 Andrew _____ the piano at the
   school concert.
   a had   b practised   c played

4 Men _____ on the moon in 1969.
   a landed   b ended   c started

5 Did she _____ a good time at the
   party?
   a has   b had   c have

6 The woman _____ open
   the door.
   a did   b didn't   c don't

7 What _____ last weekend?
   a you did   b do you did   c did you do

8 A: Did you talk to David yesterday?
   B: No, I _____ .
   a didn't   b doesn't   c don't

9 A: _____ did your cousins
      arrive?
   B: On Sunday.
   a Where   b When   c What

| | 8 |

3 Correct the mistakes

In each sentence there is a mistake with the past simple. <u>Underline</u> the mistake and write the correct
sentence.

1 We <u>watch</u> a great programme last night.   *We watched a great programme last night.*

2 They traveled to the USA in 2002. _____

3 Why you did open the window? _____

4 I not wanted to go swimming yesterday. _____

5 Where she parked the car? _____

6 John and Melanie enjoyed the film last night? _____

7 No, they didn't liking it at all. _____

8 I tryed to phone you, but you weren't at home. _____

9 Lisa and her family was born in Spain. _____

| | 8 |

How did you do?

Total: | 25 |

| ☺ | Very good 20 – 25 | ☺ | OK 14 – 19 | ☹ | Review Unit 14 again 0 – 13 |

15 Where did they go?

1 Remember and check

🔊 Can you complete the dialogue about Lord Lucan? Complete the sentences. Then listen and check.

> know   children   opened   tried   kill   killed
> woman   wife   dead   house

Interviewer: Sandra Rivett? Who was she?

Professor: She was the young ¹ _____ who looked after Lord Lucan's ² _____ . And on November 7 1974, somebody killed her in a room in Lord Lucan's ³ _____ .

Interviewer: Lord Lucan? Did he ⁴ _____ her?

Professor: Well, we don't ⁵ _____ for sure. But we do know that Lord Lucan's ⁶ _____ , Lady Lucan, was in the house that day. She heard a noise and went downstairs. She ⁷ _____ the door, saw Sandra dead. Then somebody ⁸ _____ to kill her too, and ran away. But Lady Lucan wasn't ⁹ _____ . The police think that Lord Lucan wanted to kill his wife, and ¹⁰ _____ Sandra Rivett by mistake.

2 Grammar

Past simple – irregular verbs

a Fill in the crossword with the past simple forms of the verbs.

Across	Down
1 leave	2 find
3 become	3 begin
4 eat	6 write
5 know	8 go
7 see	10 have
9 run	12 get
11 think	
13 give	
14 take	

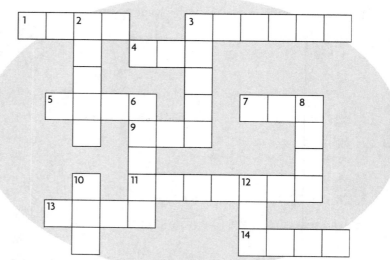

b Complete the sentences. Use past simple verbs from Exercise 2a.

1 **Tina:** I _had_ lunch at the café today.

   Lynn: Did you see Adam?

   Tina: No, but I _____ Liz and Charlie.

2 **Harry:** Why wasn't Mum here this afternoon?

   Carol: She _____ shopping with Dad. They _____ home at 2.30.

3 **Karen:** Our French teacher _____ us a test today.

   Dad: Was it OK?

   Karen: Yes, I _____ it was easy.

4 **John:** Sam _____ five pages for his History project.

   Mark: Yes, I know. He _____ a lot of information from the library.

5 **Tom:** I _____ someone's wallet in the park yesterday.

   Claire: What did you do with it?

   Tom: I _____ it to the police station.

c What did Angela do on Saturday morning? Look at the pictures and complete the sentences.

Angela ¹ _____ at 8.30 and she ² _____ for a walk. After breakfast she ³ _____ . She ⁴ _____ at 12.00 and then she ⁵ _____ to her friend Zoë. Angela and her family ⁶ _____ at 1.15.

d Complete the sentences. Use the negative form of the verbs in the box.

> became   went   heard   gave   left   ran   ~~ate~~   came

1 Barbara _*didn't eat*_ much for breakfast because she wasn't hungry.

2 Terry knew it was my birthday yesterday, but he _____ me a present.

3 We told Sue and Jill about our party on Saturday, but they _____ .

4 Richard _____ a doctor because he didn't pass his university exams.

5 We got to the station at 9 o'clock, but the train _____ until 10.15.

6 Alan shouted for help, but his friends _____ him.

7 I'm not scared of snakes, so I _____ away.

8 Jane _____ to school on Thursday because she was ill.

e Complete the questions in the dialogue.

Jason: _*What did you do*_ (do) last night?

Sylvia: We went to the cinema and saw the new Spielberg film.

Jason: ¹ _____ (begin)?

Sylvia: At 6.30.

Jason: ² _____ (go) after the film?

Sylvia: We went to the Riverview Restaurant.

Jason: ³ _____ George _____ (have) dinner with you?

Sylvia: Yes, he did.

Jason: ⁴ _____ (sit) outside?

Sylvia: No, it was a bit cold, so we sat inside.

Jason: ⁵ _____ (have) for dinner?

Sylvia: I had fresh fish with potatoes and salad.

Jason: ⁶ _____ (be) good?

Sylvia: Yes, it was delicious.

Jason: ⁷ _____ (get) home?

Sylvia: At about 11.30.

3 Pronunciation

Past simple questions

🔊 Listen to the questions. <u>Underline</u> the words that are stressed. Listen again and repeat.

1 Did she <u>know</u> the <u>answer</u>?
2 Did they give you a present?
3 When did he write to you?
4 What did she think of the book?
5 Where did you get your jacket?
6 Why did they leave on Sunday?

4 Vocabulary

Adverbs

a Complete the table.

Adjectives	Adverbs
1 strange	*strangely*
2 brilliant	
3 easy	
4 nice	
5 unhappy	
6 real	
7 mysterious	
8 noisy	

b Complete the sentences. Make adverbs from the adjectives in the box.

angry   careful   sudden   quick   ~~quiet~~   slow

1 He came in _____*quietly*_____ .

2 She wrote _____ .

3 He ran _____ .

4 She shouted _____ .

5 They walked _____ .

6 A ghost _____ appeared.

c Adjective or adverb? <u>Underline</u> the correct words.

1 We knew we were late, so we went out *quick / quickly*.
2 Come in *quiet / quietly*, please. Don't make a lot of noise.
3 Stella is *brilliant / brilliantly* at music. She plays four different instruments.
4 Please be *careful / carefully* with my glasses. I don't want you to break them.
5 The test wasn't difficult. I could answer all the questions *easy / easily*.
6 There were *mysterious / mysteriously* sounds on our roof last night.
7 'I don't think Anna likes me,' said Peter. He was very *unhappy / unhappily*.
8 The child didn't make a sound for five minutes. Then *sudden / suddenly* she started to cry.

d What do you think happened in Mr Brown's apartment? Write three sentences giving your ideas. Use *probably*, *maybe* and *perhaps*.

5 Everyday English

Look at the <u>underlined</u> words and write the complete questions.

1 Louise: <u>Want to come to my place?</u>

   Do you want to come to my place?

   Catherine: Yes – great. See you soon.

2 Patrick: I think I'm ready to leave.

   Dad: <u>Got your passport?</u>

   Patrick: Yes, everything's here.

3 Rachel: I can't do any more work tonight.

   Mum: <u>Tired?</u>

   Rachel: Yes. It's time for bed.

4 Robert: My CD player isn't working very well.

   Andy: <u>Want me to have a look at it?</u>

   Robert: Oh, yeah – thanks, Andy.

5 Judy: I had my last exam this morning.

   Daniel: <u>Feeling good?</u>

   Judy: Yeah – fantastic!

6 Study help

Self-assessment

When you make mistakes, don't worry! You can learn from your mistakes.

● What words do you often forget? What are your 'favourite' grammar mistakes? Make a note of them in your Vocabulary notebook. Use different colours so they are easy to see.

● Think about the vocabulary and grammar topics in the Student's Book. Which ones do you know well? Which ones do you need to work on?

Fill in the table for topics in Units 14 and 15.

✓✓✓ I know this very well
✓✓ I know this quite well
✗ I need to work on this

Topic	My self-assessment
past simple (regular verbs) – positive	
past simple (regular verbs) – negative	
past simple (regular verbs) – questions	
past simple (irregular verbs)	
adverbs	

Skills in mind

7

Read

Read the text and mark the statements *T* (true) or *F* (false).

Map showing Florida, Atlantic Ocean, Bermuda, Bermuda Triangle, Puerto Rico

The mystery of the Bermuda Triangle

The Bermuda Triangle is a small part of the Atlantic Ocean between Florida, Bermuda and Puerto Rico. A lot of people believe that there's something very strange about this place.

Between 1940 and 1990, 50 ships disappeared while sailing through the 'triangle'. But not only ships – there were aeroplanes too. In 1945, five American planes disappeared there. When a sixth plane went to look for them, it never came back. Nobody saw the planes or their 27 crew members again. We don't know what really happened to the planes and ships.

But people give different reasons for their disappearance.

▲ Perhaps they disappeared because of stormy weather in the Bermuda Triangle. It's certainly true that there are lots of big storms in the area.

▲ In 1945 the commander of the five planes probably became confused in bad weather and they went in the wrong direction. When they no longer had any petrol, they crashed into the sea.

▲ Some people say that mysterious UFOs came from another planet, and they took the ships and boats away with them.

▲ Another strange idea is that there are 'holes' in our world. Some people say that the ships and planes disappeared into one of these holes and went to another world.

Scientists are sure there's a good reason for the disappearances in the Bermuda Triangle – but people love mysteries, and there's still a lot of interest in this part of the Atlantic.

1   The Bermuda Triangle is a country in the Atlantic Ocean. ☐
2   In 1990, 50 ships disappeared there. ☐
3   There is often bad weather in the Bermuda Triangle. ☐
4   In 1945, the commander of the planes probably didn't know where they were. ☐
5   People sometimes think that UFOs came to the Bermuda Triangle. ☐
6   Scientists think that the planes and ships disappeared into a hole. ☐

Write

Imagine you were on a ship or plane which disappeared in the Bermuda Triangle – but you lived to tell the story. Describe what happened. Think about these questions:

● When were you there?
● What was the weather like?
● How did you know that something was wrong?
● What happened next?
● How did you get away?

Writing tip

Checking your work

● When you finish writing, check your story carefully. Think about your 'favourite' mistakes.

● Exchange stories with a friend. Help each other to find mistakes.

● You can use a code to show mistakes in your story or your friend's story. For example: gr = grammar mistake, sp = spelling mistake.

Can you work out what the mistakes are here?

     gr   *sp*
I (were) in a quiet ship with 38 other (poeple) in 2001.

                                               sp
We entered ⌄ Bermuda Triangle on 23(th) Febuary ...

Unit check

1 Fill in the spaces

Complete the sentences with the words in the box.

| had | went | didn't | know | ~~heard~~ | slowly | got | thought | could | looked |

Peter was in bed when he ___heard___ strange noises in the garden. He [1] _____ up quietly, found his glasses and [2] _____ to the window. When he looked out, he [3] _____ see an animal under the tree. At first he [4] _____ it was a dog – but it [5] _____ very long ears and small red eyes. Peter didn't [6] _____ what it was. As he watched, the animal suddenly [7] _____ up at his window. Then it turned. It [8] _____ run, but walked [9] _____ to the end of the garden and disappeared.

☐ 9

2 Choose the correct answers

(Circle) the correct answers, a, b or c.

1 Elise _____ speak English when she was five years old.
   a (could) b knew c was

2 She _____ a nurse in 1997.
   a came b became c began

3 Jack ran very _____ , so of course he didn't win the race.
   a slowly b quietly c quickly

4 I _____ a fight with my sister yesterday.
   a have b has c had

5 The teacher didn't _____ us about the test.
   a tell b telled c told

6 _____ they take the dog to the park?
   a Does b Did c Were

7 What _____ in the box?
   a found you b you found c did you find

8 Kate was at the cinema, so she _____ saw us there.
   a probably b perhaps c maybe

9 Please be _____ when you drive the car.
   a suddenly b carefully c careful

☐ 8

3 Correct the mistakes

In each sentence there is a mistake with the past simple or with adverbs. Underline the mistake and write the correct sentence.

1 I <u>writed</u> postcards to all my friends. _I wrote postcards to all my friends._

2 Sara goes swimming yesterday afternoon. _____

3 He looked at her angryly and left the room. _____

4 My grandfather can juggle when he was young. _____

5 I ran quick to the phone and called the police. _____

6 You ate all the chocolate? _____

7 Ben not said goodbye to me. _____

8 He didn't maybe have time. _____

9 When your parents got home last night? _____

☐ 8

How did you do?

Total: ☐ 25

| 😊 | Very good 20 – 25 | 😐 | OK 14 – 19 | 🙁 | Review Unit 15 again 0 – 13 |

16 Now and then

1 Remember and check

(a) 🔊 Think back to the exercise with Lucy (L) and her grandfather (G). Match the two parts of the sentences. Then listen and check your answers.

1 G: When I was young, of course,
2 G: I think school life is more
3 G: I think perhaps
4 L: Some things now
5 L: I'm sure that now life is
6 L: There are a lot more

a are difficult for my granddad.
b cars these days.
c difficult now, certainly.
d faster than in the 1950s.
e we didn't even have television!
f she's happier than I was!

(b) Find pairs of opposites in the box.

| ~~exciting~~ young |
| crowded   different |
| fast difficult empty |
| happy   slow ~~boring~~ |
| sad   easy   the same |
| old |

_____exciting_____   _____boring_____
....
....
....
....
....

2 Grammar
Comparison of adjectives

(a) Complete the table.

Adjectives	Comparative adjectives
1 hard	_harder_
2 hot	
3 happy	
4 difficult	
5 unhappy	
6 expensive	
7 good	
8 hungry	
9 mysterious	
10 bad	

A

B

(b) Look at the picture and answer the questions. Write *A* or *B*.

1 Which dog is smaller? ....
2 Which one is older? ....
3 Which one has got longer ears? ....
4 Which one has got curlier hair? ....
5 Which one is more excited? ....
6 Which one do you think is nicer? ....

c Read the information about Brian and Rebecca, then complete the sentences. Use the comparative form of the adjectives in the box.

bad good tall interesting young big

	Rebecca	Brian
Age:	16	15
Height:	1.7 m	1.6 m
Brothers and sisters:	4	1
Maths results:	75%	70%
French results:	38%	41%
Art project:	☆	☆☆☆

1 Brian is 15. He's .... than Rebecca.

2 Rebecca is 1.7 metres. She's .... than Brian.

3 Rebecca's family is .... than Brian's.

4 Rebecca's Maths results are .... than Brian's.

5 But her French results are .... than Brian's.

6 Brian's Art project is .... than Rebecca's.

d Look at the pictures and write sentences. Use the comparative form of the adjectives.

1 (cold) *Today's colder than yesterday.*

2 (expensive) *The dress*

3 (interesting) ....

4 (busy) ....

5 (fast) ....

6 (good) ....

e Write true sentences comparing these things.

1 me – my best friend

_____

2 my street – my friend's street

_____

3 my town – (another place)

_____

4 school days – weekends

_____

5 comedy programmes – news programmes

_____

6 History – English

_____

4 Vocabulary
Adjectives

a Match the two parts of the sentences.

1 Some snakes
2 I didn't finish the book because it
3 She couldn't sleep because the traffic
4 We loved the film – it
5 Don't climb on the roof – it
6 You can travel very fast
7 I'm watching this programme, so please
8 Computers from the 1980s

a be quiet.
b look really old-fashioned now.
c in a modern train.
d was very noisy.
e isn't safe.
f are dangerous.
g was boring.
h was really exciting.

b Complete the sentences. Use six of the adjectives from Exercise 4a.

1 It was an _____ race.
2 A: Is this river _____ for swimming?
   B: No! There are alligators here!
3 A: What is it?
   B: It's an _____ washing machine.
4 They've got a _____ kitchen.
5 Don't go in there. It's

   _____ .
6 A: Oh! It's very

   _____ !
   B: What? I can't hear you.

Comparisons

🔊 Listen to the sentences. Underline the words that are stressed. Listen again and repeat.

1 She's younger than him.
2 You're happier than me.
3 The bank is older than the bookshop.
4 Maths is more difficult than Science.
5 The book was more interesting than the film.
6 The shoes were more expensive than the trainers.

(c) Think of an example for each of these descriptions.

1 a dangerous road ....

2 a modern building ....

3 a safe place to ride a bicycle ....

4 an old-fashioned shop ....

5 an exciting pop group ....

6 a noisy person in my class ....

5 Culture in mind

(a) Correct these false statements.
Check your answers with the text on page 114 of the Student's Book.

1 Butlin's camps became popular in the 1970s.

Butlin's camps became popular in the 1950s. ....

2 The camps were in cities.

....

3 They were quieter and less comfortable than Center Parcs.

....

4 Center Parcs are smaller than Butlin's camps, but they're more expensive.

....

5 People were freer to choose what they wanted to do at Butlin's.

....

6 At Center Parcs it's always cold at night.

....

(b) Which do you think is a better place for a holiday, Butlin's or Center Parcs? Why?

....

....

6 Study help

Revision

When you're revising, try working with a friend. Make tests for each other.
For example:

- Write sentences with a mistake in each one. Correct the mistakes in your friend's sentences. Here's one to practise. Can you see the mistake?

  My brother Ned is older then me.

- Write sentences and leave empty spaces for one or two words. Fill in the words in your friend's sentences. Here's one to practise.

  Our cooker is .... modern than our fridge.

Skills in mind

7 Listen

🔊 Listen and write the names of the people on the picture.

Tim   Frank   Anne   Lisa   Dad   Uncle Bill   Sandy   Pablo

1 _____
2 _____
3 _____
4 _____
5 _____
6 _____
7 _____
8 _____

Listening tip
Revision

For revision, use your Workbook recording. Practise the pronunciation exercises and listen to the dialogues.

- Play the recording often at home. For example, you can listen when you're getting dressed in the morning, or for ten minutes before you go to sleep.

- If possible, also play the recording when you're out. Listen on your way to school or when you're sitting in the bus.

8 Write

Write a paragraph comparing the two living rooms.

Alan's room is smaller than Peggy's and it's got more modern furniture ...

Alan

Peggy

Unit check

1 Fill in the spaces

Complete the sentences with the words in the box.

| difficult | busier | ~~lived~~ | more | modern | crowded | easier | was | town | old-fashioned |

My family ___*lived*___ in the city for a long time, but in 1998 we moved to an old house in a small
[1] _____ called Kingslea. Of course it [2] _____ strange at first. London was a lot
[3] _____ and [4] _____ exciting than Kingslea. We missed the [5] _____
streets and the big shops. In our house we had an [6] _____ cooker so it was [7] _____
to cook, and the toilet was at the end of the garden. But later, when we got a [8] _____ kitchen
and bathroom, life was [9] _____ , and now we love the place.

☐ 9

2 Choose the correct answers

(Circle) the correct answers, a, b or c.

1 Helen is taller _____ Wendy.
   a that   b (than)   c then

2 This is a _____ road. There are lots
   of accidents here.
   a quiet   b safe   c dangerous

3 That radio is 60 years old, so it's very

   _____ .
   a funny   b old-fashioned   c noisy

4 Sorry, I can't talk to you now – I'm very

   _____ .
   a busy   b important   c difficult

5 Joe is twelve, so he's _____ than
   William.
   a younger   b newer   c more modern

6 This is terrible. The weather was awful
   yesterday and today it's _____ .
   a bigger   b better   c worse

7 I was a _____ person before I
   came to this town.
   a more happy   b happier   c happyer

8 My sister is taller than _____ .
   a I   b me   c she

9 A: Great! This T-shirt's only £3.50.
   B: Yes, and the white one's

   _____ cheaper.
   a lot   b more   c even

☐ 8

3 Correct the mistakes

In each sentence there is a mistake with making comparisons. <u>Underline</u> the mistake and write
the correct sentence.

1 The bank is <u>modern</u> than the post office. *The bank is more modern than the post office.* _____

2 I think English is easer than German. _____

3 Buses are more cheaper than trains. _____

4 My mother is more old than my aunt. _____

5 It's hot today, but it was hoter last week. _____

6 My bike is good, but Sam's bike is gooder. _____

7 The jeans are expensive than the trousers. _____

8 Exercise 1 was OK, but Exercise 2 was difficulter. _____

9 Oh no! This hotel's more bad than the last one! _____

☐ 8

How did you do?

Total: ☐ 25

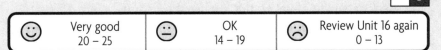

| ☺ | Very good 20 – 25 | ☺ | OK 14 – 19 | ☹ | Review Unit 16 again 0 – 13 |

Grammar reference

Unit 1
Plurals

1 We usually make a noun plural by adding *s*.
   house – houses   teacher – teachers   film – films

2 If a noun ends with consonant + *y*, the ending is *ies*.
   *city – **cities**   party – **parties***

3 If a noun ends with *sh, ch, s* or *x*, the ending is *es*.
   *bush – bush**es**   match – match**es**   bus – bus**es**   box – box**es***

4 Some nouns have irregular plurals.
   *man – **men**   woman – **women**   child – **children**   person – **people***

Adjectives

1 Adjectives come before nouns.
   *a **new** film   an **interesting** video*

2 Adjectives don't have a plural form.
   ***big** hotels   **good** teachers*

a and *an*

1 We use *a/an* before singular nouns.
   *It's **a** museum.   It's **an** expensive restaurant.*

2 We use *a* when the next word begins with a consonant sound.
   a hotel   a book

   We use *an* when the next word begins with a vowel sound.
   ***an** expensive hotel   **an** interesting book*

Units 2 and 3
be: present simple

1 We form the present simple of *be* like this:

Singular	Plural
I am	*we are*
you are	*you are*
he/she/it is	*they are*

2 In speaking and informal writing we use short forms.
   I'm   you're   he's   she's   it's   we're   they're.

3 We use the verb *be* before a noun or an adjective.
   *He's an **actor**.   They're **footballers**.   I'm **American**.*

4 We make the negative by adding *not*.
   *I am **not**   you are **not***

   In speaking and informal writing we use short forms.
   *I'm **not**   you **aren't**   he **isn't**   she **isn't**   it **isn't**   we **aren't**   they **aren't***

5   To make questions we put the verb before the subject.

Am I right?	*Yes, you **are**. / No, you **aren't**.*
Are you British?	*Yes, I **am**. / No, I'**m not**.*
Is he an actor?	*Yes, he **is**. / No, he **isn't**.*
Is she from Poland?	*Yes, she **is**. / No, she **isn't**.*
Are we late?	*Yes, we **are**. / No, we **aren't**.*
Are they singers?	*Yes, they **are**. / No, they **aren't**.*

Unit 2

Question words

Who ...? questions ask about a person/people.
   Who are they?   *They're my friends.*
What ...? questions ask about a thing/things.
   What's this?   *It's a computer game.*
When ...? questions ask about a time.
   When's the concert?   *It's at seven o'clock.*
   When's your music lesson?   *It's on Monday.*
Where ...? questions ask about a place.
   Where's Moscow?   *It's in Russia.*
How old ...? questions ask about age.
   How old are you?   *I'm fifteen.*
How many ...? questions ask about a number.
   How many students are in your class?   *Twenty-six.*

Unit 3

Object pronouns

1   Here is a list of pronouns.

Subject	I	you	he	she	it	we	they
Object	me	you	him	her	it	us	them

2   We use object pronouns after the verb, instead of a noun.

*I like **the music**.*	*– I like **it**.*
*I love **my mother**.*	*– I love **her**.*
*They don't like **you and me**.*	*– They don't like **us**.*
*I want to see **Jack and Sue**.*	*– I want to see **them**.*

Unit 4

Present simple

1   We use the present simple for things that happen regularly or are normally true.

*We **watch** TV after school.*	*He **goes** shopping at the supermarket.*
*They **live** in Australia.*	*She **speaks** French.*

2   Usually the present simple is the same as the base form of the verb. But with a third person singular subject (*he, she, it*) we use an *s* ending.

*I **play** tennis.*	*She **plays** tennis.*
*My parents **work** in London.*	*My brother **works** in London.*

If a verb ends with *o, sh, ch, ss* or *x*, we add *es*.

*go – it go**es**   finish – he finish**es**   watch – she watch**es**   miss – he miss**es**   fix – she fix**es***

If a verb ends with consonant + *y*, we change the *y* to *i* and add *es*.

*study – she stud**ies**   carry – he carr**ies**   fly – it fl**ies***

3 We make the negative with *don't* (*do not*) or *doesn't* (*does not*) + base form of the verb.

*I **don't like** football.*   *He **doesn't like** football.*
*My cousins **don't live** in Italy.*   *Gina **doesn't live** in Italy.*

4 We make questions with *Do* or *Does* + base form of the verb.

***Do** you **like** me?*   ***Does** Helen **go** to school?*
***Do** we **know** the answer?*   ***Does** he **listen** to the radio?*
***Do** your parents **work**?*   ***Does** this shop **sell** chocolate?*

Possessive 's

1 We put *'s* after a noun to say who something belongs to.

Mum's car   John's family   Susan's bicycle
the dog's bed   my brother's problem   your sister's friend

2 We <u>don't</u> usually say ~~the family of John~~, ~~the car of my father~~, etc.

Possessive adjectives

1 Here is a list of possessive adjectives.

Subject pronoun	I	you	he	she	it	we	they
Possessive adjective	**my**	**your**	**his**	**her**	**its**	**our**	**their**

2 We use these adjectives before a noun to say who something belongs to.

***My** name's Steve.*   *I like **your** parents.*
*He's rich. Look at **his** car!*   *We love **our** dog.*
*She's a good teacher. We like **her** lessons.*   *They ride **their** bicycles to school.*
*The video isn't in **its** box.*

Unit 5

there's / there are

1 We use *there's / there are* to say that something exists.

***There's** a bank in South Street.*
***There are** two parks in my town.*   ***There are** lots of good restaurants here.*

2 The full form of *there's* is *there is*. In speaking and informal writing we usually say *there's*.

3 In positive sentences, we use *there's* + *a/an* + singular noun and *there are* + plural noun.

***There's a** parcel on the table.*
***There's an** interesting film on TV.*
***There are** good clothes at the market.*

4 In questions and negative sentences, we use *a/an* + singular noun and *any* + plural noun.

***Is there** a railway station here?*   ***There isn't** a railway station here.*
***Are there** any cafés in this street?*   ***There aren't** any cafés in this street.*

Positive imperative

1 We use the imperative when we want to tell someone to do something.

2 The positive imperative is the same as the base form of the verb.

***Turn** left into Spring Street.*   ***Sit** down on that chair.*   ***Be** quiet, please!*

Prepositions of place

We use prepositions of place to say where something or someone is.

*My pen is **in** my bag.*
*The box is **on** the table.*

*Our car is **in front of** the post office.*
*There's a garden **behind** the house.*
*There's a table **next to** my bed.*
*The bookshop is **between** the chemist and the newsagent.*

Unit 6

Why ...? Because ...

Why ...? questions ask about the reason for something that happens. We usually answer the question with *Because* ...

Why *do you want to see this band?*   **Because** *their music is fantastic.*

has / have got

1   We use the verb *have got* to talk about things that people own.

2   Normally we use *have got*. But with a third person singular subject (*he, she, it*) we use *has got*. In speaking and informal writing we use the short forms *'ve* and *'s*.

*I'**ve got** two brothers.*   *Ben'**s got** a new computer.*
*They'**ve got** a DVD player.*   *My sister'**s got** fair hair.*

3   The negative form is *haven't got / hasn't got*.

*You **haven't got** a big family.*   *Alison **hasn't got** a mobile phone.*
*We **haven't got** a computer at home.* *My brother **hasn't got** fair hair.*

4   To make questions we use *Have/Has* + subject + *got*.

Have *you **got** a bicycle?*   **Has** *she **got** blue eyes?*

Have *we **got** a problem?*   **Has** *your uncle **got** a car?*

5   People sometimes use *have / has* without *got* – this is normal in the USA.

*I **have** a bicycle.* **Do we have** *a problem?*   *She **doesn't have** a mobile phone.*

Unit 7

Countable and uncountable nouns

1   Nouns in English are countable or uncountable. Countable nouns have a singular and a plural form.

apple – apples   tomato – tomatoes   book – books   question – questions   man – men

2   Uncountable nouns don't have a plural form – they are always singular.

food   fruit   rice   bread   milk   music   money   hair   homework
*This **food is** delicious.   The **music is** awful!   Your **hair is** lovely.   My **homework is** in my bag.*

3   Some nouns can be countable or uncountable.

*I want to buy two **chickens** at the market.   (= two whole birds, countable)*
*Roast **chicken** is my favourite meal.   (= a type of meat, uncountable)*

4   With countable nouns, we can use *a/an* + singular noun and *some* + plural noun.

*There's **a café** next to the cinema.   I'd like **some strawberries**.*
*I often have **an egg** for breakfast.   There are **some** good **CDs** in that shop.*

5   With uncountable nouns, we use *some*.

*I'm hungry. I want **some food**.   Please buy **some milk** at the supermarket.*

We <u>don't</u> use *a/an* with uncountable nouns ~~a bread~~   ~~an information~~

this/that/these/those

1   We use *this* or *that* + singular noun. We use *these* or *those* + plural noun.

    this fruit   **that** book   **these** clothes   **those** apples

2   We use *this* or *these* to point out things that are close to us. We use *that* or *those* to point out things that are at some distance from us.

    *Come and look at **this** letter.*   *Mmm! **These** strawberries are delicious.*
    ***That** man on the corner is our teacher.*   *Can you see **those** people over there?*

I'd like ... / Would you like ...?

1   We use *would like* to ask for things or to offer things. *Would like* is more polite than *want*.

    *I'd **like** two kilos of apples, please.* ***Would** you **like** vegetables with your meal?*

2   The full form of *I'd like* is *I would like*, but in speaking and informal writing we use the short form.

Unit 8
Adverbs of frequency

1   Adverbs of frequency are words that say how often we do things.

    always   usually   often   sometimes   hardly ever   never

2   Adverbs of frequency come <u>after</u> the verb *be*, but <u>before</u> other verbs.

    *I'm **usually** tired after school.*   *I **usually have** breakfast at 7.30.*
    *He's **always** late.*   *She **always arrives** before me.*
    *We're **never** bored.*   *We **never go** to that restaurant.*

Unit 9
Negative imperatives

We form the negative imperative with *Don't* + base form of the verb.

    ***Don't buy** those eggs – they aren't fresh.*   ***Don't cry** – it's OK.*   ***Don't be** stupid!*

Unit 10
can/can't (ability)

1   We use *can/can't* to talk about someone's ability to do something. The form is *can/can't* + base form of the verb.

    *I **can swim** 3 kilometres.*   *My little sister **can count** to 100.*   *We **can walk** on our hands.*
    *They **can't run** fast.*   *My father **can't ride** a horse.*   *We **can't speak** Chinese.*

2   To make questions we use *Can* + subject + base form of the verb.

    ***Can** your brother **swim**?*   ***Can** you **use** a computer?*   ***Can** they **play** the violin?*

    We <u>don't</u> use the verb *do* for questions or negatives.

like / don't like + -ing

1   We often use the *-ing* form of a verb after *like, enjoy, love* and *hate*.

    *He likes cycl**ing**.*   *I love swimm**ing**.*   *They enjoy watch**ing** tennis.*
    *Anne doesn't like ski**ing**.*   *She hates play**ing** computer games.*

2   If a verb ends in *e*, we drop the *e* before adding *ing*.

    *live – liv**ing**   ride – rid**ing***

If a short verb ends in 1 vowel + 1 consonant, we double the final consonant before adding *ing*. We do the same if the verb ends in 1 vowel + *l*.

get – getting   shop – shopping   swim – swimming   travel – travelling

Unit 11
Present continuous

1   We use the present continuous to talk about things happening at the moment of speaking.

*The girls **are doing** their homework now.*
*Alex is in the bathroom. He**'s having** a shower.*
*Don't make a noise. I**'m listening** to the radio.*

2   We form the present continuous with the present simple of *be* + *-ing* form of the verb.

*I**'m having** lunch.*   *You**'re shouting**!*
*He**'s playing** volleyball.*   *We**'re sitting** in the garden.*
*It**'s raining**.*   *They**'re studying** in the library.*

3   We make questions and negatives with the question/negative form of *be* + *-ing* form of the verb.

*I**'m not watching** TV.*   ***Are** you **speaking** to me?*
*You **aren't listening** to me!*   ***Is** he **doing** his homework?*
*She **isn't playing** well today.*   ***Are** they **travelling** in France?*

4   Some verbs aren't normally used in the present continuous, for example:

understand   know   like   hate   remember   forget   want

5   Look at the difference between the present continuous and the present simple.

*I usually **do** my homework in my bedroom, but today I**'m doing** it in the dining room.*
*My father hardly ever **watches** TV, but this afternoon he**'s watching** the football.*
*I **listen** to music every day. At the moment, I**'m listening** to the new Alanis Morissette CD.*

Unit 12
Prepositions of time: *at, in, on*

1   We use *at* with times, and with the word *night*.

*The lesson starts **at nine o'clock**.*
*I get up **at 6.30**.*
*My uncle works **at night**.*

2   We use *in* with parts of the day (but not with *night*), and with months and seasons.

*I go to school **in the morning**.*   *I often read **in the evening**.*
*Her birthday is **in September**.*   *We go on holiday **in August**.*
*It's always cold **in winter**.*   *I like going to the beach **in summer**.*

3   We use *on* with days of the week.

*We have an English lesson **on Monday**.*   *I usually go to the cinema **on Saturday**.*

Asking for permission: *Can I ...? / Yes, you can. / Sorry, you can't.*

1   We often use *Can I ...?* to ask for permission to do something.

***Can I** leave now, please?*   ***Can I** go to the party on Saturday?*

2   To give or refuse permission we use *can* or *can't*.

***Can I** borrow your jacket?*
*Yes, you **can**.*   *No, sorry, you **can't**. I want to wear it tonight.*

one/ones

We use *one* or *ones* when we don't want to repeat a noun. We use *one* instead of a singular noun and *ones* instead of a plural noun.

> *My bicycle's very old. I want a new **one**. (= bicycle)*
> *I've got a CD by Britney Spears, but it's an old **one**. (= CD)*
> *I'd like two chocolate ice creams and two strawberry **ones**. (= ice creams)*
> *Do you know those boys – the **ones** in the café? (= boys)*

Unit 13

Past simple: *was/wasn't, were/weren't*

1   We use the past simple form of *be* to talk about actions and events in the past.

2   We form the past simple like this:

*I **was***	*we **were***
*he/she/it **was***	*you **were***
	*they **were***

> *I **was** in town on Saturday.*   *He **was** tired after the match.*   *It **was** hot last week.*
> *You **were** late yesterday.*   *We **were** at the cinema last night.*   *They **were** angry.*

3   We make the negative by adding *not* (*was not, were not*). In speaking and informal writing we use short forms: *wasn't* and *weren't*.

> *I **wasn't** here last year.*   *The film **wasn't** interesting.*
> *You **weren't** at school yesterday.*   *They **weren't** at the concert.*

4   To make questions we put the verb before the subject.

> ***Were** you in town on Saturday?*   ***Was** James happy about the test?*

5   We often use time expressions with the past simple.

> *yesterday   yesterday morning   yesterday afternoon   yesterday evening*
> *last night   last Friday   last week   last weekend   last month   last year*

Unit 14

Past simple – regular verbs

1   We use the past simple to talk about actions and events in the past.

2   With regular verbs we form the past simple by adding *ed*. The form is the same for all subjects.

> *I walk**ed** to school yesterday.*   *She open**ed** the door.*   *The concert start**ed** at 8 o'clock.*
> *You finish**ed** before me.*   *We play**ed** cards last night.*   *They watch**ed** the news on TV.*

3   If a verb ends with consonant + *y*, we change the *y* to *i* and add *ed*.

> *study – stud**ied**   marry – marr**ied**   carry – carr**ied***

If a short verb ends in 1 vowel + 1 consonant, we double the final consonant before adding *ed*. We do the same if the verb ends in 1 vowel + *l*.

> *stop – sto**pped**   hop – ho**pped**   travel – trave**lled***

4   We make the negative with *didn't* (*did not*) + base form of the verb.

> *I **didn't walk** to school yesterday.*   *She **didn't open** the door.*
> *You **didn't finish** before me.*   *We **didn't play** cards last night.*

5   We make questions with *Did* + subject + base form of the verb.

> ***Did** I **start** before you?*   ***Did** he **open** the window?*
> ***Did** you **walk** to school yesterday?*   ***Did** they **play** volleyball last week?*

Unit 15

Past simple – irregular verbs

1   A lot of common verbs are irregular. This means that the past simple forms are different –
    they don't have the usual *ed* ending.

    *go – **went**   see – **saw**   find – **found**   write – **wrote**   think – **thought***

    There is a list of irregular verbs on page 122 of the Student's Book.

2   We make questions and negatives in the same way as for regular verbs.

    *I **went** to town, but I **didn't go** to the bookshop.*   ***Did** you **go** to the newsagent?*
    *We **saw** James, but we **didn't see** Jonathan.*   ***Did** you **see** Alison?*

Unit 16

Comparison of adjectives

1   To compare two things, or two groups of things, we use a comparative form + *than*.

    *I'm **older than** my brother.*
    *France is **bigger than** Britain.*
    *TVs are **more expensive than** radios.*
    *Your computer is **better than** mine.*

2   With short adjectives, we normally add *er*.

    *old – old**er**   cheap – cheap**er**   quiet – quiet**er***

    If the adjective ends in *e*, we add only *r*.

    *nice – nice**r**   safe – safe**r**   free – free**r***

    If the adjective ends with consonant + *y*, we change the *y* to *i* and add *er*.

    *easy – eas**ier**   early – earl**ier**   happy – happ**ier***

    If the adjective ends in 1 vowel + 1 consonant, we double the final consonant and add *er*.

    *big – big**ger**   sad – sad**der**   thin – thin**ner***

3   With longer adjectives, we don't change the adjective – we put *more* in front of it.

    *expensive – **more** expensive   difficult – **more** difficult   interesting – **more** interesting*

4   Some adjectives are irregular – they have a different comparative form.

    *good – **better**   bad – **worse***

Acknowledgements

The publishers are grateful to the following for permission to reproduce photographic material:

AA World Travel Library for pp. 32, 68; AP Photos for p. 58 Michael Dwyer;
Bananastock / Alamy for pp. 74(br), 98(inset r); Bubbles Photo Library for p. 14 Pauline Cutler; Corbis for pp.70(m), 75(r), 82; Getty Images for pp. 56, 70(b), 98 (inset l), ©Timothy N. Holt 2003 www.phatfotos.com for pp. 73, 74(m); Hulton Archive for pp. 75(l), 80; Image Source / Alamy for p. 20(tl);
London Aerial Photo Library for p. 14; Londonstills.com for p. 74(tr); Mirrorpix for pp. 97(t & b); Naturepl.com for p. 34 Anup Shah; Photofusion Picture Library / Alamy for p. 74(l); Rex Features for p. 20(r); Topfoto for pp. 70(tl) Imageworks, 88 UPP; Janine Wiedel Photography / Alamy for p. 52;
This book contains Royalty Free images on pp. 29(montage), 60 (items 1 to 8).

All other photographs taken by Gareth Boden Photography.

The publishers are grateful to the following illustrators:

Yane Christensen, c/o Advocate Illustration pp. 6, 8, 13, 26, 42, 53, 71, 84: Mark Duffin pp. 5, 29, 60, 67, 91, 98; Martha Gavin pp 26, 41, 77, 89, 95: Janos Jantner c/o Beehive Illustrations pp 29, 38, 40, 66; Graham Kennedy pp 4, 5, 7, 8, 11, 17, 25, 28, 35, 40, 46, 50, 54, 59, 61, 62, 65, 72, 78, 95, 98; Kathy Lacey pp. 12, 30, 31, 49, 68, 86, 92; Lee Montgomery pp 18, 36, 86; David Shenton pp. 10, 12, 22, 23, 30, 34, 37, 44, 48, 83, 90, 94; Kath Walker 16, 42, 47, 58, 89, 96.

The publishers are grateful to the following contributors:

Sarah Ackroyd: CD-ROM exercises
Bee2 Ltd: multimedia developer
Gareth Boden: commissioned photography
Kevin Brown: picture research
Annie Cornford: editorial work
Pentacor Book Design: text design and layouts
Anne Rosenfeld: audio CD audio recordings
Sally Smith: photographic direction
Hanna Yadi and Alex Bird: CD-ROM audio recording

The CD-ROM photographs are from Ingram Publishing, digital image © 1994–2001 Hemera Technologies Inc., © istockphoto.com or taken by Cambridge University Press

Notes

CD instructions

Audio CD
Play the CD in a standard CD player, or on your computer.

CD-ROM
No installation – simply insert the disc into your CD-ROM drive and the application will start automatically. Close any media applications (for example, Microsoft® Windows Media® Player) before inserting the disc.
If the application does not start automatically, browse to your CD-ROM drive and double-click the 'EIM' icon.

Audio CD track listing

TRACK	UNIT	EXERCISE	TRACK	UNIT	EXERCISE	TRACK	UNIT	EXERCISE
1	Introduction		24	7	7a	47	14	3b
2	1	2a	25	8	5	48	14	3c
3	1	5	26	8	6b	49	14	8
4	1	6a	27	8	10a	50	15	1
5	1	6b	28	9	1	51	15	3
6	1	7c	29	9	3	52	16	1a
7	1	10	30	9	4c	53	16	3
8	2	1g	31	10	3	54	16	7
9	2	3	32	10	3b			
10	3	5a	33	10	8			
11	3	5	34	10	9a			
12	3	8	35	11	3			
13	4	3	36	11	4c			
14	5	8	37	11	7b			
15	5	2a	38	12	5a			
16	5	2b	39	12	5b			
17	5	3	40	12	5c			
18	6	3e	41	12	9			
19	6	4	42	13	4			
20	6	7	43	13	5a			
21	7	2a	44	13	5b			
22	7	4a	45	13	9			
23	7	4b	46	14	3a			

Terms and conditions of use for the English in Mind Workbook Audio CD / CD-ROM

1 **Licence**

(a) Cambridge University Press grants the customer the licence to use one copy of this CD-ROM (i) on a single computer for use by one or more people at different times, or (ii) by a single person on one or more computers (provided the CD-ROM is only used on one computer at one time and is only used by the customer), but not both.

(b) The customer shall not: (i) copy or authorise copying of the CD-ROM, (ii) translate the CD-ROM, (iii) reverse-engineer, disassemble or decompile the CD-ROM, (iv) transfer, sell, assign or otherwise convey any portion of the CD-ROM, or (v) operate the CD-ROM from a network or mainframe system.

2 **Copyright**

All material contained within the CD-ROM is protected by copyright and other intellectual property laws. The customer acquires only the right to use the CD-ROM and does not acquire any rights, express or implied, other than those expressed in the licence.

3 **Liability**

To the extent permitted by applicable law, Cambridge University Press is not liable for direct damages or loss of any kind resulting from the use of this product or from errors or faults contained in it and in every case Cambridge University Press' liability shall be limited to the amount actually paid by the customer for the product.

CD-ROM System Requirements:
- 800 x 600 resolution
- a sound card and speakers or headphones

For PC:
- Pentium 500 MHz or higher
- 256 MB RAM
- Windows 2000 or XP

For Apple Mac:
- 500 MHz processor or higher
- 256 MB RAM
- OS X 10.4